CONTROL YOUR RETIREMENT DESTINY

ACHIEVING FINANCIAL SECURITY BEFORE THE BIG TRANSITION

Dana Anspach

Apress®

Control Your Retirement Destiny: Achieving Financial Security before the Big Transition

ISBN 978-1-4302-5022-7

ISBN 978-1-4302-5023-4 (eBook)

President and Publisher: Paul Manning
Acquisitions Editor: Jeff Olson
Editorial Board: Steve Anglin, Mark Beckner, Ewan Buckingham, Gary Cornell,
    Louise Corrigan, Morgan Ertel, Jonathan Gennick, Jonathan Hassell,
    Robert Hutchinson, Michelle Lowman, James Markham, Matthew Moodie,
    Jeff Olson, Jeffrey Pepper, Douglas Pundick, Ben Renow-Clarke,
    Dominic Shakeshaft, Gwenan Spearing, Matt Wade, Tom Welsh
Coordinating Editor: Rita Fernando
Copy Editor: Corbin Collins
Compositor: SPi Global
Indexer: SPi Global
Cover Designer: Anna Ishchenko

Distributed to the book trade worldwide by Springer Science+Business Media New York, 233 Spring Street, 6th Floor, New York, NY 10013. Phone 1-800-SPRINGER, fax (201) 348-4505, e-mail orders-ny@springer-sbm.com, or visit www.springeronline.com. Apress Media, LLC is a California LLC and the sole member (owner) is Springer Science + Business Media Finance Inc (SSBM Finance Inc). SSBM Finance Inc is a Delaware corporation.

For information on translations, please e-mail rights@apress.com, or visit www.apress.com.

Apress and friends of ED books may be purchased in bulk for academic, corporate, or promotional use. eBook versions and licenses are also available for most titles. For more information, reference our Special Bulk Sales–eBook Licensing web page at www.apress.com/bulk-sales.

Any source code or other supplementary materials referenced by the author in this text is available to readers at www.apress.com. For detailed information about how to locate your book's source code, go to www.apress.com/source-code/.

Apress Business: The Unbiased Source of Business Information

Apress business books provide essential information and practical advice, each written for practitioners by recognized experts. Busy managers and professionals in all areas of the business world—and at all levels of technical sophistication—look to our books for the actionable ideas and tools they need to solve problems, update and enhance their professional skills, make their work lives easier, and capitalize on opportunity.

Whatever the topic on the business spectrum—entrepreneurship, finance, sales, marketing, management, regulation, information technology, among others—Apress has been praised for providing the objective information and unbiased advice you need to excel in your daily work life. Our authors have no axes to grind; they understand they have one job only—to deliver up-to-date, accurate information simply, concisely, and with deep insight that addresses the real needs of our readers.

It is increasingly hard to find information—whether in the news media, on the Internet, and now all too often in books—that is even-handed and has your best interests at heart. We therefore hope that you enjoy this book, which has been carefully crafted to meet our standards of quality and unbiased coverage.

We are always interested in your feedback or ideas for new titles. Perhaps you'd even like to write a book yourself. Whatever the case, reach out to us at editorial@apress.com and an editor will respond swiftly. Incidentally, at the back of this book, you will find a list of useful related titles. Please visit us at www.apress.com to sign up for newsletters and discounts on future purchases.

The Apress Business Team

To Francois Gadenne, and The View Across the Silos

Contents

About the Author

Since 2008, **Dana Anspach** has been a featured writer for About.com. She writes as their Guide to MoneyOver55 and is responsible for all the content on the About.com MoneyOver55 site. (See www.moneyover55.about.com). She also serves as the Chair of the Practitioner Peer Review Committee for the *Retirement Management Journal*, a publication issued by the Retirement Income Industry Association.

Anspach has been practicing as a financial advisor since 1995, and founded Sensible Money, LLC, in 2011. Sensible Money is a registered investment advisory firm in Scottsdale, Arizona, with a developed specialty in the area of retirement income planning. She is a Certified Financial Planner, Retirement Management Analyst, a Kolbe Certified Consultant, and a member of NAPFA (National Association of Personal Financial Advisors), FPA (Financial Planning Association), and RIIA (Retirement Income Industry Association).

As an expert in her field, she has spoken for numerous organizations, associations, and conferences on the topic of retirement planning and investing for income and interacts regularly with readers and clients on these topics. Anspach believes the retirement income planning process is not static; it is alive with choices and variables. To make the best decisions, consumers need a way to understand the interactions of the choices they make and the corresponding impact on their future. To trust the information they see, they need an independent voice that provides information free of the influence of politics, financial products, or media articles that are advertising in disguise. As her clients can tell you, Dana Anspach is that independent voice.

Acknowledgments

To my first financial planner, Les Zetmeir. You started it all. You showed me what financial planning is really all about.

To my team at Sensible Money; Jody Hulsey, Kim Morton, Brian Duvall, and Bob Burger, I could not have completed this without you. Thank you for your support, hard work, for your amazing dedication to our clients and Kim and Brian thank you for your detailed review of so many of the chapters in this book.

Francois Gadenne, this project would never have come about if it weren't for RIIA and the RMA designation. Thank you for all the work you do for our industry, and for truly offering a View Across the Silos.

Wade Pfau, Moshe Milevsky, Michael Kitces, and Carl Richards, thank you for being an inspiration to me, each in a different way.

Mike O'Connor, thank you for your detailed review of Chapter 3 on Social Security.

Joe Elsasser, thank you for always answering my Social Security questions so thoroughly and promptly and for your review of Chapter 3.

Drew Hueler at Income Solutions, thank you for gathering quotes and then even more quotes for my use in Chapter 4.

Jeff Carman, thank you for always answering my life insurance questions so thoroughly and promptly and for your review of Chapter 6.

Scott Stolz, thank you for your review and comments on the use of annuities in Chapter 8.

Dan McGrath, thank you for your review and comments on health care costs in Chapter 10.

Nicole Gurley, thank you for your input, review, quotes, contributions, and incredible thoroughness in regards to the long term care section in Chapter 10.

Jeff Olson, thank you and the team at Apress for bringing this book to life.

Preface

This book is not about saving money. It's about saving the right way. It's about doing more with what you already have. And it's about aligning your financial decisions toward a common goal; creating reliable life-long income.

You'll read stories about people just like you. You'll see examples—with numbers—explaining why something works, or perhaps doesn't work. You'll learn how to create a plan and use it to compare various financial scenarios.

You'll learn which factors you can control, and which ones you can't, so you can focus on what matters. And when you're done, you won't be done. You'll be beginning a journey—a journey of using your money as the valued resource that it is. A resource that can allow you to pursue those things that are nearest and dearest to your heart, whatever they may be.

I'd recommend you start at the beginning, and for the most part, read in order—with one exception. If you're still many, many years away from your earliest Social Security claiming age (which is 62 for most people and 60 for widow/widowers), then you may want to simply scan Chapter 3 and keep going. It gets kind of technical and the techie stuff won't apply to you till you're older. But that's the only break you get! The rest of the chapters are appropriate for all, and you're bound to learn something that is going to be valuable for you. (And even with the Social Security chapter, you may learn something that can help out a neighbor, friend or co-worker.)

So, no time to waste. Let's get started. It is time to take control of your retirement destiny.

Your Finances

Why It's Different over 50

The question isn't at what age I want to retire, it's at what income.

—George Foreman

There I was sitting across the table from Jay. He and his wife Sally were wondering if they could go from full-time to part-time work, or perhaps leave the workforce all together.

Jay said to me, "You realize if I do this, I can't go back? I won't be working anymore. We'll be living off our acorns. This has to work. It's different than when I was 40 and I had my career ahead of me. Do you understand that?"

Whenever someone says such things in my office, which is relatively often, I am amused. For the last 17 years, I have spent nearly every day helping people align their financial decisions around the goal of allowing them a smooth transition out of the workforce. The people who come to see me know this is what I do. Yet they still feel compelled to remind me that if they retire they will be living off their savings.

I understand. You save money, and then save more money. And then one day you are faced with the prospect of having to start withdrawing some of those savings each and every year. It's scary.

I try to address this scariness: "Jay, I know the transition is scary. You've saved this money your whole life. Starting to spend that savings brings up a whole slew of emotions, and it is normal to wonder how—and if—this is all going to work. I can assure you that it will, if you follow the plan we develop."

As you'll see, having a plan is the key to a successful transition out of the workforce. Your plan must encompass far more than how much you have saved and what types of investments you own. All of your financial decisions must be aligned to work together.

▥ **Note**   Having a plan is the key to a successful transition out of the work force.

This means considering taxes, Social Security, health care expenses, pensions, lifestyle decisions, home ownership, investment risks, age differences between spouses, and more. You must consider all these items in context. It makes no sense to look at them in isolation. You have to look at how they can work together to deliver a secure outcome.

The planning needs to be different when you reach 50 and beyond. You face a new set of challenges, and traditional planning often neglects to address them in a meaningful way. These challenges are:

- Longevity risk

- Sequence risk

- Inflation risk

- Overspending risk

Let's look at each of these in detail.

Challenge One: Longevity—An Unknown Time Horizon

Have you ever planned a road trip? It's fairly easy math to determine that if you are going 300 miles, your gas tank holds 15 gallons, and your vehicle averages about 20 miles per gallon, that you can get to your destination on one tank.

Yet you may want some wiggle room. Most vehicles get better mileage on the highway than in the city. If you know part of your trip will be city driving, maybe you'll want to fill up the tank halfway through the trip, just to be sure.

Now suppose you don't know how far away your destination is or how much of the driving will be city driving verses highway driving. The only thing you know is there won't be any gas stations along the way. How much gas do you take then? Do you stock up on gas or get a more fuel-efficient car? Or both?

This is the challenge you face as you plan a transition into retirement. Do you need income for 20 years or 30? What about your spouse? Is he or she significantly younger than you? What investment returns and savings rates will you experience along the way?

When making the transition to retirement, you are headed out on a road trip. You don't know how long the trip will be, nor can you predict the conditions you will encounter. It sounds scary, but really, is it all that different than it was when you turned 18? Or when you started your first job? Or had your first child?

I would argue you have an advantage now. You have years of experience to draw from and the ability to lay out a plan that leaves wiggle room for life's unknowns. It starts by creating a model, or projection, of what the future may bring.

When I do financial modeling for people, I start with a series of default assumptions. In my initial scenario I have males living to 85 and females to 90. Without fail, about once a week someone looks at me with big eyes and says, "Well, I'll never live that long."

I look back and say, "What if you do?" It is my job to think about the future you.

▨ **Note**   What might the 84-year-old you wish the 52-year-old you had done? What decisions might the 92-year-old you wish the 63-year-old you had made?

These are the questions a good planning process must ask and answer.

Longevity risk is the technical term for the challenge of charting a path into a trip of unknown duration. It is a fancy way of saying that you have a finite set of resources that must last for an unknown amount of time.

As with other forms of risk, you have your own tolerance of longevity risk. Some will want to diligently plan so the 92-year-old you will be in great shape. Others will prefer to let the 63-year-old you have a little more play money.

The choice is a personal one. To choose in a personal way, you have to explore what your road trip might look like from many angles.

There are some decisions you can make that can help protect the 92-year-old you while allowing the 63-year-old you to continue to have fun. Making these decisions appropriately takes analysis.

Many decisions can improve your ability to spend today while also increasing the likelihood that your future income remains sufficient. You must approach these decisions with an open mind.

Learning to Use the Right Tool

You must also be willing to let go of any misinformation you may have accumulated.

For example, suppose I told you that you will need a Phillips head screwdriver to accomplish your goals. In response, you exclaim, "I've heard Phillips head screwdrivers are terrible. No way would I use one." Sounds silly, right?

Yet every day I propose solutions that will work, and I get such responses, most frequently around the topics of Social Security, reverse mortgages, annuities, and stocks. These are tools too, just like a Phillips head screwdriver.

You have likely heard stories or read inaccurate information that has affected your opinion about one or more of the tools I discuss in this book. A tool is neither good nor bad. It has a function. Once you understand the function, you know when the tool is appropriate for the job at hand.

When it comes to longevity risk, there are tools that can help you achieve the dual goals of spending today while protecting the ability to continue spending later. Such tools include

- Delaying the start date of your Social Security benefits
- Working longer
- Buying an annuity
- Using a reverse mortgage
- Choosing investments that offer inflation protection

How do you employ these planning tools in an appropriate way? By the end of this book, you'll know.

REAL LIFE: TOM AND TARA

Tom came to see me at age 55. He was a successful attorney. His practice was being sold to a larger firm, and he would be continuing on in a salaried position. He had some retirement savings and a lump sum coming in from the sale of his practice.

As a high income earner, he thought it would be relatively easy to save sufficient assets for retirement over the next ten years. There was only one catch: his wife Tara was 40, and they had a two-year-old son. His income and savings needed to provide for a much longer time span than it would for a couple closer in age.

In their case, the solution was the appropriate use of life insurance along with some revised spending habits. They were used to traveling, eating out, and maintaining homes in two locations. As we developed their plan, they realized they both wanted to enjoy some retirement years together. In order to do so, they committed to making substantial changes to their current spending habits in order to save more.

Couples with such a big age difference may be rare, but it is common to see couples with a spouse three to ten years younger. Women live longer than men, so longevity risk takes on increased importance for couples where the wife is younger by several years.

What Do the Odds Tell You?

Figure 1-1 is a graph of life expectancy probabilities.[1] Based on a male and female each aged 62 today, it shows their respective probabilities of living to a particular age. Age is the horizontal axis.

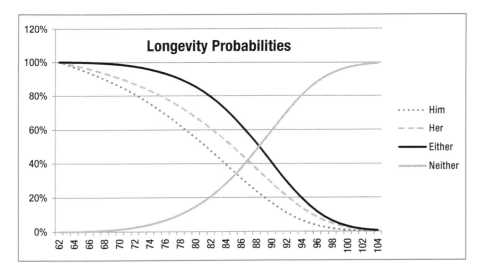

Figure 1-1. The probability of a male and female, both 62, living to a particular age, as well as the odds either or neither live to that age

Couples should focus on the Either line. You can see that, at any age, there is a higher probability that either of you will live to a particular age, which means your resources have a potentially longer time horizon when planning for two.

The crossover point—where the odds that neither of you is alive exceed the odds that one of you is alive—occurs at age 89. What decisions do you suppose your 89-year-old spouse hopes you will make?

---

[1]Figure 1-1 derived from spreadsheet developed by David E. Hultstrom of Financial Architects, LLC, using mortality data from Period Life Table, 2004.

Suppose you were the betting type. You have a decision to make, such as when to begin Social Security or whether to buy an income annuity. You want to look at the odds to see which way you should bet your money.

- The odds tell you that if you and your spouse are both 62 today, there is a 72% chance that one or the other of you will still be going strong at 84.

- The odds tell you there is a 4% probability that neither of you will still be here at 74.

You would think you would make the decision that would put you in a more secure position 72% of the time, but many people do not look at it this way. We have a tendency to place more value on a dollar of spending today than a dollar of spending in the future. That can hurt you in the long run.

When it comes to retirement planning, it's good to play the odds.

Challenge Two: Sequence Risk—The Gas Mileage Question

In addition to an unknown time horizon, you face unknown "driving" conditions. You don't know how many miles per gallon you're going to get along the way. In other words, you don't know what rate of return your savings and investments will earn.

Will you enjoy a long period of highway driving, as we saw in the 1980s and 1990s, with decent savings rates and strong returns on invested assets like stocks and bonds? Or will you suffer the inefficiency of city driving—a decade or two of low interest rates and mediocre returns?

You might have a period of great returns followed by a period of poor returns, or vice versa. The order in which your returns occur has a big impact on your future standard of living. This is called *sequence risk*, and there is no effective way to explain it without looking at the math.

History provides great examples of sequence risk. The average annualized return of the S&P 500 Index from 1973–1982 was 6.7%.[2] A software program using this average return would show funds growing, as you see in the second column of Table 1-1. Actual results are reflected in the third column.

---

[2]Unless otherwise credited, returns data throughout this book are from Dimensional Fund Advisors, *DFA Matrix Book 2012* (Austin, TX: Dimensional Fund Advisors, 2012).

Table 1-1. Year-end balances for growth of $100,000 initial investment based on 6.7% annualized returns and real historical returns

Calendar Year	End of Year Balance @ 6.7%	End of Year Balance Actual	S&P 500 Return
1973	$106,700	$85,300	−14.7
1974	$113,849	$62,696	−26.5
1975	$121,477	$86,018	37.2
1976	$129,616	$106,491	23.8
1977	$138,300	$98,823	−7.2
1978	$147,566	$105,346	6.6
1979	$157,453	$124,729	18.4
1980	$168,002	$165,141	32.4
1981	$179,259	$157,049	−4.9
1982	$191,269	$190,658	21.4

Whether using average returns or actual returns, you ended up with around $190,000.

But remember, you'll be withdrawing income. Table 1-2 shows the results after taking out $6,000 per year.

Table 1-2. Year-end balances after a year-end withdrawal of $6,000, based on $100,000 initial investment at 6.7% annualized returns and real historical returns

Calendar Year	Annual Income Withdrawn	End of Year Balance @ 6.7%	End of Year Balance Actual[3]	Difference
1973	$6,000	$100,700	$79,300	($21,400)
1974	$6,000	$101,447	$52,286	($49,161)
1975	$6,000	$102,244	$65,736	($36,508)
1976	$6,000	$103,094	$75,381	($27,713)
1977	$6,000	$104,001	$63,953	($40,048)
1978	$6,000	$104,970	$62,174	($42,796)
1979	$6,000	$106,003	$67,614	($38,389)
1980	$6,000	$107,105	$83,521	($23,584)
1981	$6,000	$108,281	$73,429	($34,852)
1982	$6,000	$109,536	$83,143	($26,393)

---

[3]Withdrawals taken at end of each year.

Average returns can provide a misleading picture of what might happen. Yet financial-planning software and online calculators often run scenarios using average returns.

In the example in Table 1-2, the difference in ending account value based on averages verses actual market returns is $26,000. The sequence, or order in which the returns occurred, left you with 24% less money than a projection based on averages said you would have. Now you know why it's called sequence risk!

A series of poor returns early in your retirement years, once you start taking income, can have an exponential effect. If you have a sequence of bad returns early on, and you are withdrawing income each year, your future portfolio will look far different than if you had a sequence of good returns early on—even if, over time, the average annualized returns for both time periods are identical.

This example illustrates the effect the order of annual returns can have, and for simplicity's sake I am basing it on one stock market index. No prudent person would invest their retirement savings in just one stock market index.

CD (certificate of deposit) investors could have experienced a poor outcome for different reasons. Table 1-3 shows CD rates, for a one-month term, from 2000–2011.

Table 1-3. One-month CD rates 2000–2011

Calendar Year	Average one-month CD rates (%)	Annual Income per $100,000
2000	6.60	$6,600
2001	4.20	$4,200
2002	1.80	$1,800
2003	1.20	$1,200
2004	1.40	$1,400
2005	3.26	$3,260
2006	5.15	$5,150
2007	5.46	$5,460
2008	3.10	$3,100
2009	0.44	$440
2010	0.24	$240
2011	0.20	$200

As you can see, planning for a stable income can be difficult when the annual interest you might earn per $100,000 of savings can vary from $6,600 to $200.

An unfortunate order of returns occurs for reasons outside your control. These can include poor economic conditions or lower interest rates. But you sometimes play a part as well, by making poor investment choices. Whatever the reason, the effect is the same.

To minimize the effect of sequence risk, you must invest differently. You have several choices:

- Take no market risk and choose only safe, guaranteed investments, which may require saving more to reach your goal.

- Segment your investments into what is needed for different legs of your trip: short, medium, and long term.

- Create a reserve account that can be used in low-return years.

- Use a disciplined rebalancing process.

All of these choices involve creating and sticking to an investment plan that is designed to reduce your exposure to sequence risk. Chapter 4 is devoted to exploring these various approaches.

Challenge Three: Inflation

There is no question prices will increase. As a result, everyone understands *inflation risk*. There is a question as to how much of an effect inflation will have on you once you are retired. You have your own unique spending patterns, and a one-size-fits-all rule won't work.

The standard rule of thumb is to assume a 3% inflation rate. In Table 1-4, you can see the effect of inflation on spending of $10,000 a year. The numbers show that it took about $23,000 in 2011 to buy what $10,000 could buy in 1982. The column listing the real inflation rate for each year shows that, indeed, over the last 30 years, inflation has averaged out to about 3% a year.

Table 1-4. Thirty years of inflation data

Calendar Year	$10,000 inflated at steady 3%	$10,000 inflated at real inflation rates	Real inflation rates (%)
1982	$10,300	$10,390	3.9
1983	$10,609	$10,785	3.8
1984	$10,927	$11,216	4.0
1985	$11,255	$11,642	3.8
1986	$11,593	$11,770	1.1
1987	$11,941	$12,288	4.4
1988	$12,299	$12,829	4.4
1989	$12,668	$13,419	4.6
1990	$13,048	$14,238	6.1
1991	$13,439	$14,679	3.1
1992	$13,842	$15,120	3.0
1993	$14,258	$15,543	2.8
1994	$14,685	$15,963	2.7
1995	$15,126	$16,394	2.7
1996	$15,580	$16,935	3.3
1997	$16,047	$17,222	1.7
1998	$16,528	$17,498	1.6
1999	$17,024	$17,970	2.7
2000	$17,535	$18,581	3.4
2001	$18,061	$18,879	1.6
2002	$18,603	$19,332	2.4
2003	$19,161	$19,699	1.9
2004	$19,736	$20,349	3.3
2005	$20,328	$21,041	3.4
2006	$20,938	$21,588	2.6
2007	$21,566	$22,473	4.1
2008	$22,313	$22,496	0.1
2009	$22,879	$23,103	2.7
2010	$23,566	$23,450	1.5
2011	$24,273	$24,153	3.0

If prices have more than doubled over the last 30 years, do retirees in their 80s and 90s spend twice as much as they did in their 60s? The answer seems to be no.

Ty Bernicke looked at U.S. Bureau of Labor's consumer expenditure data and concluded, "Traditional retirement planning assumes that a household's expenditures will increase a certain amount each year throughout retirement. Yet data from the U.S. Bureau of Labor's Consumer Expenditure Survey show that household expenditures actually decline as retirees age."[4]

▓ **Note**   My conclusions on retiree spending come not only from research but also from my experiences with real retirees. Not all research on retiree spending habits comes to the same conclusions I draw in this chapter.[5]

The decrease in spending that occurs as one moves into later decades was observed across all major categories, with the exception of health care. Health care expenditures increased as one aged, but spending in other areas declined enough to more than offset the increase in health care expenses.

Some might say this decline in spending occurs out of necessity, because retirees who have less are forced to spend less. This does not seem to be the case, however, as total spending was observed to decline even while net worth was increasing.

The conclusion: although prices on individual items will increase, retirees' overall level of spending tends to decrease, not increase, as they move into later age brackets. Planning for a steady 3%-a-year increase in total spending needs may result in oversaving for retirement.

▓ **Note**   Inflation has a bigger negative impact on low-income households than on high-income households.

Like other aspects of your plan, you need to look at inflation needs on a personal basis. If your income amply covers the basics and leaves you with spending money to spare, when prices rise you'll have room in your budget to cut back on discretionary spending items (although you may not want to).

---

[4]Ty Bernicke, "Reality Retirement Planning: A New Paradigm for an Old Science," *Journal of Financial Planning* vol. 18-6 (2005): 56.
[5]For additional analysis see Wade Pfau, "How Do Spending Needs Evolve During Retirement?" *Advisor Perspectives* (March 2012), www.advisorperspectives.com/ newsletters12/How_Do_Spending_Needs_Evolve_During_Retirement.php.

If you live on a tight budget, mild increases in prices on necessities such as food, household items, and health care may have a bigger impact on you.

Factoring the effects of inflation into your planning decisions is important. Here are some options that can improve your ability to adjust to rising prices:

- Delay the start date of your Social Security benefits.

- Grow your own food.

- Choose an energy-efficient lifestyle.

- Use savings vehicles that have an interest rate that adjusts with inflation, such as I-Bonds or TIPS (Treasury Inflation Protected Securities).

With a rapidly growing global population, you may see prices rise more quickly on food and energy items than on consumer durable items like furniture and electronics. In your post-work years, you are less likely to spend as much on furniture, electronics, and clothing; but you will most certainly be consuming food and energy.

If your financial resources are limited, you may want to focus your efforts around finding a home that is energy efficient, has access to public transportation, and has a yard conducive to growing basic food items. The time invested in such planning is likely to deliver a far higher return than trying to find the best mutual fund.

Challenge Four: Overspending

There are things you can control, and things you can't. One of my frustrations with the media—and with the financial services industry—is that they are so good at getting you to focus your efforts and energy on the wrong things.

Look at Figure 1-2, which I call the *control box*. The bottom right-hand corner represents the things that you have the least control over and that have the lowest impact on your long-term success.

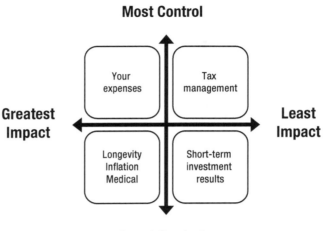

Most Control

Your expenses	Tax management

Greatest Impact ← → **Least Impact**

Longevity Inflation Medical	Short-term investment results

Least Control

Figure 1-2. The control box helps you see where to focus your financial-planning efforts

The top left-hand corner is where you have both control and impact: your expenses. It's also where a lurking problem resides for many: *overspending risk.*

Accounting for future spending is a challenge. Twenty years ago, could you have told me what you would spend each year going forward?

You may spend more in your first few years out of the work force, perhaps traveling and diving into new hobbies. Others may spend less than they did while working, perhaps by downsizing and enjoying a simpler, less-demanding lifestyle.

Estimating post-work spending is most certainly a case where a one-size-fits-all rule doesn't work. Your expenses will vary depending on your chosen lifestyle. Your choices will vary depending on your values.

Suppose after analysis you discover you can retire five years earlier if you are willing to spend $10,000 a year less? You may willingly find a way to downsize your lifestyle in order to exit the work force early. Or you may look at this trade-off and choose to work longer to insure a continued higher standard of living well into your later years.

Health care spending is another unknown. If you want to exit the work force before age 65 (when Medicare coverage begins), you must accurately estimate and account for the cost of insurance, which can be hefty.

After Medicare begins, you still have Medicare Part B premiums, and Medicare Part D drug coverage premiums, and if you want to be fully insured you'll also be paying premiums for a Medicare Supplement or a Medicare Advantage plan, as well as long-term care insurance.

When you create a model that determines how successfully your finances can meet your future needs, that model is based on a specific amount of annual spending. At some income levels, spending $5,000 a year more than what is projected in your model means your plan may not work, and the 78-year-old or 82-year-old you may be in trouble.

Overspending doesn't always come from spending too much on extras like travel, hobbies, eating out, and such. It can come from inaccurately projecting what you will need.

A successful spending plan needs flexibility built in. Just like now, in retirement you will not spend exactly the same amount each and every year. You need some wiggle room.

Here are the keys to avoiding overspending:

- Estimate current spending compared to post-work spending needs based on your lifestyle decisions
- Build in estimates for health care costs
- Track your spending in relation to your long-term plan
- Take corrective measures when overspending occurs
- Accurately project taxes in retirement

In Chapter 2, you'll begin to incorporate these actions into your plan.

A Note on Estimating Taxes

A spending plan is incomplete until it incorporates taxes. Tax management is another area in which you have some control, but accurately estimating taxes in retirement can be tricky. Many people make mistakes in this area when they run financial projections.

Here are a few areas where taxes get overlooked:

- Each withdrawal from a Traditional IRA, 401(k), or other tax-deferred account[6] is taxed at your ordinary income tax rate. These withdrawals may make more of your Social Security income taxable.

- At age 70 1/2, you are required to take withdrawals from retirement accounts like IRAs and 401(k)s. This requirement—called a required minimum distribution—creates an increase in taxable income and may cause other sources of income you have to be taxed at a higher rate.

- Upon the death of a spouse, your tax filing status changes from married to single, leaving many spouses with less after-tax income because of the change in filing status.

- If you have money in after-tax savings and in pre-tax retirement accounts, the decision about when to withdraw money from which type of account will affect the amount of taxes you pay each year.

As things stand today, many financial services companies and advisors do not incorporate tax planning into their processes. How can you deliver appropriate advice without looking at someone's entire household financial situation, including taxes? I don't think you can.

Although you can't control taxes, you can manage taxes in a way that may deliver more after-tax income.

In Chapter 5, I will teach you how to take taxes into consideration as you go forward into your transitional years and which factors play a role in reducing taxes and maximizing your after-tax income. I'm also going to encourage you to use software or seek professional advice to make sure your numbers are accurate.

---

[6]ROTH IRA withdrawals are generally tax free if you follow the rules and they are not included in the formula that determines the amount of your Social Security that will be subject to income taxes.

Summary

Your financial planning should be noticeably different as you move into your 50s and beyond. A well-designed scenario accounts for all of the following:

- *Longevity risk:* The potential for a long-lived you and/or a long-lived spouse

- *Sequence risk:* The unknown order of investment returns and interest rates

- *Inflation risk:* Increases in prices, particularly on necessities such as food, energy, and health care

- *Overspending risk:* Miscalculating what you may need to spend and thus spending down savings too quickly in retirement

To appropriately align your finances for a transition out of the work force, and to account for these new challenges, you need to look at the financial resources of your entire household. This is the only approach that makes sense.

You'll learn how to do this in Chapter 2.

Starting with Planning Basics

Balance Sheet, Income Timeline, and Spending Plan

If you don't design your own life plan, chances are you'll fall into someone else's plan. And guess what they have planned for you? Not much.

—Jim Rohn

I worked in a CPA firm for several years. One year, one of the managing partners announced he was leaving. Knowing I was responsible for financial services at the firm, and thinking I might be interested, he stopped by a few days after the announcement to tell me his story.

Barely five years back, he said, he had put together his first personal balance sheet. A simple list of everything he owned, minus everything he owed. After adding it all up, he saw he was in a hole. He earned an attractive salary, but he wasn't using the money wisely.

He started tracking his net worth diligently. He watched as he paid down debts and accumulated savings. He then started looking for investment opportunities. He was lucky enough to catch the real estate market on its upswing (yes, before 2007), and in five years his net worth went from negative to over $10 million.

We can't all get to $10 million in five years. But we can all use a personal balance sheet to improve where we're going.

■ **Tip**   Use a personal balance sheet to get to an improved place. When you focus on your numbers on a regular basis, reaching financial goals becomes much easier.

On a smaller scale, I used the same concept to dig myself out of a hole. I had taken a 100% commission job that wasn't working out so well. I had moved across the country, depleted my savings, and was rapidly racking up debt. I thought about the CPA's story.

I started adding up my debts. I had over $25,000 in credit card debt and no savings. I remember feeling physical pain as I looked at the situation. I began, every month, to track my spending diligently and pay down more debt. Each time the credit card statements came in, I dutifully recorded the new lower balance. Sometimes it seemed as if the debt was only inching down. At other times seeing the progress that was being made motivated me to pay down debt faster.

Today the credit card debt is gone, and in place of tracking debt, I track my net worth. Updating it is a simple process of recording account balances at the end of each quarter.

Sometimes getting started is painful. If you are not where you want to be at this point in your life it can be difficult to sit down and take a detailed look at your finances. If you are reluctant, work through it, and do it anyway. It's worth it.

It is also easy to get sidetracked by questions and want quick, easy answers. I receive weekly e-mail inquiries from people who want my opinion on an investment they own or an annuity they are considering. Sometimes they want to know if they should buy long-term care insurance or when they should begin their Social Security benefits.

Would you think of e-mailing a doctor you don't know and saying, "Hey doc, what medicine should I be taking?"

That's how these questions sound to me—completely out of place.

I am always tempted to respond with something along the lines of, "How the heck should I know? I don't know you."

Your money has a job to do for you. To pick an investment effectively, you must define that job and the future role that money needs to fulfill. To define the job your money has, you must start with an accurate picture of the whole spectrum of financial resources you have.

Tracking your net worth is the starting point for getting a handle on your entire household financial situation. You have to take stock of what you have to work with.

Throughout this chapter and book, you'll find exercises and examples to help you do that. You may find it beneficial to read through them without stopping to complete the worksheets and, after you have finished the book, circle back and go through the exercises one by one. Or you may feel compelled to complete the exercises as you go along. There is no right or wrong way to do it.

Whether you do the exercises now or later—and whether you use online tools, an Excel spreadsheet, Quicken or other software programs, or professional advisors—the basics matter, and this chapter is about the basics.

In addition to covering the basics, this chapter briefly introduces you to many topics that will be covered in additional depth later. When aligning your financial decisions toward a common goal, a decision in one area affects the results in another. By starting with the basics, you will begin to see how it all works. Once you have the big picture in place, you can dive into the details and complexities of individual decisions.

Your Personal Balance Sheet

A company must keep a balance sheet, a complete list of its assets and liabilities. Financial planning starts the same way, by creating a personal balance sheet. It is a snapshot of your financial situation at a given point in time.

Take a look at Figure 2-1, a personal balance sheet for Steve and Carol. Keep in mind that net worth is simply all your assets (investment accounts, house, and so on) minus all your liabilities (mortgage, credit card debt, car loan, and so forth).

Steve & Carol
Personal Balance Sheet
As of: January 1, 2013

	Asset	Liability	Net Worth
A. ACCESSIBLE SAVINGS/INVESTMENTS			
Bank Accounts			
Checking	$5,000	0	$5,000
Savings/Credit Unions	10,000	0	10,000
Certificates of Deposit	0	0	0
Consumer Debt			
Credit card	0	0	0
Other Non-Retirement Savings			
Money Market acccounts	48,000	0	48,000
Gov't Bonds (I, EE, H bonds)	0	0	0
Stocks	0	0	0
Brokerage accounts	0	0	0
Mutual fund accounts	226,000	0	226,000
Life Insurance Cash Value	0	0	0
A. TOTAL ACCESSIBLE SAVINGS	$289,000	$0	$289,000
B. RETIREMENT ACCOUNTS			
Retirement Accounts 1:			
IRA - Steve	$445,000	0	$445,000
ROTH IRA - Steve	30,000	0	30,000
Stock Options - Steve	0	0	0
Retirement Accounts 2:			
IRA - Carol	41,000	0	41,000
SEP IRA - Carol	0	0	0
B. TOTAL RETIREMENT	$516,000	$0	$516,000
C. REAL ESTATE & OTHER			
Residence	$310,000	$123,000	$187,000
C. TOTAL REAL ESTATE & OTHER	$310,000	$123,000	$187,000
TOTAL ASSETS (A+B+C)	$1,115,000	$123,000	$992,000

Figure 2-1. Steve and Carol's personal balance sheet

Once you have a personal balance sheet, you can use it to track and monitor your progress toward a goal.

To prepare your personal balance sheet, gather the following documents or have your login and password information available to access the information online:

- Bank statements
- Investment account statements
- Mortgage statements
- Retirement account statements

Use the following guidelines to list your financial resources in order of how easily accessible they are:

1. *Accessible Savings/Investments:* Start with accounts that are most accessible at the top and work your way down to accounts that are less accessible. (By *accessible* I mean accounts that do not have surrender charges or large tax liabilities associated with withdrawals.) The sample statement in Figure 2-1 lists easily accessible funds at the top, like savings, money market accounts, and mutual funds that are not inside retirement accounts. If you own Series I, H, HH, E, or EE bonds, these belong in section A also.

2. *Retirement Accounts:* Next, list retirement accounts and other tax-deferred accounts such as fixed or variable annuities. Retirement accounts are not considered as accessible because accessing the money may trigger taxes and penalties. Annuities may also assess penalties on accessing funds before age 59 1/2, which is why they belong in this section.

3. *Real Estate and Other:* When deciding what to put on your list, determine whether it is an asset that can be used for future income. For Steve and Carol, I included the net value of the home under Real Estate and Other, as this equity may be used later in the form of a reverse mortgage, or the home may be sold. "Other" assets that may someday be used for income could include gold, silver, or collectibles. One of my clients had a large gun collection, which his wife sold after his death.

4. *Liabilities:* Now add in any debts you have in the Liability column.

5. *Total Assets:* In the far right column at the bottom of your sheet, tally up what you own minus what you owe. This is your net worth.

Your goal in this exercise is not to list everything you own that has value. I noticeably left personal property off the list. The goal is to be prudent about which things you own that could reasonably be converted into income sources at some point in the future.

Sometimes determining where some items fit and whether they even belong on your personal balance sheet can be challenging. Here are a few examples:

- *Cash value life insurance*: If you plan on keeping the policy until death, than all the cash is not available for income purposes, but a portion of it may be.

- *Automobiles*: A paid-off auto you're using does not likely belong on the list. However, a collectible that may be sold one day might.

- *Automobile loans*: You can include this liability on the personal balance sheet, but typically I do not. Instead I include ongoing transportation expenses in the Spending Plan, which you'll create later.

- *Your home*: Your home equity, or a portion thereof, can be used for future income if needed. For this reason I typically do include homes on the personal balance sheet.

During your high earning years, your goal is to work toward increasing your net worth. Once you have transitioned to retirement, this goal may change.

It is not uncommon for a client to tell me that their goal is to "die with a dollar in the bank." They want to spend as much as they can without running out. They are okay with a controlled and gradual decline in their net worth.

Others would rather spend less and focus on leaving funds to future generations.

Steve and Carol's net worth is $992,000. To determine if this number is sufficient to provide their desired income once they are no longer working, they have to develop an income timeline.

MAKE THE JOB EASIER ONLINE

There are some great online resources you can use to gauge your financial well-being. Some of them are limited in scope, and some are more comprehensive. This sidebar provides a few suggestions for trusted resources.

ESPlanner Basic

ESPlanner Basic is a free financial-planning software program designed by Larry Kotlikoff. You can upgrade to an advanced version to run more detailed scenarios. The advantage to this type of program is that it runs detailed tax calculations behind the scenes, resulting in a more accurate forecast. You can learn more at http://basic.esplanner.com.

Retire Logix for iPhone and Android

For a fun way to get a general idea of how well prepared you are for a transition out of the workforce, try Retire Logix on your iPhone or Android smartphone. It's a cool program that allows you to adjust all your numbers with slide bars. You can learn more at www.retirelogix.com.

Budgeting/Spending Plan Software

I track my spending on a holistic basis. Each month I look at my total withdrawals from my bank account and record it in a spreadsheet. If my withdrawals start to run too high, I start spending less. This works better for me than keeping detailed track of where my money goes. Although my type of system might work for some, others may need more detail. Budgeting software can help. If you're looking for software, here are a few resources:

- You Need a Budget: www.youneedabudget.com

- Mint.com: www.mint.com

- Quicken: www.quicken.intuit.com

Your Income Timeline

As mentioned, a balance sheet is a snapshot in time. An income timeline is more like a movie, fluid and moving. As a result, it provides more information than the balance sheet can.

Unlike the income statement common in the business world, which focuses on a single year, an income timeline looks at what will happen over multiple years. Think about it this way: to project how your personal balance sheet may change over time, you will need to look at when you can add to savings and when you need to take withdrawals.

Eventually, you'll do this most effectively with math formulas in an Excel spreadsheet or by using other software. I suggest laying it out on paper or in a simple Excel spreadsheet first.

You'll use your income timeline for several purposes:

- To provide an estimate of the income you will need from savings on a year-by-year basis once you, your spouse, or both of you are no longer in the workforce

- To provide an estimate of total savings and investments needed to maintain a desired standard of living throughout retirement

- To help you see how much of your income will come from guaranteed sources, which will eventually help guide you toward investment choices that are most appropriate for you

Let's see how it's done.

Drawing Your Timeline

Figures 2-2 through 2-4 show Steve and Carol's income timeline. Use them and the instructions below as guidelines to create your own timeline. Across the top you'll put the calendar year and your age. Down the side you'll put income sources.

Steve & Carol, Income Timeline – Taking Social Security Now
As of: Beginning of Year 2013

# of Years	1	2	3	4	5	6	7	8	9	10
Calendar Year	2013	2014	2015	2016	2017	2018	2019	2020	2021	2022
Fixed Sources of Income										
Steve (age)	66	67	68	69	70	71	72	73	74	75
Earnings	$48,000	$48,000	$48,000	$48,000	$48,000	0	0	0	0	0
Pension	0	0	0	0	0	0	0	0	0	0
Social Security	$17,616	$26,424	$26,424	$26,424	$26,424	$26,424	$26,424	$26,424	$26,424	$26,424
Life Insurance	0	0	0	0	0	0	0	0	0	0
Other	0	0	0	0	0	0	0	0	0	0
Carol (age)	62	63	64	65	66	67	68	69	70	71
Earnings	0	0	0	0	0	0	0	0	0	0
Pension	0	0	0	0	0	0	0	0	0	0
Annuity	0	0	0	0	0	0	0	0	0	0
Social Security	$9,185	$10,020	$10,020	$10,020	$10,020	$10,020	$10,020	$10,020	$10,020	$10,020
Other	0	0	0	0	0	0	0	0	0	0
A. Total Fixed Income:	$74,801	$84,444	$84,444	$84,444	$84,444	$36,444	$36,444	$36,444	$36,444	$36,444
B. Desired Gross Income:	$80,000	$80,000	$80,000	$80,000	$80,000	$80,000	$80,000	$80,000	$80,000	$80,000
C. $ Needed from Savings: (A minus B)	($5,199)	$4,444	$4,444	$4,444	$4,444	($43,556)	($43,556)	($43,556)	($43,556)	($43,556)
D. Cumulative Savings Needed: (above line is a simple sum)	($5,199)	($755)	$3,689	$8,133	$12,577	($30,979)	($74,535)	($118,091)	($161,647)	($205,203)

Money needed today, discounted at a 2% real return, to get to ages:

	Simple sum of dollars, no discount rate:
85/81 $499,163	
90/86 $639,203	$640,763
95/91 $766,415	$858,543
99/95 $859,742	$1,076,323
	$1,250,547

Figure 2-2. Page 1 of Steve and Carol's income timeline

# of Years	11	12	13	14	15	16	17	18	19	20	21	22
Calendar Year	2023	2024	2025	2026	2027	2028	2029	2030	2031	2032	2033	2034
Fixed Sources of Income												
Steve (age)	76	77	78	79	80	81	82	83	84	85	86	87
Earnings	0	0	0	0	0	0	0	0	0	0	0	0
Pension	0	0	0	0	0	0	0	0	0	0	0	0
Social Security	$26,424	$26,424	$26,424	$26,424	$26,424	$26,424	$26,424	$26,424	$26,424	$26,424	$26,424	$26,424
Life Insurance	0	0	0	0	0	0	0	0	0	0	0	0
Other	0	0	0	0	0	0	0	0	0	0	0	0
Carol (age)	72	73	74	75	76	77	78	79	80	81	82	83
Earnings	0	0	0	0	0	0	0	0	0	0	0	0
Pension	0	0	0	0	0	0	0	0	0	0	0	0
Annuity	0	0	0	0	0	0	0	0	0	0	0	0
Social Security	$10,020	$10,020	$10,020	$10,020	$10,020	$10,020	$10,020	$10,020	$10,020	$10,020	$10,020	$10,020
Other	0	0	0	0	0	0	0	0	0	0	0	0
A. Total Fixed Income:	$36,444	$36,444	$36,444	$36,444	$36,444	$36,444	$36,444	$36,444	$36,444	$36,444	$36,444	$36,444
B. Desired Gross Income:	$80,000	$80,000	$80,000	$80,000	$80,000	$80,000	$80,000	$80,000	$80,000	$80,000	$80,000	$80,000
C. $ Needed from Savings: (A minus B)	($43,556)	($43,556)	($43,556)	($43,556)	($43,556)	($43,556)	($43,556)	($43,556)	($43,556)	($43,556)	($43,556)	($43,556)
D. Cumulative Savings Needed: (above line is a simple sum)	($248,759)	($292,315)	($335,871)	($379,427)	($422,983)	($466,539)	($510,095)	($553,651)	($597,207)	($640,763)	($684,319)	($727,875)

Figure 2-3. Page 2 of Steve and Carol's income timeline

| # of Years | 23 | 24 | 25 | 26 | 27 | 28 | 29 | 30 | 31 | 32 | 33 | 34 | 35 | 36 |
Calendar Year	2035	2036	2037	2038	2039	2040	2041	2042	2043	2044	2045	2046	2047	2048
Fixed Sources of Income														
Steve (age)	88	89	90	91	92	93	94	95	96	97	98	99	100	101
Earnings	0	0	0	0	0	0	0	0	0	0	0	0	0	0
Pension	0	0	0	0	0	0	0	0	0	0	0	0	0	0
Social Security	$26,424	$26,424	$26,424	$26,424	$26,424	$26,424	$26,424	$26,424	$26,424	$26,424	$26,424	$26,424	$26,424	$26,424
Life Insurance	0	0	0	0	0	0	0	0	0	0	0	0	0	0
Other	0	0	0	0	0	0	0	0	0	0	0	0	0	0
Carol (age)	84	85	86	87	88	89	90	91	92	93	94	95	96	97
Earnings	0	0	0	0	0	0	0	0	0	0	0	0	0	0
Pension	0	0	0	0	0	0	0	0	0	0	0	0	0	0
Annuity	0	0	0	0	0	0	0	0	0	0	0	0	0	0
Social Security	$10,020	$10,020	$10,020	$10,020	$10,020	$10,020	$10,020	$10,020	$10,020	$10,020	$10,020	$10,020	$10,020	$10,020
Other	0	0	0	0	0	0	0	0	0	0	0	0	0	0
A. Total Fixed Income:	$36,444	$36,444	$36,444	$36,444	$36,444	$36,444	$36,444	$36,444	$36,444	$36,444	$36,444	$36,444	$36,444	$36,444
B. Desired Gross Income:	$80,000	$80,000	$80,000	$80,000	$80,000	$80,000	$80,000	$80,000	$80,000	$80,000	$80,000	$80,000	$80,000	$80,000
C. $ Needed from Savings: (A minus B)	($43,556)	($43,556)	($43,556)	($43,556)	($43,556)	($43,556)	($43,556)	($43,556)	($43,556)	($43,556)	($43,556)	($43,556)	($43,556)	($43,556)
D. Cumulative Savings Needed: (above line is a simple sum)	($771,431)	($814,987)	($858,543)	($902,099)	($945,655)	($989,211)	($1,032,767)	($1,076,323)	($1,119,879)	($1,163,435)	($1,206,991)	($1,250,547)	($1,294,103)	($1,337,659)

Figure 2-4. Page 3 of Steve and Carol's income timeline

- *Fixed Sources of Income*: If married or planning with a significant other, you'll want to break out income sources separately for each of you. Each source of income should have its own line so you can adjust amounts and when they may start or stop. Note: Investment income does not belong on the income timeline. If you have an annuity that pays you guaranteed income, however, that does belong in your timeline. You'll total all sources of fixed income.

- *Desired Gross Income*: Below your annual income totals, you are going to estimate your annual gross spending needs. *Gross* means all expenditures in a year, including taxes you will have to pay. Start with a ballpark estimate, such as your current income. You'll work to revise this number later. In Steve and Carol's case, they estimate they will need about $80,000 a year.

- *$ Needed from Savings*: Calculate the annual difference between your sources of income and your expected expenses. This is the amount you would need to withdraw from savings to maintain your stated living expenses.

- *Total Savings Needed*: Sum your needed savings withdrawals through each year from now through life expectancy. This allows you to see at any given point in time the cumulative dollar amount of savings withdrawals you would need to get to that age.

In Figure 2-2, you can see that Steve plans to continue working for the next five years. During 2013, Steve will have a partial year of Social Security if he starts his benefits at his age 66 (his birthday is in April). Carol receives almost a full year of Social Security if she starts her benefits at 62, because her birthday is in January. From 2015–2017 they will be able to contribute some money to savings. After that they will need to withdraw savings to meet their desired spending level.

To get a rough estimate of their total income needs, you sum line C from now through life expectancy. I've provided a simple sum by just adding up each year's required withdrawal from savings up until the respective ages of 85/81, 90/86, 95/91 and 99/95. I provide a simple sum because you can do this at home on paper without any formulas. However, a simple sum is misleading. Here's why: Your savings will earn something. Simply adding up the amounts needed will overstate the amount of money you need today to meet your future income goals.

If you need $10,000 in 10 years, at a 3% inflation rate what you'll really need is $13,439 to buy the equivalent of $10,000 of goods and services. If you think you'll earn a 5% return on saving/investments, then you need $8,250 today earning 5% a year. That will grow into the $13,439 you need in 10 years.

To simplify the math, you can use the difference between what you think your savings will earn (5%) and what you think inflation will be (3%). This difference is often referred to as your *real return*, or the return in excess of inflation that you expect to receive.

In the examples in this book, I will use that 2% difference[1] as the *discount rate*, which means the rate needed to translate tomorrow's dollars into today's dollars.

The bottom of Figure 2-2 totals the amount needed from savings in the "Simple Sum" entry on the bottom right (row C totaled through the respective ages shown) and shows the equivalent number discounted by a real return of 2% in the "Money needed today" entry on the bottom left. Both sets of numbers are shown through the respective ages listed in Table 2-1 (numbers below are rounded down to nearest thousand).

Table 2-1. Present Value vs. Simple Sum

Ages of Couple	Money Needed Today	Simple Sum
85/81	$499,000	$640,000
90/86	$639,000	$858,000
95/91	$766,000	$1,076,000
99/95	$859,000	$1,250,000

The numbers in the "Money needed today" column are called *present values*. In this example, for a given age the number is what you would need in the bank at the beginning of 2013 earning a real rate of return of 2% to meet the stated future cash flow needs.

You can compare this present value to Steve and Carol's net worth to get a very rough estimate of how well prepared they are for a transition out of work.

Their net worth from their personal balance sheet (back in Figure 2-1) is $992,000. After discussion, they decide they do not want to include their home value as being available for future income, so that leaves them with $805,000 ($992,000 minus the $187,000 net equity in the home). This number compared to the present value of savings withdrawals needed to get to ages 90/86 would be sufficient. Compared to ages 99/95, it is not. This is longevity risk in action.

---

[1] The actual real return is calculated as $100 \times (1.05/1.03 - 1) = 1.94\%$, so when I say I am using a 2% real return, the calculations have been done using this 1.94% discount rate. Thank you, Wade Pfau, for your advice on this.

The women in Carol's family tend to be long-lived, so these numbers make Steve and Carol nervous. They want to make sure their plan sufficiently provides for Carol through age 95.

A Word of Caution

The basics are just that: basic. In Steve and Carol's analysis, I have estimated inflation and investment returns by using a 2% real return as a discount rate. I have not accounted for taxes or future changes in their spending needs. As you learn how to account for these items, the numbers will change.

You'll learn how to further refine these numbers by:

- Adding a detailed spending analysis that breaks spending into fixed and flex (flexible) components.

- Determining how you want to account for inflation.

- Adjusting how and when you claim your Social Security benefits.

- Estimating a realistic growth rate for savings and investments.

- Accounting for taxes.

The advantage of drawing out a basic scenario on paper, or in a spreadsheet, is that you gain a better understanding of what is happening. It also gives you a first draft estimate of how well prepared you may be.

If you tally up your numbers through the longest life expectancy you think reasonable, and your current net worth is more than your total income needed from savings, it is likely you are adequately prepared.

If your current net worth doesn't come close to the total income needed from savings, it may be that you will need to adjust your expectations, work longer, spend less, or do a combination of these things.

As you move through this book, you will use your timeline to visually see what decisions can improve your outcome.

A NOTE ABOUT SOCIAL SECURITY

Social Security mails annual statements to those age 60 and older, but you don't have to wait for a statement. You can create an online account to access an estimate of your future Social Security benefits at www.socialsecurity.gov/mystatement/.

Chapter 3 is devoted to Social Security. In it, I explain the information on your statement and suggest ways to make decisions concerning your Social Security benefits that are likely to increase your after-tax retirement income.

For the time being, I think it is helpful to create an income timeline that shows you what your financial picture looks like claiming Social Security when you think you should claim it. This becomes your *before* picture. Later you can create a second scenario showing how much you can improve your situation by making decisions differently—your *after* picture.

If You're Close to Leaving the Workforce: Adjusting Your Timeline for What-ifs

If you want to transition out of work sooner rather than later, you should use your income timeline to begin to see how your fixed sources of income will change based on the choices you make.

For example, you could draw out a timeline that shows what happens if you delay the start date of your Social Security benefits. You'll see what this looks like in the next chapter.

If married, you may want a timeline that shows what happens if one of you has a shorter than expected life. (Hint: At the death of the first spouse, the surviving spouse continues to receive only the larger Social Security amount; the smaller amount goes away and is no longer included in the timeline.)

If you have a pension option and are considering whether to take a single life option or an option that provides income for a surviving spouse, you could create a timeline showing both choices.

This may sound like a lot of work. But remember, retiring is something you'll (probably) only do once. Many of the decisions you'll need to make are irrevocable. Getting a solid plan in place is well worth the investment of time.

If You're Still Planning on Working for Quite Some Time

If you still have many years of contributing to savings ahead of you, the income timeline can help you see what your money can do for you in the future.

You will want to focus on saving in a tax-efficient way, increasing your earning power, and carefully choosing investments that have the best likelihood of accomplishing your goals. I cover those things in later chapters.

Regardless of your proximity to transitioning out of the workforce, accurately accounting for spending needs is critical to your success.

Your Spending Plan

My third year in college, I asked my dad for money. I can't remember what for. He asked me for a budget in return. I was mad. I didn't want to do a budget. Who wants to track where their money goes? Ugh.

In hindsight, dad taught me a valuable lesson. Banks don't hand out money without documentation, and perhaps parents shouldn't either.

I revved up both the determined and the playful side of my personality. If I was going to make a budget, by golly, it was going to be colorful. Armed with an array of multi-colored highlighters, I started going through my checkbook and bank statements. Every expense for the past six months got slotted into color-coded categories. I tallied up each category and divided by six to get a monthly average.

Budgeting has been part of my life since.

You don't have to budget to save money. Some people are naturals at spending less than they make. They don't need to track anything.

You do need a budget to make a successful transition out of the workforce. You need to know about how much you'll need to withdraw, and from where, and you can't determine that without an estimate of your spending needs.

▨ **Note** You must have a budget to make a successful transition out of the workforce.

You are going to need to break your expenses into two categories: fixed and flexed. *Fixed* expenses are necessities, such as food, health care, housing, and transportation. *Flex* expenses are extras, such as travel, eating out, entertainment, hobbies, and so on.

Later, when you match your fixed expenses with your fixed sources of income, you will learn how this can help you best select investments that are most appropriate for you.

Personally, I don't like the word *budget*. It sounds restrictive. So, I am going to call it a *spending plan* instead. A spending plan helps you make trade-offs that matter to you. For example, perhaps you think you don't have money to travel. As you begin to look at how you spend your money and create a plan, you realize you might be able to travel more by shopping less or downsizing your home or car.

There isn't a right or wrong way to spend your money. It is a matter of choosing to spend it on the things you most want to do. Many people unconsciously spend money on things that aren't that important to them. Once you create a spending plan, you can see if this is happening, and if it is, you can decide how to change it.

Honing Your Spending Plan

When starting your spending plan, I suggest that you initially guess what you think you spend in each category. Then create a second spending plan by tracking your actual spending habits. Seeing what you think you spend versus what you actually spend can be insightful.

To track actual spending habits, gather the following documents:

- One year's worth of statements from the primary checking account that you use to pay bills.

- One year's worth of statements from any credit or debit cards that you use.

If you use budgeting software, this information should be available and categorized within the software.

The sample spending plan in Figures 2-5 through 2-7 shows how to categorize expenses.

Steve & Carol Spending Plan				
	Monthly	**Annual**	**Fixed**	**Flex**
HOME				
Mortgage (Principal & Int.) or Rent	941	11,292	11,292	
2nd mortgage/Home equity line				
Real Estate taxes	175	2,100	2,100	
Homeowner's insurance	92	1,100	1,100	
Home repairs	250	3,000	3,000	
Home warranty				
Other:				
UTILITIES				
Electric	150	1,800	1,800	
Gas				
Water/Sewer/Trash	45	540	540	
Phone (Home)				
HOA:				
Other:				
HOME MAINTENANCE/UPKEEP & SERVICES				
Cable TV	100	1,200	1,200	
Internet	36	432	432	
Lawn care	100	1,200	1,200	
Pool/Garden				
House Cleaning				
Appliances (small & large)				
Other:				
FOOD				
Groceries	350	4,200	4,200	
Eating out	500	6,000	2,000	4,000
Drinks/parties				
TRANSPORTATION/VEHICLES				
Auto Payment	400	4,800	4,800	
Auto Payment				
Auto Insurance	75	900	900	
Auto Insurance	75	900	900	
Gas	150	1,800	1,800	
Maintenance	50	600	600	
Annual Registration	33	390	390	
Other:				

Figure 2-5. Page I of Steve and Carol's spending plan

MEDICAL

Health insurance premiums 1	274	3,288	3,288	
Health insurance premiums 2	718	8,616	8,616	
Health insurance (out of pocket)	100	1,200	1,200	
Doctor's visits (if not included above)				
Medicare Part B premiums	106	1,272	1,272	
Medicare Part D premiums	27	324	324	
Medicare Supplement/Advantage:				
Dental	83	1,000	1,000	
Prescriptions	50	600	600	
Eye care	17	200	200	
Chiropractic				
Other:				

OTHER INSURANCE

Life Insurance				
LTC Insurance	350	4,200	4,200	
Disability Insurance				

APPAREL

Clothing	200	2,400	2,400	
Shoes				

CHILDREN/GRANDCHILDREN

Day care				
Babysitting				
Camps/Events				
Allowance				
Lessons				
Clothing				
Current Tuition				
Savings				
Other:				

PERSONAL DEBT: List monthly payment

Credit card 1				
Credit card 2				
Personal loan				
Student loan				
Other:				

Figure 2-6. Page 2 of Steve and Carol's spending plan

OTHER EXPENSES

Cell phone	150	1,800	1,800	
Gym membership				
Monthly subscriptions	20	240	240	
Tobacco				
ATM/Cash purchases	200	2,400	2,400	
Massage				
Haircare/Haircuts	50	600	600	
Manicure/pedicure				
Drugstore/cosmetics				
Pets				
Storage Units				
Gifts (birthday/wedding/shower)	50	600	600	
Catalog/Ebay/Craigslist purchases				
Walmart/Target/Costco				
Home Depot				
Charity				
Personal Education/Union Dues				
Hobbies				
Antiquing/Photography				
Golf/Jewelry				
Season Tickets				
Cooking				
Books/Movies				
Arts/Crafts				
Tickets/events				
Airline tickets	125	1,500		1,500
Hotel	125	1,500		1,500

TAXES

Estimate income tax payments	500	6,000	6,000	
Taxes Withheld from paychecks				
Tax refund/amount owed				

	Monthly	Annual	Fixed	Flex
Grand Total:	**6,666**	**79,994**	**72,994**	**7,000**

Figure 2-7. Page 3 of Steve and Carol's spending plan

What to Watch Out For

There are certain items in your spending plan that need to be accounted for in a particular way. The suggestions I give in this section pertain to your mortgage, health care expenses, and how you might handle things if you primarily use a credit card for most of your discretionary monthly expenses.

Mortgage

If you have a mortgage, notice on the worksheet there are separate line items for principal and interest payments, real estate taxes, and homeowner's insurance. This is intentional.

Many mortgages wrap your real estate taxes and home owner's insurance into the payment. This is fine, but when your mortgage is paid off, the principal and interest payments go away, whereas the real estate taxes and homeowner's insurance expenses continue. That's an important distinction to make in a pre- and post-work budget.

In addition, mortgage interest is a tax-deductible item. If you have a large mortgage, as you pay it down, your taxes may go up. This is one of many reasons why projections that don't account for taxes are inaccurate.

Health Care Expenses

While working, your employer may be subsidizing the cost of your health insurance. Once you transition out of work, your premiums may be higher. In addition, you will likely choose a health care insurance that provides benefits that extend beyond basic Medicare coverage (Medicare is the mandatory U.S. medical coverage that begins at age 65).

In the Steve and Carol example, Steve is 65. He is on Medicare and has a Medicare supplement policy. Carol is not yet on Medicare, and her health-insurance premiums are higher than his. Their total medical expenses run about $16,500 a year, or 21% of their total spending. When a retiree is fully insured, spending 20–30% of monthly expenses on health care is not uncommon.

You can use the online health care calculator by HVS Financial (http://apps.hvsfinancial.com/hvadvisor/) to estimate your own current and future health care costs.

▨ **Caution**   In retirement, a full 20–30% of your spending may go toward health care—another reason to plan well. The online healthcare calculator at http://apps.hvsfinancial.com/hvadvisor/ will help you estimate your costs.

Many health insurance policies specify a $3,000 or $5,000 maximum amount you have to pay in any given year, with the insurance company covering expenses that exceed that amount. If an ongoing health event occurs, you may be incurring this deductible as an expense each and every year.

You need *liquid* savings (meaning not in a retirement account) to cover your deductible or out-of-pocket costs when they occur. At some point, those expenses will be incurred, and you will need to replenish the savings used. To be ultra-conservative, you could budget the entire out-of-pocket amount, or deductible amount, as if this expense will be incurred each and every year. As an alternative you could budget 25–50% of the amount as a contribution to savings (or to a Health Savings Account if you are eligible).

Credit/Debit Cards

If you are like me, you may use one or two credit or debit cards for most of your spending needs. Mine gets paid off each month.

If groceries, clothing, gas, and so forth typically go on one card, in lieu of filling in each category, you can put in your average monthly credit card expenses and leave the respective categories blank. This can be a quick and efficient way to assess overall spending. If you do this, some of this spending will need to be assigned to a fixed category (we all need to eat) and some to flex (we don't need to eat out five times a week, although we may like to).

THE FALLACY OF ONE-TIME EXPENSES

Businesses must budget too. In a former partnership, my business partner and I updated our business budget quarterly. In our first year of business, our actual expenditures always seemed higher than we had projected. There were things that would come up that we had deemed "one-time expenses," and so we didn't build them into our projections. After that first year, we put a permanent line item in our budget for one-time expenses.

The one-time expenses that get left out of personal budgets are not all that different than those that get left out of business budgets. Maybe the hot water heater had to be replaced last year. This year it might be the dishwasher, a termite problem, or a child that needs financial assistance. Make sure you include room for those one-time expenses that have a strange way of recurring every year.

Monthly, Annual, and Fixed vs. Flex

It is important to calculate each expense on a monthly and annual basis. When managing cash flow, think in terms of monthly expenses. For purposes of projecting expenses throughout a post-work era, having annual numbers to use in worksheets, spreadsheets, or software programs is helpful.

It is also helpful to take each annual expense and estimate what portion of it belongs in the fixed column verses the flex column. If you live in a modest house and plan to live there the rest of your life, the mortgage payment and associated expenses likely belong in the fixed column. If you live in a super-sized house and plan to downsize later, the portion of your mortgage and home maintenance that would be attributable to a smaller residence would belong in the fixed column, with the excess in the flex column.

Dividing expenses this way will help you evaluate trade-offs later. Some people will choose to reduce fixed expenses so they can have more flex, which for them may involve travel and hobbies. Others may choose to work longer so they can maintain both their fixed and flex expenses at their current levels.

Items That Conspicuously Go Missing

I never used to ask for detailed budgets from my clients. I mistakenly assumed that if they had been decent savers, they would have a handle on how much they spent. If they told me that in addition to mortgage and taxes, they spent about $50,000 a year, then I would use that number in their projections. Not anymore.

For some income levels, an increase of $3,000 a year in spending can mean the difference between having sufficient resources until the end of your life and not having enough.

Now I ask my clients to provide detailed information on spending. And I scour it for missing items.

Here are a few things that conspicuously go missing:

- Premiums for Medicare Parts B and D and Medicare supplement policies.

- New car purchases. If you own your car free and clear, that's great. At some point, you'll still need to replace it. That must be factored into your post-work budget.

- Replacement costs. If you own a home, at some point you'll need to replace furniture, the water heater, the roof, and so on. You must have a line item in your budget for these types of expenses.

- Annual expenses like property taxes and insurance premiums can easily be forgotten.

- Health insurance premiums for those who plan to leave the workforce before age 65. (The price tag for private health insurance between ages 55 and 65 can cause sticker shock. If you want to leave the workforce early, get quotes and factor this expense into your plan before you leave employment that subsidizes this expense for you.)

Gathering information on spending is tedious. The good news: once you spend the time creating a spending plan, updating it becomes quick and easy.

The purpose of gathering spending information is not to render judgment. We all place different values on how we spend our time and our money. The purpose is to use this information to help you make trade-offs that are based on what is important to you.

Exiting the traditional workforce early might be worth a downsized lifestyle to you. Or it might not. Once you see your options, you can decide.

Pre- and Post-Work Spending

This is the time to think about how to spend your money on things that matter the most to you. Do you want to travel more? Would you be willing to lower your fixed expenses by moving to a less expensive home?

What items in your spending plan might decrease post-work? Dry cleaning, transportation, and parking costs will decrease substantially for some.

What items in your spending plan might increase? If you plan on more airline travel to see family, account for this expense in your post-work spending plan.

You may find that your pre- and post-work spending plans total up to about the same amount, but that funds get spent on different things.

This is not an exercise where you simply fill in the blanks. Give thought to your lifestyle and to how a change in it will affect each item.

Your Spending Timeline

Your *spending timeline* helps you see when some expenses might drop off and others might appear. Here are a few examples:

- If you have a mortgage, at some point it will be paid off.

- If you are planning to leave the workforce early, you may be picking up health care premium expenses that your employer is currently paying. That expense will need to be added into your timeline at the appropriate time.

- If you want to travel during your first few years of retirement, you can use your spending timeline to account for this.

Steve and Carol's spending timeline is shown in Figures 2-8 and 2-9 as an example. Again, this is a "rough cut." It doesn't take inflation into account, for example.

Steve & Carol, Spending Timeline
As of: Beginning of Year 2013

# of Years	1	2	3	4	5	6	7	8	9
Calendar Year	2013	2014	2015	2016	2017	2018	2019	2020	2021
Ages	66/62				70/66				
Fixed Expenses									
Mortgage	$11,291	$11,291	$11,291	$11,291	$11,291	$11,291	$11,291	$11,291	$11,291
All other fixed items	$61,702	$61,702	$61,702	$61,702	$61,702	$61,702	$61,702	$61,702	$61,702
Total Fixed:	$72,993	$72,993	$72,993	$72,993	$72,993	$72,993	$72,993	$72,993	$72,993
Flex									
Flex items	$7,000	$7,000	$7,000	$7,000	$7,000	$7,000	$7,000	$7,000	$7,000
Total Flex:	$7,000	$7,000	$7,000	$7,000	$7,000	$7,000	$7,000	$7,000	$7,000
Total Desired Spending	$79,993	$79,993	$79,993	$79,993	$79,993	$79,993	$79,993	$79,993	$79,993

Figure 2-8. Page 1 of Steve and Carol's spending timeline

# of Years	10	11	12	13	14	15	16	17	18	19	20	21
Calendar Year	2022	2023	2024	2025	2026	2027	2028	2029	2030	2031	2032	2033
Ages	75/71					80/76					85/81	
Fixed Expenses												
Mortgage	$11,291	$11,291	$11,291	$11,291	$11,291	$11,291	0	0	0	0	0	0
All other fixed items	$61,702	$61,702	$61,702	$61,702	$61,702	$61,702	$61,702	$61,702	$61,702	$61,702	$61,702	$61,702
Total Fixed:	$72,993	$72,993	$72,993	$72,993	$72,993	$72,993	$61,702	$61,702	$61,702	$61,702	$61,702	$61,702
Flex												
Flex items	$7,000	$7,000	$7,000	$7,000	$7,000	$7,000	$7,000	$7,000	$7,000	$7,000	$7,000	$7,000
Total Flex:	$7,000	$7,000	$7,000	$7,000	$7,000	$7,000	$7,000	$7,000	$7,000	$7,000	$7,000	$7,000
Total Desired Spending	$79,993	$79,993	$79,993	$79,993	$79,993	$79,993	$68,702	$68,702	$68,702	$68,702	$68,702	$68,702

Figure 2-9. Page 2 of Steve and Carol's spending timeline

Steve and Carol recently refinanced to a 15-year mortgage. When they did their spending timeline, they could see how this expense would drop off in the year 2028.

They took their new, revised spending numbers and went back to their income timeline. Starting in the year their mortgage would be paid off, they lowered their desired income from $80,000 to $69,000 (spending numbers rounded up to nearest one thousand), as shown in Figures 2-10 and 2-11.

The result: the amount of income needed from savings using a 2% discount rate dropped to the following (numbers rounded down to nearest one thousand):

- Age 85/81: $460,000
- Age 90/86: $564,000
- Age 95/91: $659,000
- Age 99/95: $729,000

When compared to their current net worth of $992,000, Steve and Carol are starting to feel a little more comfortable.

The next step, covered in the next section, is for them to calculate what I call a *coverage ratio*.

Your Coverage Ratio

If I were to ask you if you want guaranteed income in retirement, you would likely say yes. Yet if I were to present you with tools that could provide such guaranteed income—tools like an immediate annuity, a reverse mortgage, or a delayed start date for your Social Security benefits—it is likely that (without education) you would turn them down.

When it comes to guaranteed income, you need to start with a different question: how much guaranteed income do you need? You can answer that with your income timeline and your spending timeline. The purpose of separating your fixed expenses from your flex expense is so you can compare fixed expenses to your fixed sources of income in your post-work years.

In Steve and Carol's revised income timeline (Figures 2-10 and 2-11), you can see that in 2018, when neither expects to be working, they have $36,444 of fixed income each year if they are both collecting Social Security. On their spending timeline, their fixed expenses total up to about $73,000 per year and later go down to about $62,000 (when the mortgage is paid off).

Their fixed income sources divided into fixed expenses provide a coverage ratio of .50, which goes up to .59 when their mortgage is paid off. This ratio is now included as a line item on their timeline.

Steve & Carol, Income Timeline - Taking Social Security Now - Mortgage Expense Gone in 2028
As of: Beginning of Year 2013

# of Years	1	2	3	4	5	6	7	8	9	10	11
Calendar Year	2013	2014	2015	2016	2017	2018	2019	2020	2021	2022	2023
Fixed Sources of Income											
Steve (age)	66	67	68	69	70	71	72	73	74	75	76
Earnings	$48,000	$48,000	$48,000	$48,000	$48,000	0	0	0	0	0	0
Pension	0	0	0	0	0	0	0	0	0	0	0
Social Security	$17,616	$26,424	$26,424	$26,424	$26,424	$26,424	$26,424	$26,424	$26,424	$26,424	$26,424
Life Insurance	0	0	0	0	0	0	0	0	0	0	0
Other	0	0	0	0	0	0	0	0	0	0	0
Carol (age)	62	63	64	65	66	67	68	69	70	71	72
Earnings	0	0	0	0	0	0	0	0	0	0	0
Pension	0	0	0	0	0	0	0	0	0	0	0
Annuity	0	0	0	0	0	0	0	0	0	0	0
Social Security	$9,185	$10,020	$10,020	$10,020	$10,020	$10,020	$10,020	$10,020	$10,020	$10,020	$10,020
Other	0	0	0	0	0	0	0	0	0	0	0
A. Total Fixed Income:	$74,801	$84,444	$84,444	$84,444	$84,444	$36,444	$36,444	$36,444	$36,444	$36,444	$36,444
Fixed Expenses	$72,993	$72,993	$72,993	$72,993	$72,993	$72,993	$72,993	$72,993	$72,993	$72,993	$72,993
Coverage Ratio	1.02	1.16	1.16	1.16	1.16	0.50	0.50	0.50	0.50	0.50	0.50
B. Desired Gross Income:	$80,000	$80,000	$80,000	$80,000	$80,000	$80,000	$80,000	$80,000	$80,000	$80,000	$80,000
C. $ Needed from Savings: (A minus B)	($5,199)	$4,444	$4,444	$4,444	$4,444	($43,556)	($43,556)	($43,556)	($43,556)	($43,556)	($43,556)

Money needed today, discounted at a
2% real return, to get to ages:

85/81	$460,230
90/86	$564,903
95/91	$659,988
99/95	$729,745

Simple sum of dollars, no discount rate:

$585,763
$748,543
$911,323
$1,041,547

Figure 2-10. Page 1 of Steve and Carol's revised income timeline

# of Years	12	13	14	15	16	17	18	19	20	21	22	23
Calendar Year	2024	2025	2026	2027	2028	2029	2030	2031	2032	2033	2034	2035
Fixed Sources of Income												
Steve (age)	77	78	79	80	81	82	83	84	85	86	87	88
Earnings	0	0	0	0	0	0	0	0	0	0	0	0
Pension	0	0	0	0	0	0	0	0	0	0	0	0
Social Security	$26,424	$26,424	$26,424	$26,424	$26,424	$26,424	$26,424	$26,424	$26,424	$26,424	$26,424	$26,424
Life Insurance	0	0	0	0	0	0	0	0	0	0	0	0
Other	0	0	0	0	0	0	0	0	0	0	0	0
Carol (age)	73	74	75	76	77	78	79	80	81	82	83	84
Earnings	0	0	0	0	0	0	0	0	0	0	0	0
Pension	0	0	0	0	0	0	0	0	0	0	0	0
Annuity	0	0	0	0	0	0	0	0	0	0	0	0
Social Security	$10,020	$10,020	$10,020	$10,020	$10,020	$10,020	$10,020	$10,020	$10,020	$10,020	$10,020	$10,020
Other	0	0	0	0	0	0	0	0	0	0	0	0
A. Total Fixed Income:	$36,444	$36,444	$36,444	$36,444	$36,444	$36,444	$36,444	$36,444	$36,444	$36,444	$36,444	$36,444
Fixed Expenses	$72,993	$72,993	$72,993	$72,993	$61,702	$61,702	$61,702	$61,702	$61,702	$61,702	$61,702	$61,702
Coverage Ratio	0.50	0.50	0.50	0.50	0.59	0.59	0.59	0.59	0.59	0.59	0.59	0.59
B. Desired Gross Income:	$80,000	$80,000	$80,000	$80,000	$69,000	$69,000	$69,000	$69,000	$69,000	$69,000	$69,000	$69,000
C. $ Needed from Savings: (A minus B)	($43,556)	($43,556)	($43,556)	($43,556)	($32,556)	($32,556)	($32,556)	($32,556)	($32,556)	($32,556)	($32,556)	($32,556)

Figure 2-11. Page 2 of Steve and Carol's revised income timeline

WHAT ABOUT THE MORTGAGE?

Steve and Carol will have several options with regard to their mortgage. They can

- Use non-retirement savings to pay it off all at once or through systematic withdrawals

- Use a reverse mortgage to pay it off

- Use a term certain immediate annuity to guarantee income available to pay the mortgage

Later chapters evaluate these choices in detail.

A coverage ratio of 1.0 means all your fixed expenses are covered by guaranteed sources of income. I am tempted to suggest you strive for a coverage ratio as close to 1.0 as possible. However, that is a rule of thumb that would not apply to everyone.

Rather than use the coverage ratio to define a target to shoot for, use it as a tool for having discussions about risk. If you overspend early in retirement and have a low coverage ratio later, and thus must make forced lifestyle changes to reduce spending, is that acceptable to you? Some will say yes. Others will prefer to lock in a higher minimum floor of guaranteed income.

■ **Tip** Coverage ratio is simply your fixed income divided by fixed expenses. If this ratio is 1.0 or higher, it means you have enough guaranteed income to offset all of your fixed expenses.

Steve and Carol are concerned about the gap between their guaranteed sources of income and their fixed expenses. They decide they would feel more comfortable with an additional $1,000 a month of guaranteed income. They will now need to explore the various ways of accomplishing this. Their initial thought is to buy an immediate annuity which guarantees income for life.

That is one possible solution. However, before they buy products, there are choices they may be able to make with their Social Security benefits that will improve their coverage ratio. I explore these choices in Chapter 3, where I look at an alternate version of their timeline.

Using Your Coverage Ratio to Make Better Investment Decisions

Calculating your coverage ratio can help lead you to an appropriate investment choice—a choice based on your plan and your concerns rather than on what a salesperson wants you to see.

Historically the focus has been on increasing returns or investing for upside during working and saving years. In your post-work years, the focus needs to be on defining an outcome. Comparing your fixed sources of income to your fixed expenses helps you define risks. Then you can begin to make decisions objectively and select investments that best cover those risks.

After evaluating risks, you may feel comfortable investing in a traditional portfolio of index funds (discussed in Chapter 4). Or you may want to secure your income with guaranteed choices. A combination of both can work too.

Making It Better

Once you have a basic scenario in place, the next step is figuring out how to make it better. Improving your baseline scenario has two components: planning decisions and lifestyle decisions. I frequently tell people, "I can show you the numbers. You have to bring your values to the table and decide what's right for you."

It is my job to share with you the planning decisions that can improve your outcomes. Each decision affects another. For example, the age at which you take Social Security affects how much you need to withdraw from savings, which affects how much in taxes you will pay. It is your job to define what *better* looks like to you from a lifestyle perspective. I can show you how to crunch the numbers, but I can't tell you whether you'll be happier working longer and having more post-work income or having more free time sooner, which in turn may mean driving a less-expensive car and living in a smaller home.

Each family has its own values, and faced with the same set of financial circumstances different people make different decisions. This is part of what makes us human. It is also what makes planning fun. You have a choice, and your choice may be different than your neighbor's.

There is one decision that almost every U.S. worker looking at a transition out of the workforce will be faced with. That is the decision about when to begin your Social Security benefits. For the most part, it is an irrevocable decision.

Every day, people begin their benefits without prudently considering their choices. In many cases, one choice can yield far more lifetime income than another. About half of Social Security recipients rely on Social Security to provide more than half their total income. For many, it is the most important post-work financial decision they make. That is the decision we'll look at next, in Chapter 3.

Summary

By creating a few basic financial schedules, you can begin to play with alternate futures and choose a path that best suits you. This chapter provided examples of the following to get you started:

- Personal balance sheet
- Income timeline
- Spending plan
- Spending timeline

These schedules will give you a 30,000-foot view on how well prepared you are to live off your acorns. You can then use these schedules to compare choices and see how to improve the view.

Social Security

How to Make the Most of It

> We can never insure one-hundred percent of the population against one-hundred percent of the hazards and vicissitudes of life. But we have tried to frame a law which will give some measure of protection to the average citizen and to his family against the loss of a job and against poverty-ridden old age.
>
> —Franklin D. Roosevelt

Since 2008, I have been writing an online advice column called MoneyOver55. At my first annual review, my editor asked me to write more about Social Security. I began reading everything I could find on the topic and writing as much as I could about it. It soon became my most popular topic.

As I added content, readers began asking me questions. Many questions are from informed readers who are trying to employ a suggestion in one of my articles, but when they go to the Social Security office they are told they cannot do what I say they can do. They write to me asking for a link to the source of my information. I send them back a link to Social Security's own web site. I love it when they share their stories with me. Here is a thank-you note I received from one reader:

> Dana,
>
> I just wanted to thank you again for your reference. I signed up for Social Security today based on my husband's benefits and will leave mine to accumulate. **So you were right**. And a note, the guy at Social Security said he has been working there for 25 years and never heard of this. At first he said I was wrong, as did his supervisor, but after reading his own web site (from your reference), and talking

to the regional management, he agreed that I had a choice and it got done. Thanks for your help.[1]

Even today, after years of reading and writing about it, Social Security makes my head hurt. The rules are far more complex than a glance at your Social Security statement would lead you to believe.

Making an uninformed choice can mean less income for the rest of your life. The decision about when to begin Social Security benefits is one of the biggest financial decisions many people ever make.

SOCIAL SECURITY STATISTICS

For those collecting benefits in 2010:[2]

- Social Security provided 90% or more of total income for 23% of marrieds and 46% of singles.

- Social Security provided 50% or more of total income for 53% of marrieds and 74% of singles.

What Your Benefits Are Worth

What would you guess your Social Security benefits are worth? A few hundred thousand dollars, maybe? Would it surprise you to know that the average single person living 25 years after retirement could receive $500,000 or more in total Social Security benefits? Many married couples will receive more than $1 million dollars in total benefits. It's a big pot of money. By making a wise decision, you can increase the size of the pot.

MORE SOCIAL SECURITY STATISTICS

According to the Social Security Administration, in 2010 the average monthly Social Security retirement benefit was $1,230 a month.[3] That's $14,760 a year. Starting in 1975, Social Security benefits have had a cost-of-living adjustment (COLA) applied to them, which means your benefits increase as prices rise (prices as measured by the Consumer Price Index, called the CPI-W).[4]

[1] http://moneyover55.about.com/b/2010/01/29/think-the-social-security-office-gives-you-the-right-answer-think-again.htm
[2] Size of Income, 1962 and 2010, www.ssa.gov/policy/docs/chartbooks/fast_facts/2012/fast_facts12.html#page5
[3] http://ssa-custhelp.ssa.gov/app/answers/detail/a_id/13/~/average-monthly-social-security-benefit-for-a-retired-worker
[4] www.ssa.gov/oact/cola/colaseries.html

Historically, benefits have increased at an annual rate in excess of 4%. If your $14,760 a year increases at just 2.5% a year for 25 years, you could expect to receive $504,168 in total benefits.

People miss out on thousands in benefits because they talk to a neighbor, friend, family member, well-intentioned-but-uninformed accountant or financial advisor, or even the Social Security office and get, often unintentionally, bad advice.

The decision about when to start your Social Security benefits has been examined by academics from numerous angles, and there is overwhelming evidence that, for most people, taking benefits at the earliest possible claiming age is not the wisest choice.

Let's look at a simple example. You can see Steve and Carol's possible Social Security benefit amounts in Table 3-1.

Table 3-1. Steve and Carol's Social Security Benefits

Age	Steve	Carol
62	----[5]	$835
66	$2,202	$1,114
70	$2,906	$1,470

Let's assume for a minute that Carol is single, and, as stated before, women in her family tend to live long. She thinks it is quite likely she'll live to 90 or beyond.

- If she starts benefits at 62 and lives to 90, she'll get $10,020 a year for 28 years, for a total of $280,560 (not including inflation increases).
- If she starts at 70, she'll get $17,640 a year for 20 years for a total of $352,800 (not including inflation increases).

Common sense tells you that if you are getting more total income from Social Security, you will spend less of your own money to have the same lifestyle.

Suppose Carol needs $25,000 a year in total income. Initially, like most people, she wants to take Social Security early.

---

[5]Steve is 65, so the amount he would have gotten at 62 is no longer relevant.

- If she does take it early, as already shown she gets $10,020 a year, which means she'll need to withdraw $14,980 a year from savings. Over 28 years that's $419,440 of savings withdrawals.

- If she waits to take Social Security until age 70, in her first eight years she must withdraw the full $25,000 a year from savings for a total of $200,000. Then for the remaining 20 years she only needs to withdraw $7,360 a year ($25,000 needed minus the $17,640 of Social Security starting at age 70) for a total of $147,200. Her total withdrawals are $347,200.

- Conclusion: by delaying the start date of her Social Security, Carol gets to spend the exact same amount, $25,000 a year, but needs to use $72,240[6] less of her savings to do it.

This is a simple example that does not include inflation increases that apply to Social Security benefits or an interest rate that would apply to savings. Nor does it factor in how your Social Security benefits are taxed (which in some cases can make delaying benefits look even more attractive).

I provide more detailed examples throughout this chapter. I can assure you, after running scenarios for years, that in a low-interest-rate environment, the answer does not materially change. When viewed in the context of your life expectancy (if married over your joint lives), delaying the start date of your Social Security benefits can result in preserving more of your own savings.[7]

WHO BENEFITS FROM DELAYING SOCIAL SECURITY?

According to economists John B. Shoven and Sita Nataraj Slavov, "The gains from delaying are greater at lower interest rates, for married couples relative to singles, for single women relative to single men, and for two-earner couples relative to one-earner couples."[8]

---

[6]Adding in the time value of money would change this number, although many argue the rate of return to use on an investment that is a fair comparison to Social Security would be the TIPS yield, which is currently about zero.

[7]For detailed research on how your Social Security decision affects your portfolio values, see William Meyer and William Reichenstein, Ph.D., CFA, "How the Social Security Claiming Decision Affects Portfolio Longevity," *Journal of Financial Planning* (April 2012).

[8]John B. Shoven and Sita Nataraj Slavov, "The Decision to Delay Social Security Benefits: Theory and Evidence," NBER Working Paper No. 17866 (February 2012).

Social Security Basics

If I could administer a quiz before allowing people to begin their benefits, I would. The point of the quiz would be to prevent people from unknowingly making a decision that would hurt them financially by making sure they knew the following:

- Your benefit amount is determined by looking at each year you worked, indexing what you earned for inflation, and then using the highest 35 years of earnings[9] to create what is called your Average Indexed Monthly Earnings. This number is put into a formula that, in combination with the age at which you begin benefits, determines how much you receive.

- You can begin taking your Social Security benefits as early as age 62, but you will receive a reduced benefit amount if you do so.

- You receive your full benefit amount at your full retirement age, which varies by year of birth. For those born January 2, 1943 to January 1, 1954, the full retirement age is 66.

- You can receive the maximum monthly benefit amount by waiting until age 70 to begin benefits. The increases you receive by delaying benefits between your full retirement age and age 70 are called *delayed retirement credits*.

- If you begin to receive Social Security benefits before you reach your full retirement age and you continue to work, your benefits will be reduced if you earn too much. This reduction in benefits no longer applies once you reach your full retirement age.

- Your Social Security benefits are subject to income taxes based on a formula that takes into account your other sources of income.

- If you are married, the date you begin receiving your own benefits will affect your spouse's choices, and vice versa. It is important to understand all the claiming combinations available as a married couple *before* either one of you starts receiving benefits.

---

[9] If you have only 30 years of earnings, 5 of the years will have a value of "zero." That will have the effect of lowering your average indexed monthly earnings. If you have 40 years of earnings, the 5 years with the lowest values (after earnings are indexed for inflation) will be dropped and not used in the formula.

- Your retirement date and the start date of your Social Security benefits are not synonymous. You do not have to start your benefits just because you stop working. In many cases, it is better to use savings to supplement your income needs and delay the start date of your Social Security benefits.

- Once you begin benefits, you can change your mind within the first 12 months if you are willing to repay what you've received. If you are at full retirement age or older, you also have the option of requesting a voluntary suspension of your benefits. You can put them on hold and then restart them later at a higher amount.

- If you have a previous marriage that lasted at least ten years, you may be able to claim a benefit based on your ex-spouse's earnings record and then later switch to your own benefit, or vice versa. (This has no effect on your ex's benefit.)

It is easiest to understand the rules by looking at how they apply to you. Start by getting out a copy of your Social Security statement.

Your Social Security Statement

If you are 60 or older and not currently collecting Social Security, Social Security will mail you an annual statement about three months before your birthday.[10] You can also access your statement online at any time.[11] Your statement provides an estimate of the benefits you might receive at age 62, at your full retirement age, and at age 70.

Some people mistakenly look at their statement and think that if they don't begin benefits at 62, they must wait until 66, and that if they don't begin at 66, they must wait until 70. This is not true. You can begin benefits anytime at 62 or later (age 60 if you are eligible for a widow or widower's benefit). The formula that determines what you get is recalculated monthly, so your benefit increases for each month you wait.

Your statement also provides information on how your benefits are estimated and what assumptions are used. If you have not done so, get a copy of your statement, grab a cup of coffee (water or tea if you're not a coffee drinker), and read all four pages.

---

[10]Social Security is also mailing a one-time paper Social Security statement to individuals three months before they turn age 25.
[11]www.socialsecurity.gov/mystatement/

Here are a few key things to know:

- The closer you are to retirement, and the more working years you have behind you, the more accurate the statement's estimates are.

- If you are farther away from retirement or had many years of no or low earnings and are now earning more, your actual benefit amount may end up being higher than what you see on your statement.

- The estimates on your statement are based on the assumption that you continue to work and make about the same income that you did in the year prior to your statement date.

- The amounts shown on your statement are stated in today's dollars. A cost of living adjustment will be applied as time goes by. For example, if you are 62 today, and your statement estimates you will receive $1,000 at age 66, and inflation is 3% a year, your age 66 benefit amount with inflation adjustments will be $1,126 (assuming that all other factors used to estimate your benefits, such as earnings between age 62 and 66, stay constant).

- If you receive a pension from earnings on which you did not pay Social Security taxes (most frequently this is from work for a federal, state, or local government, nonprofit, or foreign employment), the estimated benefit amount on your Social Security statement may be completely inaccurate. This is due to two provisions: Windfall Elimination Provision (WEP) and Government Pension Offset (GPO). More information on these provisions is provided later in the chapter.

The most important decisions you'll make are the age you begin your benefits and, if married, how you coordinate your claiming decisions with your spouse.

Age When You Begin Benefits

Your full retirement age (FRA) is assigned to you based on the year you were born. A lot of things hinge on your FRA. Sometimes FRA is called *normal retirement age*. The FRA[12] schedule is listed below.

---

[12]According to the Social Security Administration: "If your birthday is on January 1st, we figure your benefit as if your birthday was in the previous year. If you were born on the 1st of the month, we figure your benefit (and your full retirement age) as if your birthday was in the previous month." www.socialsecurity.gov/retire2/agereduction.htm

For each year, the year technically runs from a birth date of January 2 of that year to January 1 of the following year. For example, if you were born from January 2, 1955 to January 1, 1956, your FRA is the one listed after 1955, which would be 66 and 2 months. If you were born January 1, 1955, your FRA would be considered as if you were born in 1954, which would be 66.

- If you were born in 1937 or earlier, FRA is 65.
- 1938: 65 and 2 months.
- 1939: 65 and 4 months.
- 1940: 65 and 6 months.
- 1941: 65 and 8 months.
- 1942: 65 and 10 months.
- 1943–1954: 66.
- 1955: 66 and 2 months.
- 1956: 66 and 4 months.
- 1957: 66 and 6 months.
- 1958: 66 and 8 months.
- 1959: 66 and 10 months.
- If you were born in 1960 or later, FRA is 67.

Your Social Security benefit amount is calculated relative to what you will receive at your FRA. There is a formula that lowers your benefit if you begin before this age, and a different formula increases your benefit if you begin after this age.

Starting Benefits Before or After Full Retirement Age

If you claim benefits before your full retirement age, your FRA benefit is reduced based on a formula that is recalculated monthly.

This formula is described below by Michael Kitces in the September 2009 issue of *The Kitces Report*:

> If an individual chooses to begin Social Security retirement benefits before normal retirement age, then those benefits are reduced by 5/9ths of 1% for each month the benefits begin early, up to a maximum of 36 months. If benefits are started more than 36 months before normal retirement age, then each additional early month beyond the first 36 causes benefits to be further reduced, but only by 5/12ths of 1% per month.[13]

---

[13]Michael E. Kitces, *The Kitces Report* (September 2009). Verification can be found in the Social Security Handbook, section 724.1.A.

In plain English, this means for each month you wait, you get a little more, or for each month you claim early, you get a little less.

Here are a few examples of how this formula affects you based on your year of birth:

- For someone with a FRA of 66, the age 62 benefit amount will be 75% of their age 66 benefit amount.

- From someone with a FRA of 67, the age 62 benefit amount will be 70% of their age 67 benefit amount.

If you want to get to 100%, you have to wait until your FRA to begin benefits. If you want to get more than 100%, you have to wait even a bit longer.

Starting After Full Retirement Age

If you claim benefits after your FRA, delayed retirement credits apply, and your FRA benefit is increased by 2/3 of 1% per month,[14] or 8% a year.

As you'll learn in a bit, delayed retirement credits are one of the features that married couples can take advantage of in a way that singles can't.

Table 3-2 shows you how the Social Security reductions or delayed retirement credits affect someone who has a full retirement age of 66 (January 2, 1943–January 1, 1955), and someone with a full retirement age of 67 (January 2, 1960 or later), both with a full retirement age benefit amount of $1,000.

Table 3-2. Benefit Amount After Applicable Reductions or Credits

Born in 1943–1954		Born in 1960 or later	
Age	Benefit after reduction or credit ($)	Age	Benefit after reduction or credit ($)
62	750	62	700
63	800	63	750
64	867	64	800
65	933	65	867
66	1,000	66	933
67	1,080	67	1,000
68	1,160	68	1,080
69	1,240	69	1,160
70	1,320	70	1,240

[14]For those born in 1943 or thereafter. For those born prior to 1943, the formula provides a lower increase for delaying. Data in the Social Security Handbook, section 720.3.C.

Increasing the benefit amount is not the only reason to delay benefits. People who begin benefits before FRA frequently get caught off guard by a rule that takes some of their benefits back if they go back to work.

Working and Collecting Benefits Before Full Retirement Age

Occasionally I receive e-mails from readers who begin their Social Security benefits early because they are laid off from work. A year or two later, they get a job opportunity and go back to work. At the end of the year, they are shocked when they receive a notice that they owe some of their Social Security benefits back. This happens if three conditions are present:

- You are collecting your Social Security retirement benefit, and

- You have not yet reached your FRA, and

- Your income from earnings exceeds the Social Security's earnings limit. (The earnings limit is $15,120 in 2013. The year you reach FRA, the earnings limit increases to $40,080.[15] These limits are indexed to inflation.)

The amount of the reduction depends on how old you are relative to your FRA, as follows:

- If you are younger than FRA for the full year, than benefits are reduced $1 for every $2 earned above the $15,120 earnings limit.

- If you reach FRA during the year, then benefits are reduced $1 for every $3 you earn above $40,080 limit. There is a special rule for the year you reach FRA—you get a full Social Security check for any whole month you are FRA or older, regardless of yearly earnings. This means only earnings in months prior to your reaching FRA count toward the earnings limit.

- Once you reach FRA, you can earn any amount, and the reduction in benefits does not apply.

Bill and Jess provide a good example of how these rules can catch you off guard. They took Social Security in 2011 before they reached their FRA,

---

[15]The year you reach full retirement age, only earnings prior to your reaching FRA count toward this limit. To learn more, see *How Work Affects Your Benefits*, SSA Publication No. 05-10069, ICN 467005 (January 2013). Find it online at www.ssa.gov/pubs/10069.html#a0=2.

expecting to have $20,000 a year of benefits plus self-employment income from a small business they started.

They earned $34,000 in net income in 2011 from their business. They received a notice to repay $9,920 of their Social Security benefits ($1 for every $2 over the 2011 earnings limit, which was $14,160). They would receive no benefits until this amount was "repaid."

If you have benefits withheld because of the earnings limit, your early retirement reduction factor will be recalculated at your FRA so you don't get penalized for months that you didn't actually receive benefits. This recalculation does not constitute a replacement of lost benefits.[16]

In many cases, even after facing a layoff, it can be to your benefit to use savings to supplement your income and delay the start of your Social Security. The exception to this may be if you have dependents eligible for a benefit based on your earnings record.

Social Security for Married Couples

This is where the rules get complicated. Married couples have choices regarding their Social Security benefits that singles don't have. Studies show that these choices are not well understood.

In a 2008 study titled "When Should Married Men Claim Social Security Benefits?",[17] the authors conclude:

> Most married men claim Social Security benefits at age 62 or 63, well short of the age that maximizes the expected present value of the average household's benefits. That many married men "leave money on the table" is surprising. It is also problematic. It results in much lower benefits for surviving spouses and the low incomes of elderly widows are a major social problem. If married men delayed claiming Social Security benefits, retirement income security would significantly improve.

Technically, the last sentence of the quote above should be changed to, "If the higher earner of the two delayed claiming Social Security benefits, retirement income security would significantly improve."

---

[16]If you retired at 62 and exceeded the earnings limit in all 48 months until FRA, the recalculation would restore your benefits to what they would have been without the early retirement reduction factor applied.

[17]Steven A. Sass, Wei Sun, and Anthony Webb, Center for Retirement Research at Boston College (March 2008). Find it online at www.globalaging.org/pension/us/2008/Married.pdf.

The higher earner, whether that is the husband or the wife, has the ability to make choices that leave the couple in a more secure financial situation whether they are both long-lived or if only one is long-lived. It is not about being male or female; it is about developing a plan to get more income as a couple.

Claiming strategies for married couples offer so many possibilities because of two features of Social Security benefits that apply only to married couples:

- *Spousal benefits:* As a spouse, you are eligible for a spousal benefit that is equal to 50% of your spouse's benefit at their FRA or your own benefit amount, whichever is higher. Depending on the relative ages of you and your spouse, you may be able to use this feature to claim a spousal benefit for a few years, while letting your own benefit amount accumulate delayed retirement credits, and then switch to your own benefit at age 70. For example, when Carol reaches her full retirement age of 66, she could collect a spousal benefit of $1,101, which is half of Steve's full retirement age benefit of $2,202 (as shown in Table 3-1)—or she could collect a benefit of $1,114 based on her own earnings record. Initially, because her own benefit is larger, Carol thinks that is what she should take. In her case, however, if she collects the monthly spousal benefit of $1,101 at age 66, when she reaches age 70 she can switch to her own age 70 benefit amount of $1,470 (which would have increased with any cost of living adjustments). Although she would get slightly less monthly income for four years (age 66 through 69), she would get quite a bit more from age 70 on.

- *Widow/Widower benefits:* Once you are both claiming Social Security, when one spouse dies, it is the higher of the two Social Security benefit amounts that the surviving spouse continues to receive. By planning to get the most out the highest earner's benefits, you can provide a significant survivor benefit to a spouse.

In Steve and Carol's case, if Steve waits until age 70, he gets $2,906 per month. This higher monthly amount is then locked in as the survivor benefit for either spouse. If Steve collects at age 66, the lower $2,202 becomes the survivor benefit and would represent a permanent, life-long reduction for either spouse, or both, who may be long-lived.

▓ **Note** The maximum spousal benefit payable is 50% of the earner's benefit at the earner's FRA. Spousal benefits do not participate in delayed retirement credits. If you are not eligible for your own benefit, but only for a spousal benefit, there is no benefit to waiting beyond your FRA to apply for your spousal benefit.

To use Social Security rules for spousal and widow/widower benefits, you have to learn about your ability to:

- File and suspend or request a voluntary suspension of benefits.
- File a restricted application.

File and Suspend

Filing and suspending allows your spouse to collect a spousal benefit while your own benefit continues to accumulate delayed retirement credits. You can only file and suspend once you are full retirement age or older.

For example, suppose you and your spouse are both age 65, and your FRA is 66, at which point you will receive $1,000 a month. After doing your homework, you decide that you do not want to start benefits until age 70. When you reach age 66, you can file and suspend your benefits, which then allows your spouse at their FRA to begin collecting a benefit of $500 a month (50% of your age 66 benefit amount). Because you have suspended your benefits, they will continue to accumulate delayed retirement credits. When you reach age 70, you can begin your age 70 benefit amount of $1,320[18] (which will have increased a bit more due to inflation adjustments).

File a Restricted Application

Filing a restricted application allows you to collect just a spousal benefit (or widow/widower benefit) while your own benefit continues to accumulate delayed retirement credits. If married, this only works once you are full retirement age or older. If widowed, or if looking at collecting spousal benefits on an ex-spouse's record, you may also need to restrict the scope of your application to preserve your ability to switch benefit strategies later.

For example, in Carol's case, if she wants to collect a spousal benefit at her age 66, she will need to file a restricted application so she can collect the spousal benefit based on Steve's earnings record.

---

[18]Using numbers from Table 3-2 as an example.

- If she does not file a restricted application, she will be deemed to be filing for both her own and a spousal benefit and will automatically be given the larger of the two.

- If she does file a restricted application, she can choose which one to apply for, thus preserving her ability to later switch and apply for the other option.

Carol would choose the restricted application, because then at age 70 she can file for her own benefit amount, which will be higher based on her delayed start date.

■ **Note** You do not have the option to file this type of restricted application before you reach your FRA.

Factoring all this in is challenging. Larry Kotlikoff, professor of economics at Boston University, had this to say about it in his column in *Forbes*:

> Suppose the couple are the same age. The husband can apply for his spousal benefit in any of 48 months between 62 and 66. Same with the wife. They can both apply for their retirement benefits in any of 96 months between 62 and 70. But in all 48 months between 66 and 70 each spouse can suspend his/her retirement benefit collection and then restart it again later. This gives us 48 × 48 × 96 × 96 × 48 × 48 × 48 × 48 = 112.7 trillion combinations to consider .... [M]y point is that we have a system that not only redefines complexity, but also defies understanding.[19]

The rules are quite complex, and Larry and several other industry experts have designed software to calculate your claiming options for you. If I were married or eligible for a benefit on an ex-spouse's record, I would not even think about starting benefits without first running an analysis using such software.

Even when using software, it still helps to understand the rules so you know why one option might be preferable to another. Let's examine spousal benefit and widow/widower benefits in greater detail and see how these items affect the total amount of income you and your spouse may receive.

Spousal Benefits

This is one area where I see misinformation coming out of the Social Security Administration on a regular basis. The rules are complex, and your average

---

[19]Larry Kotlikoff, "Thomas Jefferson Is Rolling in His Grave—A Rant on Social Security's Complexity," *Forbes Online* (August 2012)

Social Security office worker may not know all of them. They are trained to deal with the most common situations.

If you have been married for at least one year, or if you have a previous marriage that was at least ten years in length, you are eligible for a spousal benefit (assuming your spouse or ex-spouse is eligible for their own Social Security benefit).

Even if you have your own earnings history, and your own projected Social Security benefit, you still have the ability to collect a benefit based on your spouse's (or ex-spouse's) record and later switch to your own benefit, or vice versa. Table 3-4 shows how this works in Steve and Carol's situation.

Here are the two basic rules you need to know:

- If you file for benefits before you reach your FRA, you forgo your ability to switch between spousal and your own benefits. Why? When you file early, you are deemed to be filing for both your own benefits and a spousal benefit, and Social Security automatically gives you the larger of the two. You cannot choose which to take.

- If you wait until your FRA, you have choices. You can file a restricted application and just collect a spousal benefit for a few years. This may be advantageous if your age 70 benefit amount would be higher, because you could switch over from a spousal benefit to your own at that point.

You can increase your benefits by using these complex rules, but you may need to go in to the Social Security office armed with printouts from its own web site to implement some of the choices available to you.[20]

Let's put some of these rules in action by looking at Steve and Carol's choices.

LENGTH OF MARRIAGE RULES

- *9 months*: To be eligible for a survivor's benefit on your spouse's record

- *1 year*: To be eligible for a spousal benefit

---

[20]Visit the Retirement Planner: Benefits For Your Spouse section of the Social Security web site at www.socialsecurity.gov/retire2/yourspouse.htm#a0=0 if you need references to help you follow your claiming plan.

- *2 years*: If your divorced spouse is 62, but has not yet filed, you must be divorced two years before you can claim a spousal benefit based on their record. If they have already filed for benefits, there is no two-year requirement for claiming on an ex-spouse's record.

- *10 years*: To claim a spousal benefit on an ex-spouse's record

Your Spouse and Collecting Benefits Before Full Retirement Age

Steve and Carol, whose benefit amounts are in Table 3-1, provide a good example of how both spousal rules and widow/widower rules can be leveraged to your benefit.

Steve was born April 10, 1947, which makes him 66 in 2013. Carol was born January 2, 1951, which makes her 62 in 2013. They both have an FRA of 66.

I met Steve and Carol before Steve turned 66. He thought he should begin benefits at age 66. I was able to show him how making a different choice would put him and Carol in a more secure position.

Table 3-3 shows Steve and Carol's yearly benefit amounts based on what they thought they should do. Table 3-4 shows an alternate strategy they could choose.

On the right-hand side of the tables, you see two columns under the Cumulative section. The first, labeled "Sum of benefits received," is a running total of the benefits without accounting for inflation or a *discount rate* (potential rate of return that savings and investments would earn). The far right column, labeled "Discounted @ 2% ($)," is a present value calculation.

Here's how it works. Assume that your benefits would increase with an inflation rate of 3% a year, and your savings could earn a 5% return. Your real rate of return is therefore 2%.[21] This column shows you the value of your benefits in today's dollars by discounting them back to today using this 2% real rate of return. In other words, for Steve's age 75 in Table 3-3, in the far right column the present value of the benefits received is $318,932. That means if Steve and Carol had $318,932 in the bank today, earning a 2% real rate of return, that would be equivalent to the stream of benefits to be received up through Steve's age 75.

---

[21]As mentioned in a footnote in Chapter 2, to discount at the equivalent of a 2% real return, I use a discount rate of 1.94%.

Table 3-3. Steve and Carol Claiming Social Security Now

Steve		Carol			Cumulative	
Age	Benefit ($)	Age	Own Benefit ($)	Widow Benefit ($)	Sum of benefits received ($)	Discounted @ 2% ($)
66	17,616	62	9,185		26,801	26,291
67	26,424	63	10,020		63,245	61,361
68	26,424	64	10,020		99,689	95,764
69	26,424	65	10,020		136,133	129,512
70	26,424	66	10,020		172,577	162,617
71	26,424	67	10,020		209,021	195,093
72	26,424	68	10,020		245,465	226,951
73	26,424	69	10,020		281,909	258,202
74	26,424	70	10,020		318,353	288,859
75	26,424	71	10,020		354,797	318,932
76	26,424	72	10,020		391,241	348,433
77	26,424	73	10,020		427,685	377,372
78	26,424	74	10,020		464,129	405,761
79	26,424	75	10,020		500,573	433,609
80	26,424	76	10,020		537,017	460,928
81	26,424	77	10,020		573,461	487,727
82	26,424	<u>78</u>	10,020		609,905	<u>514,015</u>
83	26,424	79	10,020		646,349	539,803
84	26,424	80	10,020		682,793	565,101
85	26,424	81	10,020		719,237	589,917
86		82		26,424	745,661	607,568
87		83		26,424	772,085	624,882
88		84		26,424	798,509	$641,868
89		85		26,424	824,933	$658,530
90		86		26,424	851,357	$674,875
91		87		26,424	877,781	$690,909
92		88		26,424	904,205	$706,637
93		89		26,424	930,629	$722,067
94		90		26,424	957,053	$737,202
95		91		26,424	983,477	$752,050
96		92		26,424	1,009,901	$766,615
97		93		26,424	1,036,325	$780,903
98		94		26,424	1,062,749	$794,919

Now let's look at a better plan for Steve and Carol (Table 3-4).

Table 3-4. Steve and Carol Claiming Benefits According to a Plan

Steve		Carol			Cumulative	
Age	Benefit ($)	Age	Spousal benefit ($)	Own/Widow benefit	Sum of benefits received ($)	Discounted @ 2% ($)[22]
66		62			0	
67		63			0	
68		64			0	
69		65			0	
70	23,248	66	12,111		35,359	32,120
71	34,872	67	13,212		83,443	74,968
72	34,872	68	13,212		131,527	117,001
73	34,872	69	13,212		179,611	158,234
74	34,872	70	1,101	16,170	231,754	202,097
75	34,872	71		17,640	284,266	245,429
76	34,872	72		17,640	336,778	287,937
77	34,872	73		17,640	389,290	329,635
78	34,872	74		17,640	441,802	370,541
79	34,872	75		17,640	494,314	410,667
80	34,872	76		17,640	546,826	450,030
81	34,872	77		17,640	599,338	488,644
82	34,872	<u>78</u>		17,640	651,850	<u>526,523</u>
83	34,872	79		17,640	704,362	563,682
84	34,872	80		17,640	756,874	600,133
85	34,872	81		17,640	809,386	635,890
86		82		34,872	844,258	659,184
87		83		34,872	879,130	682,034
88		84		34,872	914,002	704,450
89		85		34,872	948,874	726,439
90		86		34,872	983,746	748,010
91		87		34,872	1,018,618	769,170
92		88		34,872	1,053,490	789,927
93		89		34,872	1,088,362	810,289
94		90		34,872	1,123,234	830,264
95		91		34,872	1,158,106	849,859
96		92		34,872	1,192,978	869,081
97		93		34,872	1,227,850	887,937
98		94		34,872	1,262,722	906,434

[22]As previously discussed, the actual discount rate used is 1.94%, which equates to a 2% real return (5% return on savings/investments, 3% savings rate).

About the time Steve reaches 82 and Carol reaches 78, as you can see, the cumulative numbers in the far right column of Table 3-4 exceed the cumulative numbers at the same ages in Table 3-3. For each year they live past 82/78, the Table 3-4 claiming plan becomes more and more attractive.

In Chapter 2, Figures 2-2 through 2-4 showed the first income timeline for Steve and Carol. Using a 2% discount rate, they would need $499,000 of savings to use to supplement their fixed sources of income to Steve's age 85 (and higher amounts to reach later ages).

After adjusting their spending needs to account for the lower amount needed once the mortgage was paid off, that number went down to $460,000 (as shown in Figures 2-10 through 2-11). Both of these timelines showed Steve claiming his Social Security benefits at his age 66 and Carol at her age 62.

Figures 3-1 and 3-2 present a third income timeline showing the claiming strategy depicted in Table 3-4. In this timeline, Steve is claiming his own benefits at age 70. Carol is claiming a spousal benefit based on Steve's record at her age 66 and then switching to her own benefit at her age 70. This change means now Steve and Carol only need $414,000 of present value savings to achieve their income goals through Steve's age 85.[23] Following their Social Security plan helps Steve and Carol keep $46,000 more of their own savings, while spending the same amount each year. Through Carol's age 86, following their Social Security plan means they keep $97,000 more of their own savings (or they could spend more along the way).

---

[23]In Tables 3-3 and 3-4 I have set Steve's life expectancy at age 85. In Figures 2-2 through 2-5, and 2-8 through 3-2, I show both Steve and Carol with extended longevity.

Steve & Carol, Income Timeline: Claiming Social Security Benefits According to a Plan, Mortgage Gone in 2028
As of: Beginning of Year 2013

# of Years	1	2	3	4	5	6	7	8	9	10	11
Calendar Year	2013	2014	2015	2016	2017	2018	2019	2020	2021	2022	2023
Fixed Sources of Income											
Steve (age)	66	67	68	69	70	71	72	73	74	75	76
Earnings	$48,000	$48,000	$48,000	$48,000	$48,000	0	0	0	0	0	0
Pension	0	0	0	0	0	0	0	0	0	0	0
Social Security	0	0	0	0	$23,248	$34,872	$34,872	$34,872	$34,872	$34,872	$34,872
Life Insurance	0	0	0	0	0	0	0	0	0	0	0
Other	0	0	0	0	0	0	0	0	0	0	0
Carol (age)	62	63	64	65	66	67	68	69	70	71	72
Earnings	0	0	0	0	0	0	0	0	0	0	0
Pension	0	0	0	0	0	0	0	0	0	0	0
Annuity	0	0	0	0	0	0	0	0	0	0	0
Social Security - Spousal	0	0	0	0	$12,111	$13,212	$13,212	$13,212	$1,101	0	0
Social Security - Own	0	0	0	0	0	0	0	0	$16,170	$17,640	$17,640
Other	0	0	0	0	0	0	0	0	0	0	0
A. Total Fixed Income:	$48,000	$48,000	$48,000	$48,000	$83,359	$48,084	$48,084	$48,084	$52,143	$52,512	$52,512
Fixed Expenses	$72,993	$72,993	$72,993	$72,993	$72,993	$72,993	$72,993	$72,993	$72,993	$72,993	$72,993
Coverage Ratio	0.66	0.66	0.66	0.66	1.14	0.66	0.66	0.66	0.71	0.72	0.72
B. Desired Gross Income:	$80,000	$80,000	$80,000	$80,000	$80,000	$80,000	$80,000	$80,000	$80,000	$80,000	$80,000
C. $ Needed from Savings: (A minus B)	($32,000)	($32,000)	($32,000)	($32,000)	$3,359	($31,916)	($31,916)	($31,916)	($27,857)	($27,488)	($27,488)

Money needed today, discounted at a 2% real return, to get to ages:		Simple sum of dollars, no discount rate:	Advantage over Figure 2-10 to 2-11 (real returns):
85/81	$414,257	$495,614	$45,973
90/86	$467,268	$578,054	$97,635
95/91	$515,424	$660,494	$144,564
99/95	$550,753	$728,446	$178,992

Figure 3-1. Page 1 of Steve and Carol's income timeline with a Social Security plan

# of Years	12	13	14	15	16	17	18	19	20	21	22	23	24	25	26
Calendar Year	2024	2025	2026	2027	2028	2029	2030	2031	2032	2033	2034	2035	2036	2037	2038
Fixed Sources of Income															
Steve (age)	77	78	79	80	81	82	83	84	85	86	87	88	89	90	91
Earnings	0	0	0	0	0	0	0	0	0	0	0	0	0	0	0
Pension	0	0	0	0	0	0	0	0	0	0	0	0	0	0	0
Social Security	$34,872	$34,872	$34,872	$34,872	$34,872	$34,872	$34,872	$34,872	$34,872	$34,872	$34,872	$34,872	$34,872	$34,872	$34,872
Life Insurance	0	0	0	0	0	0	0	0	0	0	0	0	0	0	0
Other	0	0	0	0	0	0	0	0	0	0	0	0	0	0	0
Carol (age)	73	74	75	76	77	78	79	80	81	82	83	84	85	86	87
Earnings	0	0	0	0	0	0	0	0	0	0	0	0	0	0	0
Pension	0	0	0	0	0	0	0	0	0	0	0	0	0	0	0
Annuity	0	0	0	0	0	0	0	0	0	0	0	0	0	0	0
Social Security - Spousal	0	0	0	0	0	0	0	0	0	0	0	0	0	0	0
Social Security - Own	$17,640	$17,640	$17,640	$17,640	$17,640	$17,640	$17,640	$17,640	$17,640	$17,640	$17,640	$17,640	$17,640	$17,640	$17,640
Other	0	0	0	0	0	0	0	0	0	0	0	0	0	0	0
A. Total Fixed Income:	$52,512	$52,512	$52,512	$52,512	$52,512	$52,512	$52,512	$52,512	$52,512	$52,512	$52,512	$52,512	$52,512	$52,512	$52,512
Fixed Expenses	$72,993	$72,993	$72,993	$72,993	$61,702	$61,702	$61,702	$61,702	$61,702	$61,702	$61,702	$61,702	$61,702	$61,702	$61,702
Coverage Ratio	0.72	0.72	0.72	0.72	0.85	0.85	0.85	0.85	0.85	0.85	0.85	0.85	0.85	0.85	0.85
B. Desired Gross Income:	$80,000	$80,000	$80,000	$80,000	$69,000	$69,000	$69,000	$69,000	$69,000	$69,000	$69,000	$69,000	$69,000	$69,000	$69,000
C. $ Needed from Savings: (A minus B)	($27,488)	($27,488)	($27,488)	($27,488)	($16,488)	($16,488)	($16,488)	($16,488)	($16,488)	($16,488)	($16,488)	($16,488)	($16,488)	($16,488)	($16,488)

Figure 3-2. Page 2 of Steve and Carol's income timeline with a Social Security plan

Figures 3-1 and 3-2 show Steve and Carol doing the following:

- Steve begins his own benefit at age 70.

- Carol files for a restricted application for a spousal benefit based on Steve's earning's record at her FRA.

- Carol switches to her own benefit at her age 70.

By coordinating when and how they each claim their benefits, Steve and Carol have increased the amount of guaranteed income in their plan without buying an annuity or any other investment product.

- Now, at their respective ages 75/71, they will have $52,512 of guaranteed income versus $36,444 if they claim Social Security now.

- When their mortgage is paid off, their fixed expenses will be about $62,000 a year. At ages 81/77, their coverage ratio has increased from .59 to .85, putting them in a more secure position.

When looking at a delayed Social Security choice, people often ask me, "Yeah, but what if I die early?"

I am known to say, "Well, you'll be gone. You won't know the difference."

Larry Kotlikoff put it more appropriately when he said, "With Social Security, you won't feel regret by delaying Social Security and then dying before collecting benefits, because you won't be around anyway. Regret comes when you live a long life and think about how your situation would have been improved through delay."[24]

With couples, you must also think about your other half. If Steve does not end up having as long a life as he hopes for, he has now locked in his higher benefit amount as a survivor benefit for Carol. This life-insurance-like feature of Social Security benefits is often overlooked by couples.

Before deciding on a Social Security plan, many couples ask, "What happens if the higher earner delays benefits but dies before they start collecting?" The short answer is that the decision still benefits the survivor. The long answer requires looking into how widow/widower benefits work.

Widow/Widowers Benefits

Developing a plan for how and when to collect your Social Security benefits is not only smart, it can be one of the most cost-effective ways to provide life insurance.

---

[24]Wade Pfau, "Kotlikoff on Social Security," Retirement Researcher Blog (August 20, 2012) www.globalaging.org/pension/us/2008/Married.pdf.

Upon the death of a spouse, you do not get to collect your own benefits and a widow/widower benefit, but you can collect one type of benefit for a while and then switch to the other.

The surviving spouse keeps the higher benefit amount, so it make sense to create a plan that makes the most of the higher earner's benefit amount. To understand how it all works, let's take a look at the rules, which apply as long as you've been married for at least nine months.

The amount of a widow/widower benefit depends on a few things:

- Whether you have started your benefits, and if you have, whether you started before or after your FRA

- The amount of your benefit at your FRA (which I may refer to as your PIA, or Primary Insurance Amount)

- Whether your surviving spouse has reached his/her FRA

Let's look at the potential scenarios and how a widow/widower benefit amount would be affected by the death of one spouse or the other.

If you start benefits before your full retirement age

> Your surviving spouse will be eligible for a widow/widower benefit that is the larger of what you were receiving or 82.5% of your PIA.

The 82.5% rule was put in place to protect a minimum benefit amount for a surviving spouse whose husband or wife began their own benefits early.

For example, if John has an FRA of 66 and was expected to receive $1,000 at his FRA, but he began benefits at age 62, he would receive $750. If John passes away, his wife Beth would be eligible for a survivor benefit of $825 based on the 82.5% rule. (This amount can be further reduced if the surviving spouse begins the benefit prior to reaching their own FRA.[25]) Beth might choose to collect this survivor benefit and then later switch to her own benefit amount at her age 70, if her own would be higher at that point.

If you start benefits after your full retirement age

> Your survivor is entitled to whatever you were receiving.

Again using John as an example, if he started benefits at 66 and is receiving $1,000 a month, his wife is entitled to the same $1,000 a month as a survivor benefit. If John waited until age 70, his benefit would be $1,320 per month, and this would also be the survivor amount his wife could receive. (This amount can be further reduced if the surviving spouse begins benefits prior to reaching their own FRA.)

---

[25]FRA for widow/widower benefits is defined by a different schedule than FRA for your own benefits. Find the schedule at www.ssa.gov/survivorplan/survivorchartred.htm.

If you have not started your benefits yet and have not reached your full retirement age

> Your surviving spouse can receive what you would have received at your FRA. (This amount can be further reduced if the surviving spouse begins benefits prior to reaching their own FRA.)

Let's say John passes away at 64 and has not started his benefits yet. His wife Beth could begin benefits now and be eligible for the full $1,000 a month that John would have gotten at his FRA. This amount would be reduced if Beth claims benefits before her own FRA.

▨ **Note**   One of the unique options available to widows and widowers is the ability to claim a widow/widower benefit and then later switch to your own benefit, or vice versa, even if you claim before you have reached FRA. This means multiple potential claiming strategies should be examined before a surviving spouse decides which claiming plan is best for them.

If you have not started your benefits yet and you are full retirement age or older

> Your surviving spouse can receive the amount you would have received had you begun benefits at the time of your death. This applies if you delay the start date of your retirement benefits and pass away between your FRA and age 70.

This works because delayed retirement credits are applied to your PIA[26] for the purposes of calculating the widow/widower benefit amount, even if you had not started your benefits yet.

Let's say John passes away at 69. He had not begun benefits. If he had, his benefit amount would be $1,240. (This is his FRA benefit amount of $1,000 plus an 8% a year increase attributable to delayed retirement credits.) Beth can collect $1,240 (which may be reduced if she has not reached her FRA).

In all of these scenarios, if Beth is also eligible for her own benefit, she does not get to collect her own benefit and a survivor benefit simultaneously.

---

[26]Remember, your PIA is your Primary Insurance Amount, which is about the amount you would receive at your FRA without reductions or credits applied.

If you and your spouse have both already started your benefits

The surviving spouse can continue the larger benefit amount, but not both benefits. In Steve and Carol's scenario, one possible future we must account for is Steve passing away early and Carol living long. If Steve were to start benefits at 70 and then pass away a year later, what happens?

Carol would be able to continue his age 70 benefit amount of $34,872 a year, but her spousal benefit and her own benefit amount would go away.

How does this compare to their financial state if Steve had started benefits at 66?

You can model both scenarios using the income timelines.

In Figures 2-10 and 2-11 and Figures 3-1 and 3-2, what you do is simply take out Carol's benefit amounts at Steve's hypothetical age of death. Figures 3-3 and 3-4 show the first page of the results for each.

Here is a summary of the relative benefits to Carol:

- *Carol's age 81:* –$31,000
- *Carol's age 86:* –$4,000
- *Carol's age 91:* +$20,000
- *Carol's age 95:* +$38,000

If they should both pass away young, the claiming plan had a minimal negative effect on their remaining assets. If either lives long, the Social Security plan puts the long-lived spouse in a more secure position.

Tip Another thing to account for when you create a plan: fixed expenses will often decrease at the death of the first spouse from the reduction in health insurance premiums, transportation costs, and less food and fewer household items. You can model this in your income timeline by lowering fixed expenses by a reasonable amount at the death of the first spouse in your what-if scenarios.

Steve & Carol, Income Timeline - Taking Social Security Now, Steve with Short Longevity
As of: Beginning of Year 2013

# of Years	1	2	3	4	5	6	7	8	9	10	11
Calendar Year	2013	2014	2015	2016	2017	2018	2019	2020	2021	2022	2023
Fixed Sources of Income											
Steve (age)	66	67	68	69	70	71	72	73	74	75	76
Earnings	$48,000	$48,000	$48,000	$48,000	$48,000	0	0	0	0	0	0
Pension	0	0	0	0	0	0	0	0	0	0	0
Social Security	$17,616	$26,424	$26,424	$26,424	$26,424	0	0	0	0	0	0
Life Insurance	0	0	0	0	0	0	0	0	0	0	0
Other	0	0	0	0	0	0	0	0	0	0	0
Carol (age)	62	63	64	65	66	67	68	69	70	71	72
Earnings	0	0	0	0	0	0	0	0	0	0	0
Pension	0	0	0	0	0	0	0	0	0	0	0
Annuity	0	0	0	0	0	0	0	0	0	0	0
Social Security - Own	$9,185	$10,020	$10,020	$10,020	$10,020	$26,424	$26,424	$26,424	$26,424	$26,424	$26,424
Social Security - Survivor	0	0	0	0	0	$26,424	$26,424	$26,424	$26,424	$26,424	$26,424
A. Total Fixed Income:	$74,801	$84,444	$84,444	$84,444	$84,444	$26,424	$26,424	$26,424	$26,424	$26,424	$26,424
B. Desired Gross Income:	$80,000	$80,000	$80,000	$80,000	$80,000	$80,000	$80,000	$80,000	$80,000	$80,000	$80,000
C. $ Needed from Savings: (A minus B)	($5,199)	$4,444	$4,444	$4,444	$4,444	($53,576)	($53,576)	($53,576)	($53,576)	($53,576)	($53,576)

Money needed today, discounted at a
2% real return, to get to her age:

81	$577,713
86	$714,602
91	$838,952
95	$930,179

Simple sum of dollars, no
discount rate:

$736,063
$948,943
$1,161,823
$1,332,127

Figure 3-3. Steve and Carol's income timeline, claiming Social Security at 66/62, Steve with short longevity

Steve & Carol, Income Timeline - Taking Social Security Later, Steve with Short Longevity
As of: Beginning of Year 2013

	1	2	3	4	5	6	7	8	9	10	11	12
# of Years / Calendar Year	2013	2014	2015	2016	2017	2018	2019	2020	2021	2022	2023	2024
Fixed Sources of Income												
Steve (age)	66	67	68	69	70	71	72	73	74	75	76	77
Earnings	$48,000	$48,000	$48,000	$48,000	$48,000	0	0	0	0	0	0	0
Pension	0	0	0	0	0	0	0	0	0	0	0	0
Social Security	0	0	0	0	$23,248	0	0	0	0	0	0	0
Life Insurance	0	0	0	0	0	0	0	0	0	0	0	0
Other	0	0	0	0	0	0	0	0	0	0	0	0
Carol (age)	62	63	64	65	66	67	68	69	70	71	72	73
Earnings	0	0	0	0	0	0	0	0	0	0	0	0
Pension	0	0	0	0	0	0	0	0	0	0	0	0
Annuity	0	0	0	0	0	0	0	0	0	0	0	0
Social Security - Spousal	0	0	0	0	12,111	$34,872	$34,872	$34,872	$34,872	$34,872	$34,872	$34,872
Social Security - Survivor	0	0	0	0	0	0	0	0	0	0	0	0
A. Total Fixed Income:	$48,000	$48,000	$48,000	$48,000	$83,359	$34,872	$34,872	$34,872	$34,872	$34,872	$34,872	$34,872
Fixed Expenses	$72,993	$72,993	$72,993	$72,993	$72,993	$72,993	$72,993	$72,993	$72,993	$72,993	$72,993	$72,993
Coverage Ratio	0.66	0.66	0.66	0.66	1.14	0.48	0.48	0.48	0.48	0.48	0.48	0.48
B. Desired Gross Income:	$80,000	$80,000	$80,000	$80,000	$80,000	$80,000	$80,000	$80,000	$80,000	$80,000	$80,000	$80,000
C. $ Needed from Savings: (A minus B)	($32,000)	($32,000)	($32,000)	($32,000)	$3,359	($45,128)	($45,128)	($45,128)	($45,128)	($45,128)	($45,128)	($45,128)

Money needed today, discounted at a 2% real return, to get to ages:
81	$609,159
86	$718,886
91	$818,562
95	$891,688

Simple sum of dollars, no discount rate:
$746,561
$917,201
$1,087,841
$1,224,353

Advantage over Figure 3-3 (real returns):
($31,446)
($4,284)
$20,390
$38,491

Figure 3-4. Steve and Carol's income timeline with a Social Security plan, Steve with short longevity

If I'm the survivor and have not started my benefits yet

> If you are the widow or widower, and you have not started your own benefits yet, you will have a choice. You can start your own and then later switch to a widow/widower benefit, or vice versa.

This is a situation where you want to calculate out which option provides you the most income over your lifetime. Then, when you apply, you may need to restrict the scope of your application so that you can specify whether you are applying for your own retirement benefit or the survivor's benefit.

Social Security for Ex-Spouses

The same widow/widower benefits described for a spouse are available for an ex-spouse if you were married at least ten years and did not remarry prior to age 60.

In addition, spousal benefits are available based on an ex-spouse's record. The Social Security representatives may not be able to advise you on how to use such benefits to your advantage. I saw this first-hand with Mary.

Mary went to the Social Security Administration office to inquire about claiming a benefit based on her ex-spouse's record. Social Security told her that if she did so, the benefit amount would be about the same as if she claimed her own benefit. They told her it probably didn't make sense for her to do this. They were right, and they were wrong.

All the rules discussed on spousal benefits also apply for benefits based on an ex-spouse's record—with one important difference. When married, your spouse must have filed for their own benefits in order for you to be eligible for a spousal benefit. When it is your ex-spouse, this rule does not apply. As long as they have reached age 62, even if they have not filed for their own benefits, you are still eligible for a spousal benefit (if they haven't applied for benefits yet you must be divorced for two years before you can apply for a spousal benefit on an ex-spouse's record).

The same rules about full retirement age apply:

- If you file before your own FRA, and your ex-spouse is 62 or older, you will be automatically given the larger of your own reduced benefit or a reduced spousal benefit. If you are receiving a reduced benefit, it has nothing to do with your ex-spouse's age; the reduction is based on the fact that you are not yet at FRA (see Table 3-2). If your ex-spouse is not yet age 62, then you are not eligible for the spousal benefit yet, so you would only be applying for your own benefit amount.

- If you wait until your FRA to file, you will be able to file a restricted application, claim a spousal benefit, and then later switch to your own benefit. Table 3-5 shows an example of this.

Table 3-5. Mary's Social Security Claiming Options

Mary's age	Mary's benefit ($)	Cumulative Benefits Discounted @ 2% ($)	`Spousal benefit ($)	Mary's Benefit at her age 70 ($)	Cumulative Benefits Discounted @ 2% ($)
66	16,080	15,774	13,464		13,208
67	16,080	31,248	13,464		26,164
68	16,080	46,427	13,464		38,874
69	16,080	61,318	13,464		51,342
70	16,080	75,925		21,216	70,615
71	16,080	90,254		21,216	89,520
72	16,080	104,310		21,216	108,066
73	16,080	118,099		21,216	126,260
74	16,080	131,625		21,216	144,106
75	16,080	144,894		21,216	161,614
76	16,080	157,911		21,216	178,788
77	16,080	170,680		21,216	195,635
78	16,080	183,206		21,216	212,161
79	16,080	195,493		21,216	228,374
80	16,080	207,547		21,216	244,277
81	16,080	219,371		21,216	259,878
82	16,080	230,970		21,216	275,182
83	16,080	242,348		21,216	290,195
84	16,080	253,510		21,216	304,922
85	16,080	264,460		21,216	319,369
86	16,080	275,201		21,216	333,540
87	16,080	285,738		21,216	347,443
88	16,080	296,074		21,216	361,080
89	16,080	306,213		21,216	374,458
90	16,080	316.160		21,216	387,582

To be eligible for a spousal (or widow/widower) benefit on an ex-spouse's record, you must meet the following criteria:

- You had a previous marriage that was at least ten years in length.

- You are currently unmarried or you are remarried, but only remarried after age 60.

- You are 62 (if your ex-spouse is deceased, you are eligible for a widow/widower benefit on their record as early as age 60).

When you collect a benefit based on an ex-spouse's record, it does not affect their benefit in any way. If you have an ex-spouse who collects benefits based on your earning's record, it will not affect your benefit in any way.

Mary was going to reach her FRA in a few months. Her benefit amount was going to be $1,340 a month. If she claimed a spousal benefit, she would get $1,122 a month. Mary thought she should claim her own benefit amount.

A better choice would be for Mary to file a restricted application for a benefit based on her ex-spouse's record, claim the $1,122 a month for four years, and then switch to her own age 70 benefit amount, which would accumulate to $1,768 a month.

By the time Mary reaches age 72, her Social Security plan will have outperformed her initial choice, which was to collect her own benefit at age 66.

▓ **Note** To claim a benefit on an ex-spouse's record, be prepared to provide documentation such as a copy of your marriage certificate and divorce decree.

Social Security for Single People

Conceptually, the Social Security formula was designed so that if you live to your life expectancy, you should get about the same amount no matter when you begin your benefits.

In a February 2012 article in *Investment News* titled "Social Security and the Single Retiree," Mary Beth Franklin writes:

> Ironically, assuming that a single person lives to 80, it makes almost no difference when he or she begins drawing benefits. The cumulative lifetime benefits from Social Security will be about the same whether reduced benefits begin at 62, full benefits are taken at 66 or enhanced benefits start at 70.[27]

---

[27]www.investmentnews.com/article/20120226/REG/302269976 (access requires free registration)

Let's see how this works. Using Carol as an example, if Carol lives to age 80, the following are the total amounts she receives, depending on what age she starts benefits (not including inflation adjustments or discount rates):

- *Age 62:* $835 × 12 × 18 = $180,360
- *Age 66:* $1,114 × 12 × 14 = $187,152
- *Age 70:* $1,470 × 12 × 10 = $176,400

But today, people are living longer than ever. Advances in health care are occurring at a staggering rate. So if Carol lives to age 84, the answer changes:

- *Age 62:* $835 × 12 × 22 = $220,440
- *Age 66:* $1,114 × 12 × 18 = $240,624
- *Age 70:* $1,470 × 12 × 14 = $246,960

Additional factors such as interest rates and longevity should be part of the decision for singles. A 2012 National Bureau of Economic Research paper states:

> In general, women benefit more from delaying benefits, due to their longer life expectancies. For real interest rates of 0.8 percent or below, women maximize expected present value by delaying until age 70; on the other hand, even for a real interest rate of zero, men with average mortality risk maximize present value by delaying only until age 69. Delays of any length no longer increase present value for interest real rates above 3.5 percent for men and 4.2 percent for women.[28]

The interest rate component in that quote is important. The examples in this chapter are assuming either a 0% real rate of return or a real rate of return of 2%. If the economy moves back into a higher interest rate environment, where real interest rates are expected to be 4% or higher, it will change the answer for whether it makes sense to follow a particular plan or not.

Right now, we are in a low interest rate environment, and I ask singles to consider all the following regarding their Social Security decision:

- Will you work prior to reaching your full retirement age? If yes, and if there is likelihood you will earn in excess of the earnings limit, then why mess with potentially having to repay benefits? Wait until you reach full retirement age to begin benefits.

---

[28]John B. Shoven and Sita Nataraj Slavov, "The Decision to Delay Social Security Benefits: Theory and Evidence," NBER Working Paper No. 17866 (February 2012).

- What story does your family health history and personal health history tell? Social Security provides inflation-adjusted income as long as you live. The 84-year-old you will have an increased level of security if the 62-year-old you delays the start date of benefits. Is this important to you?

- Do you have other savings you could use to supplement your income while delaying the start of your Social Security benefits? Sometimes you have no other options and must start benefits early. If you do have other options, have you explored them and run a plan showing how these choices play out over time?

- Do you have dependents that may be able to claim a benefit based on your record? You should consider total family benefits when you evaluate your choices.

- Will you be eligible for a pension for work where you received earnings that were not covered by Social Security? If so, your Social Security benefit amounts may be significantly reduced from what you see on your statement, or your spousal or widow/widower benefit may be reduced.

There is an additional consideration: risk. Immediate annuities are often a recommended investment for securing retirement income for singles. By delaying Social Security, you are in effect buying an inflation-adjusted annuity from Social Security.

In a Center for Retirement Research paper,[29] one key finding says, "Buying an annuity from Social Security is generally the best deal in town, especially in today's low interest-rate environment."

If it's the best deal in town, make sure you take advantage of it before using your savings to go buy a lesser deal.

Social Security When You Have a Pension from Work Not Covered By Social Security

To fund Social Security while working, you and your employer pay a portion of your wages into the Social Security system. Social Security by nature is designed to replace a higher percentage of pre-retirement income for lifetime low-wage earners than for lifetime high-wage earners.

---

[29]"Should You Buy an Annuity From Social Security?" Center for Retirement Research of Boston College (May 2012), www.ssa.gov/survivorplan/survivorchartred.htm.

If you worked for an employer that provides you a pension for years of work, and that work was not covered by the Social Security system (meaning no Social Security payroll taxes were paid on those years of earnings), then a modified formula is used to determine the amount of your Social Security benefits.

This modification is designed to prevent a "windfall" that may occur for those who have only minimal Social Security coverage and will receive a pension based on years of work that wasn't covered by Social Security.[30]

If you answer yes to any of the following questions, this section may apply to you:

- Did you work for a government agency (federal, state or local)?

- Did you work for an employer in another country?

- If yes to either question, do you receive a pension from this government agency or employer in another country?

▦ **Note**   If you were a federal employee after 1956 and were covered under the Civil Service Retirement System (CSRS) this provision affects you. If you were a federal employee covered under the Federal Employees' Retirement System (FERS) where Social Security taxes are withheld, this provision does not affect you.

There are two different rules:

- *Windfall Elimination Provision (WEP):* If you receive a pension from work that was not subject to Social Security taxes, WEP may reduce your own Social Security benefit and may affect your dependents' benefits that are based on your earning's record.[31]

---

[30]See Social Security Handbook, Windfall Elimination Provision (WEP), section 718.
[31]The WEP calculation affects your PIA. Dependent benefits are calculated based on your PIA. However, in the case of a widow/widower, when the worker dies, the WEP reduction is removed. For details, see Effect of the Windfall Elimination Provision on Dependents and Survivors at http://ssa-custhelp.ssa.gov/app/answers/detail/a_id/1266/~/effect-of-the-windfall-elimination-provision-on-dependents-and-survivors.

- *Government Pension Offset (GPO)*: If you receive a pension from work that was not subject to Social Security taxes, then GPO may reduce the Social Security spousal benefit you receive (or benefit you receive as an ex-spouse) and may reduce the widow/widower benefit you receive.

WEP and GPO most commonly affect educators, firefighters, police officers, and other public employees whose work is covered under a state pension system but is not also covered under Social Security. Let's take a closer look at these rules.

Windfall Elimination Provision

If you qualify for a pension based on work that paid you earnings not covered under Social Security, and you also had years of work with earnings that were covered under Social Security and qualify for a Social Security benefit, then the Windfall Elimination Provision (WEP) may reduce the amount of Social Security that you qualify for.

This situation can apply to teachers who work in states where teacher's wages are not covered under Social Security but have their own pension system instead.[32] My mom, for example, was a teacher in Missouri, and her Social Security benefits were reduced because of WEP.

In this situation, your Social Security statement will not reflect the deduction that may apply under WEP rules. Many people are caught off guard, expecting to receive both their full pension from government or foreign employment and their full Social Security benefit.

The amount of the reduction depends on how many years of work you had that were covered under Social Security and how much you made.

The WEP section of the Social Security web site[33] provides an excellent description of how this provision works and describes the reduction formula.

I say *excellent* because it explains the provision in language that you can actually understand. If you think WEP applies to you, I suggest you go online and read it.

---

[32]"Fourteen states ... do not provide Social Security coverage for teachers. These states have so-called 'independent' retirement systems for teachers and, in some cases, other public employees." They are: Alaska, California, Colorado, Connecticut, Illinois, Kentucky, Louisiana, Maine, Massachusetts, Minnesota, Missouri, Nevada, Ohio, Texas. Judith S. Lohman, OLR Research Report (September 7, 2006), www.cga.ct.gov/2006/rpt/2006-R-0547.htm.

[33]Windfall Elimination Provision, SSA Publication No. 05-10045 (January 2012) ICN 460275. Find it online at www.socialsecurity.gov/pubs/10045.html#a0=0.

If WEP does apply to you, you'll need to use your reduced Social Security amounts to build your plan and to decide on a claiming strategy.

Government Pension Offset

The Government Pension Offset (GPO) does not affect the Social Security benefit you receive on your earnings record but does affect the benefit you might receive as a spouse, ex-spouse, or widow/widower.

As with the Windfall Elimination Provision, GPO applies if you receive a pension for years of work where you received earnings that were not subject to Social Security taxes.

If GPO applies to you, your spousal or widow/widower benefit will be reduced by two-thirds of the amount of your pension.

You can learn more on the Government Pension Offset page of the Social Security web site.[34]

Social Security When You Have Dependents

In today's modern families, it is more and more common to have parents of traditional retirement age who may still have dependent children, stepchildren, or grandchildren.

If you...

- have a dependent child, stepchild, adopted child, grandchild, or step-grandchild, or in some cases, an illegitimate child who is under the age of 18 (or between 18 and 19 if they are a full-time elementary or high school student), or

- are caring for a child under age 16, and your spouse is deceased,

...then contact your Social Security office when you turn 62 to explore the total amount of family benefits you are eligible for.

For those who qualify for additional family benefits based on dependents, delaying Social Security may not be as advantageous. You need to evaluate your claiming choices side by side to see what choices lead to the most benefits for you and your family.

---

[34]Government Pension Offset, SSA Publication No. 05-10007 (June 2012) ICN 451453. Find it online at www.ssa.gov/pubs/10007.html.

To dig into the rules, I recommend the current-year edition of *Social Security &
Medicare Facts* by Joseph F. Stenken, published by the National Underwriters
Association, which provides great detail on family benefits as well as details on
all aspects of Social Security.

Help! I Already Started Social Security—Can I Change My Mind?

Maybe you or your spouse already started Social Security. After reading
through this chapter, you may be thinking you could have followed a better
plan. Joe Elsasser, developer of the software program Social Security Timing,
has the following four options on how you can fix things:[35]

Option 1: Pay It Back

If you change your mind within the first 12 months of electing benefits, you
can file a form 521 to withdraw the application and pay back any benefits.
If benefits were received by auxiliaries, such as a spouse or children, those
benefits would also need to be repaid. Once benefits have been repaid, you
are treated as though you never elected, which means you will not receive an
actuarial reduction due to the original filing, and can file a restricted application for spousal benefits.

Option 2: Go Back to Work

If you are outside the 12-month window and decide you want to go back to
work between the ages of 62 and Full Retirement Age (FRA), your benefits
will be subject to an Earnings Test. The 2012 earnings test exempt amount is
$14,640 ($38,880 in the year you turn FRA). Social Security will withhold $1 in
benefits for every $2 of earnings in excess of that amount. This is not a tax!

Let's say you elected benefits at 62 and were receiving an $1,800 monthly bene-
fit (75% of $2,400) and now you want to go back to work at 63 earning $90,000
per year. $90,000 - $14,640 is $75,360. Divide that by two and the earning
penalty would be $37,680. Since that is greater than the total Social Security
benefit of $21,600, you would not receive any Social Security for this period.

The reason we want to be very clear that the "earnings penalty" is not a tax is
because Social Security would adjust the reduction on your benefits for each

---

[35]Joe Elsasser, "Social Security: How to Fix a Mistake" www.socialsecuritytiming.
  com/sstiming.cfm?page=advisors&logic=how-to-fix-a-social-security-
  mistake&cobrand=sst. Used by permission.

month in which you didn't receive a check due to the earnings test. If you actually received benefits for the 12 months you were 62, but then worked and did not receive any further benefits until age 66, SSA would go back to your record and adjust your benefit upwards. They will treat it as if you had originally elected at 65 instead of 62, so you would then begin receiving a check for $2,240 plus any Cost of Living Adjustments that had accrued.

Option 3: Voluntarily Suspend

There is another option for those who don't want to go back to work. Once you reach FRA, you can voluntarily suspend benefits. You simply need to call or visit a Social Security office and request a voluntary suspension. You can even call in advance of FRA with instructions to suspend at FRA.

Here's where it gets interesting. See if you can follow the math here. By electing at age 62 to receive benefits, you basically reduced your monthly benefit to 75% of what you would have received if you had elected at FRA. By suspending benefits at age 66, you will increase your monthly benefit by 8% per year until age 70, for a total of 32%. So, if you increase 75% by 32% you get 99% ($.75 \times 1.32 = .99$). In other words, you can take Social Security from 62-66, suspend from 66-70 and still get 99% of the benefit you would have gotten had you simply waited until full retirement age.

This should not be viewed as a claiming strategy, only as a means for minimizing the damage of a mistake. There are several reasons one wouldn't want to elect at 62 with the intent of suspending at FRA. First, if you die between 62 and FRA, your widow/widower would be permanently stuck with a substantially reduced benefit. Second, you would forfeit any future option of claiming a restricted spousal benefit, because once you file for your own benefit, even if it is in suspension, your spousal benefit is reduced as if you were actually receiving your benefit. If your own suspended benefit is higher than your spousal benefit, you will not receive a spousal benefit.

Option 4: Maximize Benefits for your Spouse who has not yet elected.

When you are married and one of you has already elected benefits and the other has not yet elected benefits, your best option is to identify the best of the remaining strategies for the spouse who has not yet elected.

The strategies to consider include the possibility of having the spouse who has already elected choose a voluntary suspension once he or she reaches full retirement age.

> **REAL LIFE EXAMPLE: I FELL FOR THE BIGGEST CON THERE IS**
>
> George is one of the smartest clients I have ever worked with. He has numerous advanced degrees and enjoys digging into the details of decisions. He and his wife Chris came to see me when both were 63 because they wanted an expert opinion on when he might be able to transition to part-time work.
>
> A year prior, he thought he had done all his homework on Social Security, and after seeking advice elsewhere, he had Chris begin her benefits at age 62. She began receiving about $700 a month. He knew he would delay the start date of his own benefits.
>
> He thought when Chris reached her FRA she would be able to switch and begin collecting a spousal benefit on his record, which would be about $1,100 a month. I had to be the bearer of bad news. Because Chris filed before she reached her own FRA, this switching strategy was not an option.
>
> George's response was, "I fell for the biggest con there is. Free advice." He had gotten his earlier advice for free from a representative of a large, well-known mutual fund company and had followed the strategy they recommended. Because it had been more than 12 months since Chris had filed, there was no way to undo the decision.
>
> In their case, the "fix" was to have Chris request a voluntary suspension at her FRA and then resume her benefits at her age 70, which would bump her benefit up to about $900 a month. When George reached his FRA, he would collect a spousal benefit on Chris' record and then switch to his own benefit at his age 70. George was both thankful for the fix and frustrated, as he realized this mistake would likely mean they would receive less total benefits than if he had been given the right advice initially.
>
> I cannot overemphasize the importance of doing a thorough analysis before you claim.

Social Security Software and Calculators

As you've learned, Social Security is complex. I'd advise you use an online tool or calculator to help you evaluate your options. It is beyond the scope of this book to provide a comprehensive analysis of the different methods that online Social Security calculators use. Some tools use different methodologies than others, which can change the advice. In addition, online tools are continuously being improved, so at different times in the software development cycle, one tool may have more advanced capabilities than another, but that can change rapidly. This section contains a brief list of online resources that includes the tools I am most familiar with at the time of writing.[36]

---

[36] As new Social Security calculators and tools become available I do my best to add them to my online list at: http://moneyover55.about.com/od/socialsecuritybenefits/tp/Best-Social-Security-Calculators.htm.

- *From the Social Security Administration*: You can download a free, detailed Social Security calculator from the Social Security web site (www.ssa.gov/OACT/anypia/anypia. html). However, it does not evaluate claiming options for you and a spouse. You may find it useful for understanding the factors that affect your own benefits.

- *From the AARP*: AARP offers a free calculator (www.aarp. org/work/social-security/social-security-benefits-calculator/) that can help you see some of your claiming options. It does not allow you to see the numbers that lead to the final recommendation, nor at the time of writing does it deliver some of the more advanced claiming strategies that some of the fee-for-service software products provide.

As for software that charges a fee, there are a few options:

- *Maximize My Social Security*: Maximize My Social Security (www.maximizemysocialsecurity.com) was developed by Boston University economics professor Laurence Kotlikoff, software engineer Richard Munroe, and other professionals at Economic Security Planning, Inc., which markets personal financial-planning programs. This calculator covers all the Social Security claiming scenarios one might encounter: retiree, spousal, survivor, divorcee, parent and child benefits, as well as calculations for the windfall elimination provision and government pension offset. (These will affect you if you receive a pension from an employer who did not withhold Social Security tax from your earnings, such as state employers.)

- *Social Security Solutions*: Social Security Solutions (www.socialsecuritysolutions.com) was developed by William Meyer and Dr. William Reichenstein, who holds the Pat and Thomas R. Powers Chair in Investment Management at Baylor University. Together, they have published numerous papers on Social Security claiming strategies as well as the book *Social Security Strategies: How to Optimize Retirement Benefits* (2011). You can access their calculator directly. Kiplinger also offers a branded version of their software (www.kiplinger.socialsecuritysolutions.com).

Financial advisors have a few options as well:

- *Social Security Timing*: Social Security Timing (www.socialsecuritytiming.com) was developed by Joe Elsasser, an Omaha-based financial planner. Joe is also the Director of Advisory Services for Senior Market Sales, Inc. In his work as a financial advisor, Joe began testing a variety of Social Security calculator tools in search of a solution that would help his clients make the best decision about when to elect to take Social Security benefits. What he found was that every tool he tested, including the government's, was woefully incapable of providing a thorough analysis that took all of the election strategies for married couples into account. This calculator provides a free look into what is at stake between a poor claiming choice and a planned claiming choice and generates three strategies you may want to consider. To see the full strategy and the full report, you have to agree to be contacted by an advisor who subscribes to the full version of the software.[37]

- *Social Security Analyzer*: Social Security Analyzer (www.ssanalyzer.com) is the financial advisor version of the consumer calculator Social Security Solutions listed earlier.

Taxes on Your Social Security Benefits

If Social Security is your sole source of income, you do not pay taxes on it. If you have sources of income in addition to Social Security, up to 85% of your Social Security benefits may become subject to federal income taxes.

The formula used to determine the amount of taxes you might pay is complex, and I cover it in Chapter 5.

When you learn how to factor in taxes, you see that many people have their plan completely backwards. They take Social Security early and leave their retirement money alone, waiting until age 70 1/2, when required minimum distribution rules require them to begin taking withdrawals. From a tax perspective, for some people this can be one of the worst strategies. It is beyond the scope of this chapter to get into the details of why, but I cover it in Chapter 5.

What If Social Security Goes Away?

When I read online articles about Social Security claiming strategies, I always find it fascinating to read the comments from readers. A number of them attempt

---

[37]Author disclosure: at the time of writing, I subscribe to Social Security Timing.

to negate the information in the article by suggesting that Social Security won't be around, and therefore you should take your money and run.

Often, the same people who say this have their money in the bank (backed by FDIC insurance, which is backed by the U.S. Government), collect unemployment or other forms of benefits, or own U.S. bonds of some kind. Why would you be willing to count on the government for one form of sustenance but not another?

Yes, there will likely be changes to the Social Security system to make it viable for younger generations. Small changes like adjusting the full retirement age up by one month can have a big impact on the overall system but a negligible impact on any one person. Those are the types of changes I foresee.

No one is required to stay in the United States. If you find another country which you believe provides more security, and you can juggle the visa requirements and immigration laws to make it happen, then go. That is your right. It is also you right to say whatever you want as publicly as you wish. If you are near retirement age today, it is my right to think you are a fool if you are making your decision about Social Security based on a belief that it is going to go away.

Summary

The Center for Retirement Research offers a short brochure called "The Social Security Claiming Guide." On the front page it says, "A guide to the most important financial decision you'll likely make."[38]

It is important to do analysis before you make this important and often irrevocable decision.

A smart Social Security decision that is integrated with the rest of your retirement plan can help provide a solid floor of guaranteed income.

The evidence is clear that everyone has something to gain from developing a Social Security plan, with married couples, or singles eligible for a benefit on an ex-spouse's record, potentially having the most to gain.

I think it is important to use software to advise you on your options. The rules are complex, and important nuances can easily be missed by trying to work through this decision on your own.

Be smart and design a claiming plan. Build it into your income timeline. Then you can begin to align your investment decisions around your plan. I examine potential investment choices in Chapter 4.

---

[38]http://crr.bc.edu/special-projects/books/the-social-security-claiming-guide/

Investing

How Much Risk to Take

The safe way to double your money is to fold it over once and put it in your pocket.

—Frank Hubbard

Many years ago, I was sitting on a flight headed to see my family in Des Moines, Iowa. As we were waiting to take off I noticed the guy sitting in the seat next to me reading a publication called *Computerized Investing*, published by the American Association of Individual Investors. I hadn't seen this publication before, so I asked him if I might take a look at it when he was done. He said sure. Then he asked me a question that, at the time, I hated. It's a common enough question, but all the same, it is one I hated.

"So, what do you do for a living?"

I could feel a cringe creep over me as I replied, "I'm a financial advisor."

Why is it that I cringed at this oh-so-normal question? I am certainly not ashamed of what I do. I am, however, ashamed at the way a lot of so-called financial advisers do what they do. A lot of misconceptions arise in people's minds when they hear the term *financial advisor*.

Most people assume that if I'm a financial advisor, I sell investments. Somehow this also leads them to believe I might have a stock tip for them. Upon hearing my profession, they almost always ask some version of the same question: "What do you recommend people invest in right now?"

He didn't let me down. He asked, "So, what are you buying these days?"

The absurdity of the question hit me all at once, and I was silent for an uncomfortable length of time. I could not think of a rationale reply.

After the unusually long pause, I looked at my airplane buddy with a puzzled look on my face and said, "I'm really not sure how to answer that."

I'm sure he sat there thinking, "Geez, I'm glad she's not my financial advisor."

When someone asks me this question, it makes me wonder if they think they would get a different answer if they asked me tomorrow, or the day after. A good investment strategy should not change daily—or even monthly.

I can think of a hundred questions you can ask that will have a bigger impact on your financial success than asking a financial advisor what investment they are recommending. As you reach 50 and beyond, asking the right questions becomes particularly important.

The first thing you need to learn is how to measure risk. As you transition toward using your savings, your primary goal becomes the development of a strategy that delivers reliable monthly paychecks. This requires a new mindset and a new way of looking at investing. You need to have a way to compare the potential results of one strategy or investment choice to another. You need to make sure you are doing an apples-to-apples comparison, and this means you must have something objective to measure against.

Measuring Risk

Before putting your money somewhere, the first question to ask is "Can I lose all my money?" The second question is "Can I lose any money?"

Every investment can be logged somewhere on such a scale (Figure 4-1).

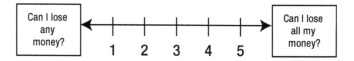

Figure 4-1. A Simple Investment Risk Scale

The investment risk scale in Figure 4-1 can help you compare the relative risk in one investment choice versus another.

However, you need to be careful with questions like "Can I lose any money?" You would think the definition of *losing money* would be simple, but it isn't always so.

Suppose you were to put all your money in a five-year, bank-issued certificate of deposit paying 2% a year. You invest $10,000. Five years later, it is worth $11,041. Inflation over those five years averaged 3% a year. If I were to ask you if you lost money, what would you say?

After adjusting for inflation, your $11,041 would buy only $9,524 of goods and services. Although you didn't lose any actual dollars, you did lose purchasing power. This is inflation risk in action.

In today's investing world, the word *risk* is often used only to refer to one type of risk: volatility. *Volatility* is the variation of returns from their average.

For example, from 1926–2011, U.S. stocks, as measured by the S&P 500 Index, averaged 9.8% a year. But that average encompassed years where it was down 43.3% (1931) and up 54% (1933),[1] as well as more recent years like 2008 when it was down 37%, and 2009 when it went up 26.5%. This variation of returns from the average in the withdrawal phase shows up as *sequence risk*. You may project one outcome based on your expected average return but experience an entirely different outcome because of the volatility of the actual returns incurred.

Nassim Taleb, in his book *The Black Swan* (Penguin, 2008), has a section called "Don't cross a river if it is (on average) four feet deep." It is a statement worth pondering. Most financial projections use averages. There is no guarantee that your investments will achieve the average return. When it comes to aligning your investments toward the objective of producing reliable income, you need to decide whether you want to rely on averages and whether you think they provide an accurate representation of risk.

James Montier, a member of GMO's asset allocation team,[2] has a definition of risk that I like. He says, "Let us forsake the false deity of volatility as a measure of risk. Risk isn't a number. It is a far more complex and multifaceted concept. Risk is the permanent impairment of capital."[3]

The real measure of risk is not losing or gaining money; it is the risk of not achieving your goals. If your money no longer buys the necessary amount of food, clothing, and shelter, conceptual views of risk—whether it is inflation risk, sequence risk, or some other form of risk—become irrelevant.

A 1–5 risk scale is useful for comparing the relative amount of risk in one investment to another, but how do you compare an investment choice against the risk of not achieving your goals?

- First you must clearly identify and quantify the goals.

- Next you must determine a risk-free way to achieve those goals.

---

[1]Dimensional Fund Advisors, *DFA Matrix Book* (2012), 12–13.
[2]GMO is a global investment management firm. As of June 30, 2012 it had $99 billion in client assets.
[3]James Montier, "The Flaws of Finance," GMO White Paper (May 2012).

- Then you can compare your alternatives relative to the risk-free choice. Once you have done this, you can decide whether the riskier alternatives potentially improve your outcome enough to warrant taking on the risk.

Identifying goals can be challenging in and of itself. We are all different.

I do not want to work and then reach a particular age and "retire." Planning toward that end is not inspiring to me. However, I do want choices, and I do realize there may come a day when I cannot work. I want to make sure I have my finances in order when that time comes.

You may be planning a traditional retirement, or you may choose to simply identify a point in time where you don't have to go to work to earn a living each day—a point where you may still choose to work, but on your terms.

Regardless of how you define your goals, you will reach a point where your financial capital needs to provide reliable income to take the place of your former paycheck. Success at this point is no longer defined as achieving a higher rate of return. You need a different measure of success and a different measure of risk.

Measuring requires something to measure against. When your goal is reliable income, start by looking at what can be achieved by using safe, guaranteed choices. Then compare alternatives relative to your risk-free choices.[4]

Benchmarking Against a Risk-Free Choice

There's only one response when someone asks you, "Hey, is that a safe investment?" And that is: "Safe compared to what?"

A benchmark gives you something to compare to.

If you are interested in having life-long inflation-adjusted income, then compare investment alternatives to risk-free choices that provide guaranteed life-long inflation-adjusted income.

This means measuring against such choices as:

- I Bonds
- TIPS (Treasury Inflation-Protected Securities)
- Inflation-adjusted immediate annuities

Let's take a look at each one of these options.

---

[4]Special thanks to Zvi Bodie for his time in our conversations about risk.

I Bonds

My interest in I Bonds started after I met Zvi Bodie, professor of economics at Boston University. We were both guest lecturing at a class for upcoming retirement management analysts. I flew in a few days before my presentation because I wanted to meet Zvi and a few other presenters.

In his presentation, Zvi said he believes that any financial advisor who does not advise their clients about the benefits of I Bonds is committing malpractice. That certainly caught my attention. As I began looking into I Bonds, I could see why he said this. They offer features that in many cases are more attractive than some of the financial products advisors sell. How can an advisor in good faith sell their client a financial product like a fixed annuity without first educating them about a free option that may have similar qualities? Let's take a look at what makes I Bonds attractive:

- I Bonds are issued directly by the U.S. Treasury and have been around since 1998.

- Their primary advantage is tax-deferred, inflation-adjusted interest and complete liquidity after 12 months.[5] In addition, interest earned is exempt from state and local taxes, making them even more attractive for those who live in states with high income taxes.

- You can buy I Bonds by opening a TreasuryDirect account online at www.treasurydirect.gov. Note that you can only buy them in non-retirement accounts (not in IRAs[6]). You do have the option to title your account as a trust.

- I Bonds are issued with a fixed interest rate that stays with the bond for its full term and a variable interest rate which is adjusted every six months based on inflation.

Table 4-1 shows historical I Bond rates. Using the bonds issued September 1, 1998 as an example, the fixed rate of 3.4% stays with the bond for its entirety, and in the right-hand column you see the inflation rate for the six-month period beginning on that date. The inflation rate is updated every six months and is applied in addition to the fixed rate.

---

[5] You cannot redeem I bonds within first 12 months of purchase. For redemptions that occur before five years of ownership, you forfeit the interest from the three most recent months.
[6] IRAs require a custodian to provide annual reporting for tax purposes. This requires additional administrative time, paperwork, and costs. It is likely not practical or cost-effective for the Treasury to go down this path and offer TreasuryDirect IRA accounts.

Table 4-1. Historical I Bond Rates[7]

Issue Date	Fixed Rate (%)	Inflation Rate (%)
1-Sep-98	3.40	0.62
1-Nov-98	3.30	0.86
1-May-99	3.30	0.86
1-Nov-99	3.40	1.76
1-May-00	3.60	1.91
1-Nov-00	3.40	1.52
1-May-01	3.00	1.44
1-Nov-01	2.00	1.19
1-May-02	2.00	0.28
1-Nov-02	1.60	1.23
1-May-03	1.10	1.77
1-Nov-03	1.10	0.54
1-May-04	1.00	1.19
1-Nov-04	1.00	1.33
1-May-05	1.20	1.79
1-Nov-05	1.00	2.85
1-May-06	1.40	0.50
1-Nov-06	1.40	1.55
1-May-07	1.30	1.21
1-Nov-07	1.20	1.53
1-May-08	0.00	2.42
1-Nov-08	0.70	2.46
1-May-09	0.10	-2.78
1-Nov-09	0.30	1.53
1-May-10	0.20	0.77
1-Nov-10	0.00	0.37
1-May-11	0.00	2.30
1-Nov-11	0.00	1.53
1-May-12	0.00	1.10

---

[7]Treasury Direct I Savings Bonds Rates and Terms at www.treasurydirect.gov/indiv/
research/indepth/ibonds/res_ibonds_iratesandterms.htm.

If you bought an I Bond in September 1998 when they were first issued and held on to it, by my calculations as of May 2012 you would have earned about a 5.9% annualized rate of return.[8]

For I Bonds bought in November 2002 and held through May 2012, the return would have been about 4.1%, and if bought November 2007 and held until May 2012, about 3.4%.

The returns have gone down as the fixed interest rates at issue have gone down.

Interestingly enough, even with a fixed rate of zero, if you look at the May 2012 I Bonds, with the inflation-adjusted rate of 1.10%, you are still earning the equivalent of an annual rate of 2.2%. When savings accounts and money markets are paying almost nothing, 2.2% on a safe investment that is completely liquid after 12 months is attractive.

In addition, even if you buy an I Bond that is issued with a fixed rate of zero, after holding it 12 months, you can cash it in and repurchase new I Bonds if the newer issues have a higher fixed rate.

The maximum purchase amount is $10,000 per year per person. You can purchase an additional $5,000 a year by directing your tax refund directly toward the purchase of I Bonds.

Because I Bonds earn inflation-adjusted interest, and their redemption value can never be less than their value the preceding month, this makes them an attractive baseline, or ruler, against which you can measure alternative strategies.

When comparing alternatives to I Bonds, or to anything, you should ask two questions:

- What return in excess of this safe, inflation-adjusted return do you think you will achieve?
- How certain is it?

For every $10,000 of I Bonds you buy today, you can be assured that they will buy $10,000 of goods and services when you cash them in years down the road. What you will forgo is potential additional return.

When comparing safe investments like I Bonds to riskier alternatives, keep in mind that there is no guarantee that a traditional portfolio of stocks and corporate bonds will earn a higher rate of return than safer options. The majority of people in the financial services industry will tell you that you must own stocks to have some growth in your portfolio—as if it is a certainty

---

[8]An I Bonds composite rate changes every six months and is determined by the following formula: [fixed rate + (2 × semiannual inflation rate) + (fixed rate × semiannual inflation rate)].

that stocks will outperform safer choices over the long term. It is not a certainty. Japan's large cap stock market index provides a good example. From the beginning of 1992 through the end of 2011, the 20-year annualized return was −.50%.[9] (This means for every $1 invested in 1992, you lost one half of one percent a year each year for 20 years.) Any sane person must acknowledge that any stock market could follow a similar path.

Personally, I believe that over the long term, stocks will provide a higher return than safer alternatives. Yet I acknowledge that my belief will not make it so. If it were a certain thing, there would be no need for safe investments.

Once you embrace an objective view of risk, you can make smarter and more personal decisions about how to allocate your money across both safe and risky choices.

TIPS: Treasury Inflation-Adjusted Securities

TIPS are another type of bond issued by the U.S. Treasury. The Treasury began issuing TIPS in 1997.

TIPS are issued with a fixed interest rate, and the principal value is adjusted upward (or downward) based on inflation. In a deflationary environment, your TIPS principal value may decline. (This is not the case for I Bonds.)

Both the interest paid and any principal increases are reported as taxable income in the year in which they occur. This makes them tax inefficient. They are best owned inside tax-deferred accounts, like IRAs, which means you need a brokerage account to purchase them for that purpose.[10] There are also mutual funds that specialize in TIPS.

Owning Individual Bonds vs. a Bond Fund

If you buy a bond when it is issued, you get the same amount back when it matures (in nominal, not real terms[11]). Your return is then composed of the interest rate, or coupon rate, that the bond pays.

---

[9]Dimensional Fund Advisors, *DFA Matrix Book* (2012), 45.

[10]You can purchase TIPS directly with a TreasuryDirect account, but only non-retirement account options are offered. To purchase them in an IRA you must have a brokerage account, which can either be a self-directed brokerage account such as one you might open with Schwab, Vanguard, Scottrade, or E*TRADE, or one you open through a traditional brokerage firm such as Merrill Lynch.

[11]*Nominal* means in today's dollars. *Real* means in inflation-adjusted dollars. If you buy a $1,000 bond today, and it matures in ten years, you get $1,000. But it may not buy $1,000 of goods and services because of price increases due to inflation.

Note, however, that between the issue date and maturity date, bond prices fluctuate.

For example, assume you buy a $1,000 bond that matures in ten years and pays an interest rate of 5%. The bond's yield to maturity[12] is 5%. Three years later, interest rates have gone down, and new bonds being issued (of similar quality and with about seven years left to maturity) are paying 3%. At that point an investor would be willing to pay you more than $1,000 for your bond because of its higher yield. This higher price would have the effect of making this bond's yield to maturity about 3%. In other words, the price increase made it equivalent to other bonds with similar characteristics being sold the day of the transaction.

On the other hand, if interest rates had gone up to 6%, and you wanted to sell your bond before maturity, an investor would offer you less than $1,000 for it because your coupon rate is lower than current rates. If you held it to maturity you would receive your $1,000.

To summarize, if you sell your bond before it matures, you may get more or less than you paid for it, which will change the total return you earn.

When you buy a mutual fund that owns bonds, your return will depend on the collective pricing and coupon rates of all the bonds the mutual fund owns, and on the timing of when those bonds are bought and sold, which is up to the management team that runs the mutual fund.

I am explaining this because it affects how you measure the return on an investment. To measure the return on a category of investments, financial companies create an index. An index is like a ruler; it is a measuring stick. The S&P 500 Index, for example, measures the collective performance of 500 large-company U.S. stocks. It is not reflective of the performance of any one stock.

There is an index for TIPS. It measures the performance of owning lots of TIPS with varying maturity dates. You can look at this index return to see how TIPS have performed, but keep in mind it is not the same as tracking the performance of buying specific individual bonds.

The annualized total return[13] for the Barclays Capital U.S. TIPS Index for the ten years from the beginning of 2002 through the end of 2011 was 7.6%.[14]

---

[12]*Yield to maturity* is a calculation that shows your expected rate of return on a bond if you hold the bond to maturity. It takes into account the current price of the bond, the interest rate, and the time left to maturity and assumes all interest is reinvested at the same rate, which in reality is not always possible.

[13]*Annualized total return* means you earned a return equivalent to earning 7.6% a year, but in reality that return was composed of some years where the TIPS Index was down (2008, for example, was down −2.4%) and other years where it was up significantly (2002, up 16.6%).

[14]Dimensional Fund Advisors, *DFA Matrix Book* (2012), 41.

A 7.6% return in a safe investment is attractive. Before you get too excited, keep in mind this is measured over a time period where interest rates have gone down, and so the corresponding increase in bond prices is included in that total return number.

TIPS have not been around long enough to measure their performance over a prolonged period of rising interest rates. If real interest rates rise (*real* meaning a rate increase beyond the rate of inflation), prices on existing TIPS bonds may go down.

To use TIPS to create future income, you could buy bonds today that mature in the year you want to spend the money. This is called *building a bond ladder*. When the bond matures you spend the principal and the interest it has accumulated. Building a bond ladder with TIPS can be challenging because you cannot always find TIPS with maturity dates that match your spending needs.

Owning TIPS by purchasing individual bonds offers an attractive and safe option for tax-deferred accounts with a guaranteed value upon maturity. However, I find that unless you have multiple millions, it can be impractical to build an effective bond ladder entirely with TIPS.

Although it takes some work, you can accomplish a laddering strategy by using TIPS along with a combination of CDs and government, agency, corporate, and municipal bonds. Using such a strategy is a smart way to guarantee the cash flows that need to come out of each account in the first five to ten years of retirement. With current cash flows guaranteed, you will never be in a position where you are forced to liquidate riskier investments at an inopportune time.

As an alternative to buying individual bonds, you can buy an index fund of TIPS. In that case, your return is dependent on the collective pricing and yields of lots of bonds. This option can provide long-term inflation protection, but there is not a guaranteed value available at a specific future date.

Both I Bonds and TIPS provide a safe investment option and protect your future purchasing power. You can use them for all of your investments, a small portion, or none of them. It's your choice regarding how much risk you want to take. Later in this chapter, you'll learn more about deciding how much to put in these types of investments.

Inflation-Adjusted Immediate Annuities

An immediate annuity is another safe option. An *annuity* is a contract with an insurance company. With an immediate annuity you give them a lump sum of money, and they pay you guaranteed life-long income. An inflation-adjusted immediate annuity pays you a lower amount initially, but then your income increases over time according to a predetermined inflation rate.

■ **Note** The term *annuity* is used to describe many different things. There are fixed annuities, immediate annuities, variable annuities, index annuities, and the type of annuity provided by a pension plan. In this section I am speaking specifically about immediate annuities. The characteristics I am describing do not apply to all types of annuities. Other annuity types will be covered in Chapter 8.

Think of an immediate annuity as a jar of cookies. You give the insurance company the whole jar, and they hand you back a cookie each year. If the jar becomes empty, they promise to keep handing you cookies anyway, for however many years you need them. In return, you agree that once you hand them the jar, you can't reach in it anymore. If one year you want three cookies, you'll have to get them from somewhere else.

This unending supply of cookies means a life payout annuity is a good hedge against longevity risk. No matter how long you live, and no matter how much of your other money you spend early in retirement, you'll still get a cookie each year.

With an inflation-adjusted immediate annuity, you start off getting a smaller cookie and it gets a little bigger each year thereafter. With a noninflation-adjusted annuity, your cookie is the same size each year.

The amount of monthly income you receive from an annuity depends on your age, whether you purchase the annuity for a single life, or joint life, and the inflation option you choose.[15]

TERM-CERTAIN ANNUITIES FOR OLDER HUSBAND/ YOUNGER WIFE SCENARIOS

You can purchase an annuity for a specific term, such as a five-year payout. This is called a *term-certain* annuity. Contrast this with a life-long annuity, which pays out for as long as you live. You can also buy an annuity that combines both options. An example of combining the two would be a single life annuity with a five-year term certain, which means the annuity will pay monthly income for as long as you live. If you die within the first five years after purchase, it is guaranteed to pay out for at least that full five years (you would name a beneficiary to receive the remaining payments). If you die after the term-certain period, the annuity stops when you stop.

---

[15]Additional features such as return of principal may be offered. These features usually reduce the effectiveness of using an immediate annuity as a hedge against longevity risk.

This can be an appropriate option for couples where the wife is much younger than the husband, because women tend to live longer. In a few such cases with the annuities offered by a pension plan, I have advised that the couple choose a life-long annuity on the wife, with a term-certain payout for 10 or 15 years. This option provides more income than a joint life annuity, and it provides a hedge, so that if the wife should die unexpectedly at a young age, the husband still has income for a specific amount of time. The risk in this option is that the wife dies first, and the husband lives many years past the term-certain period.

Here are a few immediate annuity basics to know:

- The older you are when you purchase the annuity, the more monthly income you will receive.

- Single-life annuities will have a higher payout than annuities that must cover two lives.

- Joint life annuities can be purchased for same-sex couples.

- With an immediate annuity, you are trading in your principal in return for a guaranteed income stream.

Let's look at an example. For a 65-year-old, in a low-interest-rate environment,[16] it costs about $230,000 to buy $1,000 a month of lifelong income in the form of an immediate annuity. In a higher-interest-rate environment it would cost less to purchase this income. Table 4-2 shows quotes I ran[17] that cover two different ages, as well as male, female, and joint annuity options.

Table 4-2. How Much Monthly Income Does a $230,000 Immediate Annuity Purchase Buy?

	No Inflation ($)	Inflation at 3% ($)	Inflation Tied to CPI-U ($)
Born 1/1/1948 (age 65 in 2013)			
Single Female	1,163	840	797
Single Male	1,243	914	865
Married couple	1,058	743	680
Born 1/1/1941 (age 72 in 2013)			
Single Female	1,410	1,070	1,065
Single Male	1,727	1,373	1,368
Married couple	1,231	923	888

---

[16] 2012 rates.

[17] Quotes run on incomesolutions.com platform on October 11, 2012 for nonqualified annuity purchases. Numbers rounded down to the nearest dollar.

Using Table 4-2 you can see that for a married couple, each born 1/1/1948, it takes $230,000 to purchase $1,058 a month of guaranteed income with no inflation raises, $743 a month that increases by 3% a year, or $680 a month that increases by the official inflation rate as measured by CPI-U.[18] These numbers will look significantly different in a higher-interest-rate environment.

I also ran the numbers for Steve and Carol. If they want to purchase guaranteed income, $230,000 will buy them $1,031 a month for their joint lives with no inflation raises, or $714 a month that increases by 3% a year. The inflation option that increases with the CPI-U was not an available option for Steve and Carol.[19]

Is buying the inflation-adjusted version of the annuity worth it? As discussed in Chapter 1, when studying actual retiree behavior, total spending in retirement may not keep pace with inflation as people age, particularly as they reach age 85 and beyond. Decreases in spending on travel, clothing, and entertainment seem to offset increases in spending on health care.

If you want to create a plan that allows you to spend more real dollars today, the non-inflation adjusted annuity is a better choice. You're making a choice that spending now is more important than spending later.

If you are concerned that inflation will eat away at your standard of living later, the inflation-adjusted annuity provides protection against this.

For someone who wants guaranteed income, my personal preference is for them to build a Social Security plan first, because that allows them to take advantage of the inflation-adjusted income that Social Security provides.[20] Then fill in additional needs for guaranteed income by using a noninflation-adjusted immediate annuity.

Now that you've examined three safe options for generating retirement income, you can compare riskier alternatives to these safe choices to see whether the potential additional returns are worth the risk.

The traditional, riskier alternative is the stock market. When used as part of your plan, stocks (particularly stock index funds, which I discuss in a bit) have their place in your retirement income portfolio. For stocks to be used as an effective tool, you must know where they fit into your plan and invest in

---

[18]Consumer Price Index for All Urban Consumers, a statistical measure used to monitor the change in the price of a set list of products.

[19]Inflation increases tied to the CPI-U impose a greater risk on the insurance company. If inflation is high they must pay out more versus using a fixed rate of 3%. For this reason, the CPI-U inflation option is not always available.

[20]There are discussions to amend the way the inflation adjustments are applied to Social Security benefits. If changes are made to this formula, the effectiveness of Social Security as an inflation hedge would need to re-evaluated based on the new rules.

them in such a way that the normal monthly and yearly ups and downs of the market have little to no effect on your long-term plan. I rarely see people use stocks as part of their plan in this way.

Instead, I see them used as speculative instruments. Attempting to achieve higher returns, many people fall for the big investment lie—the idea that someone out there can pick winning stocks and time the market. This approach can cause serious damage to your retirement plan.

Let's take a look at what the big investment lie is, how to avoid it, and what you can realistically expect to see if you use stocks as part of your retirement portfolio.

Don't Fall for the Big Investment Lie

In 2011, I ran an analysis for a client I'll call Bruce. As part of the analysis, I made recommendations for his investment portfolio. A year later he came back. His portfolio was entirely in cash.

"What happened?" I asked.

"I listened to one of those radio gurus who said the market was going to crash."

It is times like these when I am glad my inside voice cannot be heard. My internal commentator said:

> What? And you believed him? I gave you clear recommendations. You are a fool. You deserve to miss out on the gains that your investments would have experienced if only you had stuck with the plan. And of course the market is going to crash. The market crashes about once every four years. But no one knows exactly when it is going to happen. That's why you design your portfolio so those market movements have no effect on your cash flow.

Although I said nothing aloud, my expression must have said it all.

"I know, I know," he said.

The question I always like to ask is, why are so many people prone to believe the radio guru?

The book *Future Babble: Why Expert Predictions Are Next to Worthless—and You Can Do Better* by Dan Gardner (Dutton, 2011) may have the answer.

In a review of the book, Michael Edesess, an accomplished mathematician and economist, had this to say about predictions:

> Watching experts predict the future is like watching professional wrestling. You assume everybody knows it's a put-up job but can't resist it anyway. Then you discover that most people don't even know it's a put-up job in the first place.
>
> ... Lacking other information—as with a coin-toss—the chances of a stock outperforming its benchmark are 50-50. Whether it does so or not isn't merely a matter of the interaction of forces obeying rigid physical laws; it's the result of an even more complex interaction of economic and human forces that do not even approximately obey laws. Yet while we would be hard pressed to find a theoretical physicist claiming to be able to predict the result of a coin toss, we can readily find thousands of people who claim to know whether a stock or stock portfolio will outperform its benchmark.[21]

Every week I talk to people who believe in this put-up job. They believe someone can consistently predict the outcome of the coin toss. They seek expert opinions by subscribing to investment newsletters, searching for actively managed funds, "hot" investment managers, or the next "beat the market" strategy. They think by finding such solutions they can achieve superior returns. Think about it—if anyone could deliver these superior returns, why would they be doing it for you and not acting solely on the information for themselves?

Anyone who has read the academic work on this return-seeking behavior finds it ludicrous that so many people continue to engage in it. Edesess goes on to describe this societal need to seek expert predictions:

> Why are there so many "expert" predictions? And why do so many people believe them?
>
> One reason, Gardner points out, is that predictions get attention. If they happen to succeed, they win attention and plaudits—even celebritization if the prediction is wildly successful. And there's not much downside. If a recognized expert succeeds, he or she can make page one. If the expert fails, the story may make the back page.
>
> ... The media needs forecasters to help make the news, the public needs predictors to give them hope or an anchor for the future and experts need to believe they can predict to validate that they are experts. The fact that the whole thing is mostly a sham is almost irrelevant.

---

[21] Michael Edesess, "No More Stupid Forecasts!" *Advisor Perspectives* (July 2011). Available online at www.advisorperspectives.com/newsletters11/pdfs/No_More_Stupid_Forecasts.pdf. Used with permission.

After reading Michael's comments, I went on to read his book, *The Big Investment Lie*.[22] His introduction in the book is fabulous. He talks about his Ph.D. in mathematics and shares his thoughts on his first job with an investment firm. He didn't know anything about the stock market when he began his job, but at the time he thought . . .

> *I may as well learn about it. Besides, I should easily be able to get rich using my knowledge of mathematics, and why not? I'm smart; surely I can figure out how to beat the stock market. Little was I to know how many people I would meet over the years with the same idea, all of whom would be wrong.*

I cannot tell you how many engineers I have had walk into my office thinking the same thing. They're super smart. They understand math. They think they can chart stock patterns, moving averages or some other such thing, and instantly make a fortune. Or if they can't do it, their definition of a financial advisor is someone who can. If only it were so easy.

Michael's introduction goes on to say,

> *But within a few short months I realized something was askew. The academic findings were clear and undeniable, but the firm—and the whole industry—paid no real attention to them.*

The academic findings he refers to show that professional money managers do not add additional returns over what can be achieved by investing in a well-designed portfolio of index funds.

When I say *professional money managers*, what I mean is actively managed mutual funds and actively managed stock accounts. Actively managed means the money manager is trying to hand-pick the investments that will deliver the highest returns.

For example, you could own an S&P 500 Index fund, which owns all 500 stocks on Standard & Poor's large cap stock list, or you could own a mutual fund that tries to pick and choose among the 500 stocks to select only those that their research shows might deliver the highest returns. The active approach has higher investment fees because research and analysis costs money.

Paying more for actively managed mutual funds would be fine, if it resulted in higher returns. However, it does not. Data shows that funds with higher fees deliver lower returns.

---

[22]Michael Edesess, *The Big Investment Lie* (Berret-Koehler Publishers, 2007).

▨ **Note**   Data shows that mutual funds with higher fees have lower returns. There is no need to pay for "active management" of a stock fund.

Fund fees are measured by an expense ratio. Each fund reports its expense ratio on an annual basis. An expense ratio of .50 means the fund costs one half of one percent a year. That means, for every $100,000 invested, you are paying $500 a year.

A 2010 Morningstar study showed that expense ratios are the best predictor of fund performance. One Morningstar article concluded, "Expense ratios are strong predictors of performance. In every asset class over every time period, the cheapest quintile produced higher total returns than the most expensive quintile."[23]

Actively managed funds have high expense ratios and have been proven to collectively deliver lower performance than their lower cost peers. If you have a proven way of selecting funds that are most likely to have higher performance, why would you choose anything else? I have not found a sufficient answer to this question.

With your market-based portfolio you can avoid the big investment lie by following two rules:

1. Buy investments based on risk, not return. If you encounter someone selling you on their ability to predict what the market is going to do, run. No one can do this, and anyone who thinks they can is not the person you want giving you advice on your retirement money.

2. Buy low-fee funds (index funds make a good choice).

Let's take a look at both of these rules in more detail, starting with a look at how to classify investments according to risks rather than returns.

Risk Choices on the 1–5 Scale

The smart way to build a portfolio is by making choices based on risk. The 1–5 risk scale (Figure 4-1) is helpful in classifying the common investments you encounter. It starts with the question, can I lose any money? If the answer is

---

[23]Russell Kinnel, "How Expense Ratios and Star Ratings Predict Success," MorningstarAdvisor (August 2010). Available online at www.morningstar.com/advisor/t/42990194/how-expense-ratios-and-star-ratings-predict-success.htm.

no, the risk level is 1. The risk scale ends with the question, can I lose all my money? If the answer is yes, the risk level is 5.

This risk scale is not an industry standard; rather, it is something I use to help people develop realistic expectations. I am sure other professionals may disagree with some of my classifications, which is fine. The list is meant to be used only as a guideline to help you understand how one investment compares to another in terms of risk.

Risk Level 1: Investing for Safety

- I Bonds
- Series E/EE Bonds
- Certificates of deposit/bank savings accounts
- Money market accounts[24]
- Fixed annuities
- Fixed immediate annuities
- TIPS (Treasury Inflation-Protected Securities) and other government-issued bonds held to maturity

Risk Level 2: Investing for Safety and Some Income

- Short- or intermediate-term corporate and municipal individual bonds and bond funds using high-quality bonds.[25]
- Some funds that are classified as income funds—if the income comes from interest from short- or intermediate-term bonds, and not from stock dividends
- TIPS mutual funds. When owned in a mutual fund format, I have chosen to classify TIPS as a 2 rather than a 1.

Risk Level 3: Investing for Income

- Individual long-term corporate bonds, bond funds, and high-yield bonds and bond funds
- Long-term bond funds that are classified as income funds—if the income comes from interest from bonds and not from stock dividends
- Asset allocation funds

---

[24]Technically a money market account is not risk-free, but I do consider it to fall in the "investing for safety" category.
[25]Rated AA or better by Moody's or S&P rating services

- Balanced funds
- Retirement income funds
- International bond funds

Risk Level 4: Investing for Growth

- Stock funds
- Equity funds
- Most growth-and-income funds
- International equity funds
- Unleveraged real estate (with no mortgage)

Risk Level 5: Investing for Growth

- Individual stocks
- Leveraged real estate
- Business ownership

You can use this list to make appropriate risk-based choices.

For example, when you buy an individual stock, can you lose all your money? Of course you can. You've heard the stories of what once were great companies who went under: Bethlehem Steel, Trans World Airlines, Montgomery Ward, Enron, WorldCom, Lehman Brothers, Wachovia, Washington Mutual ... the list goes on.

What about when you own an S&P 500 stock index fund? Can you lose all your money? An S&P 500 Index fund owns stock in 500 of the largest companies in the U.S. In order for you to lose all your money, all of those companies would have to go bankrupt at once. If that happened, I think we would have bigger problems on our hands than what a portfolio might be worth.

For this reason, using the 1-5 risk scale, I rule out individual stocks as an option for the average person. If you want to build a portfolio of dividend-paying stocks, I am not saying that won't work. It might work quite well. But it takes a good deal of time and research to do it right. If you enjoy that, take classes and learn all you can before you do it. For the average person, I don't think this is the way to go. A lower-maintenance approach using index funds will fare just as well.

Index Funds

You can build a portfolio in numerous ways. If one way were certain to deliver better results, everyone would do it. I think most people are best served by a simple and effective strategy. Index funds fit the bill. Index funds allow you to invest in an entire stock or bond market, or segment of a market, with the purchase of a single fund.

Index funds are an effective way to manage risk and they have low fees. As I mentioned, low fees have been proven to be the best indicator of fund performance. You can find great index funds at the following places.

- Vanguard (www.vanguard.com)

- iShares Exchange Traded Index Funds (www.ishares.com)

- Charles Schwab Index Funds (search "Schwab index funds" to get to the index fund section of the Schwab web site)

There is one additional mutual fund company worth mentioning in this section: DFA (Dimensional Fund Advisors). DFA funds do not actually track an index, because they have their own way of defining certain sectors of the market. The funds are not actively managed and focus on low costs. DFA believes you can't "beat" the market, so its funds are much like more traditional index funds in that regard.

DFA offers its funds through fee-only advisors[26] or through institutions (such as a pension plan or as a choice in your 401k plan). I include DFA on this list because it has great educational material on its web site (www.dfaus.com). Many reputable fee-only investment advisors use DFA funds, and you may encounter them within a 401(k) plan offered by your employer. They are a great choice.

Now that you understand what the big investment lie is, and how to avoid it, let's take a look at what you might experience when using stock and bond index funds to reach your goals.

Past Performance of Index Fund Portfolios

When I started my career as a financial advisor in 1995, the other advisers and I frequently used a version of a chart like Figure 4-2 to persuade clients to invest in stock mutual funds, particularly the ones we sold.

---

[26]Fee-only advisors are not compensated by commissions on the sale of investment or insurance products. They provide advice for a fee, which may be structured as an hourly rate, project fee, or as a percentage of assets managed.

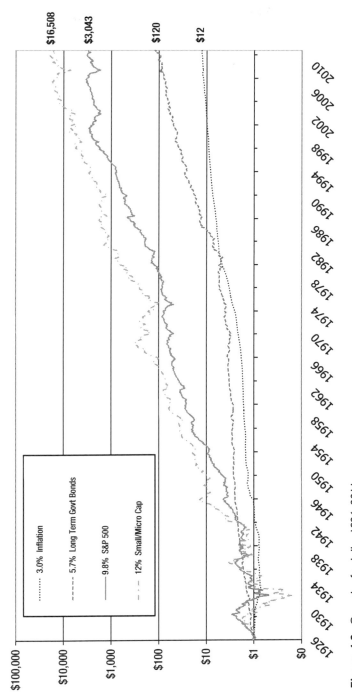

Figure 4-2. Growth of a dollar, 1926–2011

The bottom dotted line on Figure 4-2, inflation, shows you that it would take $12 at the end of 2011 to buy the same goods and services that $1 would purchase in 1926. The three lines above it show you what your dollar would be worth if you had invested it in either long-term government bonds, large-cap U.S. stocks (as measured by the S&P 500 Index), or U.S. small-cap stocks[27] (as measured by CRSP 9-10 index). The results do not reflect any deductions for transaction costs, investment management fees, or taxes.

The chart makes owning a collection of stocks look great. Why wouldn't you put all your money in the line where it grows the most?

It took me years to come to the belief I hold today: that this chart, when used on a stand-alone basis as you see it here, has caused more harm to investors than just about anything else I can think of. There is nothing on it that is not true; yet when viewing it you begin to form a set of expectations about what you might experience as an investor that is far from true.

When you zoom in and look at shorter time periods, investment results can vary significantly from the averages you see in Figure 4-2. Look at returns during the 1990s (Figure 4-3).

The solid line on the chart shows the performance of stocks listed in the S&P 500 Index. They averaged an annualized return of 18.2% a year from 1990–1999. Long-term government bonds also did well, averaging 8.9% a year.

Using that decade to set rate-of-return expectations on a portfolio that was 50% invested in stock funds and 50% in bond funds, you get the following:

- *Stocks: .50 × 18.2% = 9.1%*

- *Bonds: .50 × 8.9% = 4.5%*

- *Expected return on this portfolio:* 13.5%.[28] Net of invest-ment fees would be perhaps 12–13%, depending on the amount of fees you pay.

---

[27]*Cap* refers to capitalization or the total value of a company calculated by taking the share price multiplied by the total number of outstanding shares. Companies worth $5 billion or more are generally categorized as large cap. Small caps might be companies worth $2 billion or less. Dollar limits used for categorization can be defined differently by different organizations and may change over time.

[28]This calculation assumes half the portfolio is in stocks and half in bonds and that it is rebalanced annually. I am not saying this should be the expected return; I am saying behaviorally this is how people use past returns to begin to develop expectations about future returns.

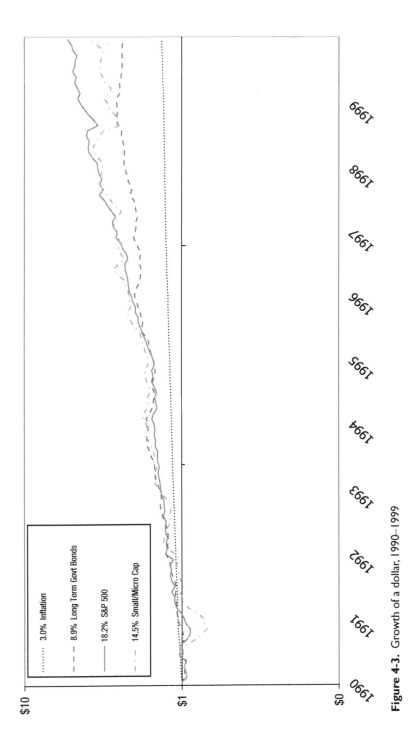

Figure 4-3. Growth of a dollar, 1990–1999

Instead of the 12–13% returns people had come to expect, the next decade delivered a mess. One of my clients shared with me her view that as a nation we are all suffering from PTSD (Post Traumatic Stress Disorder). Based on the 1990s, we all expected to be wealthy and retire at a young age. The events of the 2000–2009 decade shattered this expectation, and we are still recovering. Resetting expectations can take time.

The media occasionally refers to the ten years ending in 2009 or 2010 as "the lost decade" due to the poor performance of stocks during that time. Certainly, it was nothing like the stellar returns we became accustomed to in the 1990s, but was it truly lost? Figure 4-4 shows the returns for 2000–2009.

Notice that small-cap stocks and long-term government bonds did just fine over this lost decade. Additional asset classes such as real estate and emerging markets also did quite well.[29]

Carl Richards, author of *Behavior Gap: Simple Ways to Stop Doing Dumb Things with Money* (Portfolio/Penguin, 2012), wrote about the lost decade in his *New York Times* Bucks Blog on August 31, 2011.[30] He assumed from 2001 to 2010 an investor invested 1/5th of their portfolio in each of the following asset classes:

- U.S. large stocks (the S&P 500)

- U.S. small stocks (the Russell 2000 Index)

- U.S. real estate stocks (the Dow Jones US REIT index)

- International stocks (MSCI EAFE Index)

- Emerging markets stocks (MSCI Emerging Markets Index)

He concluded, "The return for this diversified stock portfolio ... was an annualized 8.35 percent. That is a far cry from a lost decade."

---

[29]Real estate as measured by the Dow Jones US Select REIT Index averaged 10.7% a year from 2000–2009, and emerging markets stocks as measured by the MSCI Emerging Markets Index averaged 10.1% a year.

[30]http://bucks.blogs.nytimes.com/2011/08/31/why-it-shouldnt-have-been-a-lost-decade-for-investors/

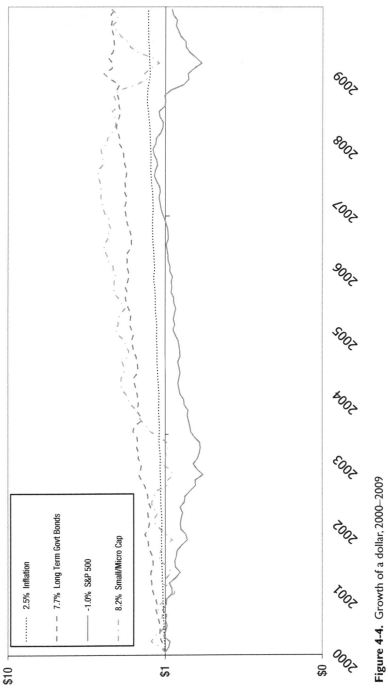

Figure 4-4. Growth of a dollar, 2000–2009

Today I often meet people who tell me that, because of recent events, they don't believe investing works. A little fact-finding often shows they've been investing in a completely illogical manner. They might own five mutual funds that all own large-cap stocks, and so their performance would have reflected only the performance of large-cap stocks, which was pretty poor.

I've been known to say, "If you're doing it wrong, of course it doesn't work. It's like trying to use a hammer to drive a screw into the wall. You get a mess. So what are you going to do, blame the hammer?"

Whether investing for accumulation or to take regular withdrawals, you must diversify. Diversifying does not mean having accounts in many different places; that does not ensure that you own a diverse portfolio.

Proper diversification involves building a portfolio model that matches your investment choices up with the point in time where you need to use the money. When done right this allocation model is aligned to your goals and tells you approximately how much money you should have in which types of investments, such as large-cap U.S., small-cap U.S., international, emerging markets, long-term bonds, short-term bonds, and so on. I can't tell you exactly how much should be where, because I don't know you. I provide one example of what a diversified index fund portfolio looks like, though.

Index Fund Portfolios with Withdrawals

Let's take a look at what happened to a retiree who was taking withdrawals from a diversified index fund portfolio over the last decade. Suppose she invested $500,000 on January 1, 2000 and withdrew $25,000 a year, each year through 2011 for a total of 12 years of withdrawals. It was the lost decade; I bet she ran out of money, right?

First, this investor built a portfolio that was 50/50 bonds and stocks, rebalanced annually,[31] and reinvested all dividends and capital gains. The bond portion of her allocation included short-, intermediate-, and long-term bonds. The stock portion included U.S. large and small cap, real estate, international large cap, and emerging markets.

Table 4-3 shows the specific index funds used, how much was allocated to each, and how much was withdrawn each year. Table 4-4 shows their remaining balances each year after taking a $25,000 withdrawal.

---

[31] As the market moves, if stocks go up and bonds stay flat, stocks may now represent more than 50% of your portfolio value. In this situation, rebalancing would involve selling stocks and buying bonds to bring the allocation back to 50/50. This would also work in reverse if stocks went down.

Table 4-3. Fund Choices, Allocation, and Amounts Withdrawn From Each[32]

Fund	Investment Amount ($)	Annual Withdrawal ($)	Rebalanced Annually to this %
Vanguard Short Term Bond Index (VBISX)	100,000	–5,000	20
Vanguard Intermediate Term Bond Index (VBIMX)	100,000	–$5,000	20
Vanguard Long Term Bond Index (VBLLX)	50,000	–2,500	10
Vanguard 500 Index (VFINX)	90,000	–4,500	18
Vanguard International Growth (VWIGX)	75,000	–3,750	15
Vanguard REIT Index (VGSNX)	30,000	–1,500	6
Vanguard Explorer (VEXPX)	30,000	–1,500	6
Vanguard Emerging Markets (VEIEX)	25,000	–1,250	5
Total:	500,000	25,000	100

Table 4-4. Portfolio Balance After Withdrawing $25,000 a Year

Calendar Year	End of Year Balance After Withdrawals ($)
2000	488,943
2001	459,451
2002	414,183
2003	468,494
2004	489,790
2005	494,517
2006	527,048
2007	540,078
2008	414,984
2009	472,964
2010	504,450
2011	488,128

[32]The numbers in Table 4-5 and Table 4-6 were run using the hypothetical illustration option in Morningstar Workstation.

This retiree has taken $300,000 of cumulative income (12 years × $25,000 a year) and has almost the same amount of principal she started with.

Using the pricing in Table 4-2, I can estimate that a noninflation-adjusted annuity that provides $25,000 a year of guaranteed income would cost about $453,000.[33] The difference is: with the market-based portfolio, you still have access to the cookie jar; at the end of the 12 years, you still have $488,000.

Now, in this example the retiree's withdrawals have not kept pace with inflation. There is a reason for this. I advise people to use a flexible approach to withdrawals from market-based portfolios. If investment returns are below expectations, be prepared to forgo inflation raises or spend more principal. If you spend principal too fast, you could run out of money later. During the recent time periods of lower-than-expected market returns, I have advised people to forgo inflation raises.

On average, I suggest if you are willing to forgo inflation raises as needed, and if you are willing to spend some principal over your life expectancy, then as a rough rule of thumb, a diversified market portfolio should deliver about $5,000 a year of income per $100,000 invested over your expected lifetime.

If you get a period of above-average returns, your $5,000 may increase with inflation, and you may retain all principal. If you get a period of below-average returns, you may need to forgo all inflation raises, take a reduction in the level of withdrawals, and/or be willing to spend principal. This decision to take inflation raises or adjust withdrawals should be evaluated each year in light of the portfolio return and future expected cash flow needs as measured over remaining life expectancy. This flexible approach makes a market-based portfolio a viable option for retirement income.

If you don't want to take the chance of forgoing inflation raises, you can buy the equivalent amount of inflation-adjusted income using the immediate annuity. Based on the pricing in Table 4-2, for a 65-year-old couple, $25,000 a year of inflation-adjusted income[34] costs about $645,000.

---

[33]From Table 4-2, I used a price of $230,000 for the married couple born 1/1/1948, which pays $1,058 a month of fixed income, or $12,696 a year. That's a price of about $18.12 per $1 of guaranteed income. $18.12 × $25,000 is $453,000. This is not as accurate as getting an actual quote, but should come pretty close.

[34]At 3%, not the CPI-U option.

To summarize outcomes:

- Noninflation-adjusted annuity providing $25,000 a year of guaranteed life-long income would cost about $453,000.
    - Advantage is a life-long guaranteed outcome.[35]
    - Disadvantages are no possibility of inflation raises and principal has been "traded in" for the income stream.
- Inflation-adjusted immediate annuity providing $25,000 a year of guaranteed income for the couple would cost about $645,000.[36]
    - Advantage is a life-long guaranteed outcome of inflation-adjusted income.
    - Disadvantage is principal has been traded in for the income stream.
- Noninflation-adjusted income of $25,000 a year based on an index fund portfolio would cost about $500,000.
    - Advantages are the possibility of inflation raises later, if market returns are higher, and the continued access to principal if needed.
    - Disadvantage is uncertainty. If you spend principal too fast, live extra long, or market returns are quite poor, you may run out of money.

There is no free lunch. Market-based portfolios that are diversified and rebalanced are an effective strategy for retirement income, but they do come with uncertainty.

Now, let's compare safer choices side by side with riskier options. Then I look at how you might combine some of these strategies to accomplish your retirement income goals.

---

[35]There is risk even with an annuity. Your guarantee is only as solid as the insurance company behind it. I discuss insurer risk in Chapter 8.

[36]From Table 4-2 I used a price of $230,000 for the married couple born 1/1/1948, which pays $743 a month of inflation-adjusted income, or $8,916 a year. That's a price of about $25.80 per $1 of guaranteed income. $25.80 × $25,000 is $645,000. This is not as accurate as getting an actual quote, but should come pretty close.

Cost of $1,000 a Month

Income isn't free. You pay a price to receive it. While working, the price of your income is your time and knowledge—what's called your *human capital*.

You may also receive benefits from the society you participate in and contribute to, such as Social Security or pensions. This is your *social capital*.

Then you have your *financial capital:* the savings and investments you have accumulated.

When considering your financial capital, you can compare alternatives by looking at how much capital you must use to generate a reliable $1,000 a month of income. The key word is *reliable*.

You may find a high-yield investment that generates a 10% dividend and decide it will only cost you $120,000 to buy $12,000 a year of income. When compared to the $230,000 price tag of an immediate annuity delivering a similar amount, this may sound great. However, the 10% is not guaranteed. The company could reduce its dividend, which would also result in a lower share price, leaving you with less income and less principal.

When comparing strategies, make sure you understand the reliability factor of the various choices you are considering and the assumptions you are making.

The estimated price of an income stream will vary, depending on the assumptions you make. The two key assumptions are the rate of return you think is achievable and your estimated life span.

- When determining realistic rates of return, think in terms of what return you will earn in excess of inflation (called your *real rate of return*). If inflation is 3%, and your portfolio earns 7%, your real rate of return is 4%.

- When determining a realistic length of life, think in terms of the longevity table in Chapter 1 and in terms of probabilities.

For example, if you think stocks will average a 7% rate of return, and bonds will average a 5% rate of return, if half of your investments are in stocks and half are in bonds, the math works like this:

- .50 × 7% = 3.5%

- .50 × 5% = 2.5%

- Total estimated annual portfolio return: 6.0%[37]

---

[37]When using realistic long-term returns, not just recent returns, I think this calculation provides an appropriate way to set long-term rate-of-return expectations based on your portfolio allocation.

You will likely have some investment fees. If you own index funds, your investment fees will run about one quarter of one percent, so your net return would be 5.75%. If you pay an investment advisor who uses actively managed funds, you may be paying fees of 2% or more a year, which reduces your net return to 4%.

Next subtract out inflation expectations. If you think inflation will be about 3%, that leaves you with a real rate of return of 1%–2.75% depending on how much in fees you pay.

To put all of this together, see Table 4-5, which was compiled by Moshe Milevsky[38] and originally published in *Research Magazine* (reprinted with permission). It outlines the costs of $1,000 a month of real income by both assumed real rate of return and estimated life span.

Table 4-5. What Size Nest Egg Do You Need?[39]

Retiring at age 65 Needing $1,000 of Monthly Income for Life					
		REAL Inflation-adjusted Investment Return (Interest Rate)			
	Age	0.0%	1.5%	4.0%	6.5%
Plan to Life Expectancy	84.2	$230,490	$200,300	$160,900	$131,600
Plan to 75th Percentile	90.1	$301,700	$251,300	$190,300	$148,600
Plan to 95th Percentile	97.1	$385,100	$305,600	$216,900	$161,700
Cost of REAL Annuity	N.A.	N.A.	$230,000[40]	N.A.	N.A.

Using Table 4-5, if you assume your real[41] rate of return is zero, meaning your savings are going to earn the rate of inflation but no more, you can see that if you live to a life expectancy of 84.2, the cost of $1,000 a month of real income is $230,490. If you live to 97.1, that cost goes up to $385,100. A real rate of return of zero would be comparable to what you might receive from I Bonds or TIPS.

---

[38]Moshe Milevsky, Ph.D., is the executive director of the Individual Finance and Insurance Decision (IFID) Centre, associate professor of finance at York University in Toronto, and author of the book *Are You a Stock or a Bond? Create Your Own Pension Plan for a Secure Financial Future* (FT Press, 2008).
[39]Data from Moshe Milevsky, "What Does Retirement Really Cost?" *Research Magazine* (September 2011). Reprinted with permission of Summit Business Media. Article available online at www.advisorone.com/2011/09/01/what-does-retirement-really-cost.
[40]Quote run in 2011 for single life, male age 65, inflation-adjusted payout.
[41]Remember, real return means the return you earn in excess of the inflation rate. Real income means income that has kept pace with inflation.

The bottom row labeled Cost of REAL Annuity is an inflation-adjusted immediate annuity quote run on a single life male. It shows that an immediate annuity that provides $1,000 a month of inflation-adjusted life-long income would cost a 65-year-old male $230,000.

In the far right column of Table 4-5, you see that if you could be assured of earning a 6.5% real rate of return (which means if inflation was 3%, your total return would be 9.5%—not something I think you should at all be assured of), the cost of achieving that same $1,000 of income goes down substantially. I think you should throw the 6.5% column out the window and focus on the remaining three columns.

You can gather your own inflation-adjusted annuity quotes[42] based on your age, marital status, and current rates and insert them into this table to compare the specific costs of your guaranteed choices to other options.

When doing such comparisons, keep in mind a bumper sticker I saw years ago. It said "Fast, Cheap, or Reliable. Pick two out of three."

With a potentially lower price come uncertainty and the possibility that you may not achieve your goals. You do not get "$1,000 a month," "life-long guarantee," and "low price." You must pick two out of those three.

Some people choose to use only safe, guaranteed options that provide a known outcome. Others prefer to invest with the goal of achieving a higher real rate of return. For most people a combination of these choices is the best solution. The question is: how do you combine them?

Asset Allocation Based on Risk Management

You can use your Social Security decision as part of a plan along with I Bonds, TIPS, immediate annuities, and a more traditional investment portfolio of stock and bond index funds to manage the different types of risk you have in retirement.

Each of these choices helps manage a different type of risk:

- Your Social Security decision provides protection against inflation risk, longevity risk, overspending risk, and sequence risk. It's an important decision.

- I Bonds and TIPS protect against inflation risk and sequence risk.

---

[42]Pricing can vary on immediate annuities, just as it can with any product. For a low-fee solution, try getting quotes through Vanguard or through a fee-only financial advisor that uses the Income Solutions platform, which is the same annuity quote platform that Vanguard uses.

- An immediate annuity insures against longevity risk, over-spending risk, and sequence risk.

- When you build a traditional portfolio of stocks and bonds, you diversify to minimize market risk with the goal of achieving a rate of return higher than a safer invest-ment. This part of your portfolio may allow you to spend more and enjoy a higher standard of living than if you choose a 100% guaranteed approach.

Using a combination of these options allows you to diversify against multiple types of risk. Let's take a look at an example. Suppose you are going to need about $36,000 a year of savings withdrawals to supplement Social Security and pensions. You could choose to allocate your investments based on the types of risk you want to protect against.

Such a strategy might work as follows:

- Hedge against inflation by using I Bonds and TIPS for $12,000 of the needed income (you may be constrained by time and the purchase amount limits on I Bonds, mak-ing it impossible to invest enough to fund this amount of income, but you could do as much as feasible). Using the zero percent real return column from Table 4-5 and planning to live until 90, you'll need to set aside about $301,000 for this purpose.

- Hedge against longevity, inflation, and overspending by using an inflation-adjusted immediate annuity to provide $12,000 of annual income. According to Table 4-5, a sin-gle male, age 65, would need to set aside $230,000 for this purpose. (As Table 4-2 shows, the cost will go down for noninflation-adjusted annuities. In addition, costs are higher for joint life expectancy and single females.)

- Retain risk and invest for additional return by building a market-based portfolio and taking $12,000 a year of with-drawals. Assuming a real return of 4% and living to 90, you would set aside about $216,000 for this purpose.

- Total savings needed to implement this approach adds up to $747,000.

Using this approach, you are allocating your investments based on the risks you expect to encounter throughout retirement.

When deciding how much income should come from which source, rather than follow a rule such as "30% of my income stream should come from guar-anteed choices," you would build your own income timeline to make choices that are based on your "sleep factor."

By *sleep factor* I mean: how comfortable are you with a given approach? The transition from saving money on a regular basis to taking regular withdrawals is scary. If the market is down, are you losing sleep? If so, maybe you would be better off with a higher allocation to lower-risk approaches. My own belief is that, given a long enough time-horizon (such as "I need this money to last the rest of my life"), a well-engineered market-based portfolio built with index funds, individual bonds, and CDs will not deliver results significantly worse than a safe, guaranteed alternative and may deliver results that far exceed safer choices. Because this is my belief, I prefer to allocate more toward the market-based portfolio because it provides the opportunity for more. However, this is not an appropriate decision for everyone. Your choices need to be based on your situation. You can use your coverage ratio and the worksheets in Chapter 2 to help you figure it out.

Using Your Coverage Ratio

Steve and Carol want to line things up now so they don't have to worry later. They want to know their fixed expenses are secure as they age. With the future secure, they feel they can enjoy traveling and spending more in their first ten years of retirement without worrying about what might happen later.

They agree to follow a Social Security claiming plan, and now we are exploring additional ways to provide guaranteed income. At their current ages, $230,000 buys them $1,031 a month of guaranteed noninflation-adjusted income that continues for whichever is longer-lived. I added this guaranteed income into their income timeline, which you can see in Figures 4-5 and 4-6 in the Annuity row listed under Carol.[43]

---

[43]The annuity is arbitrarily listed under Carol because I needed a place to put it. It is not meant to imply that the annuity is on her life only or purchased using only her money.

Steve & Carol, Income Timeline: Claiming Social Security Benefits According to a Plan, Mortgage Gone in 2028

As of: Beginning of Year 2013

# of Years	1	2	3	4	5	6	7	8	9	10	11	12
Calendar Year	2013	2014	2015	2016	2017	2018	2019	2020	2021	2022	2023	2024
Fixed Sources of Income												
Steve (age)	66	67	68	69	70	71	72	73	74	75	76	77
Earnings	$48,000	$48,000	$48,000	$48,000	$48,000	0	0	0	0	0	0	0
Pension	0	0	0	0	0	0	0	0	0	0	0	0
Social Security	0	0	0	0	$23,248	$34,872	$34,872	$34,872	$34,872	$34,872	$34,872	$34,872
Life Insurance	0	0	0	0	0	0	0	0	0	0	0	0
Other	0	0	0	0	0	0	0	0	0	0	0	0
Carol (age)	62	63	64	65	66	67	68	69	70	71	72	73
Earnings	0	0	0	0	0	0	0	0	0	0	0	0
Pension	0	0	0	0	0	0	0	0	0	0	0	0
Annuity	$12,372	$12,372	$12,372	$12,372	$12,372	$12,372	$12,372	$12,372	$12,372	$12,372	$12,372	$12,372
Social Security - Spousal	$0	$0	$0	$0	$12,111	$13,212	$13,212	$13,212	$1,101	0	0	0
Social Security - Own	0	0	0	0	0	0	0	0	$16,170	$17,640	$17,640	$17,640
Other	0	0	0	0	0	0	0	0	0	0	0	0
A. Total Fixed Income:	$60,372	$60,372	$60,372	$60,372	$95,731	$60,456	$60,456	$60,456	$64,515	$64,884	$64,884	$64,884
Fixed Expenses	$72,993	$72,993	$72,993	$72,993	$72,993	$72,993	$72,993	$72,993	$72,993	$72,993	$72,993	$72,993
Coverage Ratio	0.83	0.83	0.83	0.83	1.31	0.83	0.83	0.83	0.88	0.89	0.89	0.89
B. Desired Gross Income:	$80,000	$80,000	$80,000	$80,000	$80,000	$80,000	$80,000	$80,000	$80,000	$80,000	$80,000	$80,000
C. $ Needed from Savings: (A minus B)	($19,628)	($19,628)	($19,628)	($19,628)	$15,731	($19,544)	($19,544)	($19,544)	($15,485)	($15,116)	($15,116)	($15,116)

Money needed today, discounted at a 2% real return, to get to ages:		Simple sum of dollars, no discount rate:
85/81	$210,780	$248,174
90/86	$224,014	$268,754
95/91	$236,036	$289,334
99/95	$244,855	$305,798

Figure 4-5. Page 1 of Steve and Carol's income timeline with a Social Security plan, life annuity added

# of Years	13	14	15	16	17	18	19	20	21	22	23	24	25
Calendar Year	2025	2026	2027	2028	2029	2030	2031	2032	2033	2034	2035	2036	2037
Fixed Sources of Income													
Steve (age)	78	79	80	81	82	83	84	85	86	87	88	89	90
Earnings	0	0	0	0	0	0	0	0	0	0	0	0	0
Pension	0	0	0	0	0	0	0	0	0	0	0	0	0
Social Security	$34,872	$34,872	$34,872	$34,872	$34,872	$34,872	$34,872	$34,872	$34,872	$34,872	$34,872	$34,872	$34,872
Life Insurance	0	0	0	0	0	0	0	0	0	0	0	0	0
Other	0	0	0	0	0	0	0	0	0	0	0	0	0
Carol (age)	74	75	76	77	78	79	80	81	82	83	84	85	86
Earnings	0	0	0	0	0	0	0	0	0	0	0	0	0
Pension	0	0	0	0	0	0	0	0	0	0	0	0	0
Annuity	$12,372	$12,372	$12,372	$12,372	$12,372	$12,372	$12,372	$12,372	$12,372	$12,372	$12,372	$12,372	$12,372
Social Security - Spousal	0	0	0	0	0	0	0	0	0	0	0	0	0
Social Security - Own	$17,640	$17,640	$17,640	$17,640	$17,640	$17,640	$17,640	$17,640	$17,640	$17,640	$17,640	$17,640	$17,640
Other	0	0	0	0	0	0	0	0	0	0	0	0	0
A. Total Fixed Income:	$64,884	$64,884	$64,884	$64,884	$64,884	$64,884	$64,884	$64,884	$64,884	$64,884	$64,884	$64,884	$64,884
Fixed Expenses	$72,993	$72,993	$72,993	$61,702	$61,702	$61,702	$61,702	$61,702	$61,702	$61,702	$61,702	$61,702	$61,702
Coverage Ratio	0.89	0.89	0.89	1.05	1.05	1.05	1.05	1.05	1.05	1.05	1.05	1.05	1.05
B. Desired Gross Income:	$80,000	$80,000	$80,000	$69,000	$69,000	$69,000	$69,000	$69,000	$69,000	$69,000	$69,000	$69,000	$69,000
C. $ Needed from Savings: (A minus B)	($15,116)	($15,116)	($15,116)	($4,116)	($4,116)	($4,116)	($4,116)	($4,116)	($4,116)	($4,116)	($4,116)	($4,116)	($4,116)

Time Segmented Approach

	Withdrawals Needed	Discount Rate	PV of Withdrawals Needed:
Years 1 - 10	($152,014)	0%	$152,014
Years 11 - 20	($96,160)	1%	$83,623
Years 20 - 34	($57,624)	2%	$33,534

Figure 4-6. Page 2 of Steve and Carol's income timeline with a Social Security plan, life annuity added

When looking at Figure 4-6, you can see that their coverage ratio is now 1.05 when Steve reaches 81. Research shows cognitive abilities decline as we age.[44] In addition, one spouse often handles the finances. For both these reasons, I think it makes sense to build a plan that provides a higher coverage ratio later. It protects you against a future self that may not be able to make decisions as soundly as you can today, and if you are married, it protects a spouse who may not be as money-savvy as you. (You can also protect your future self and your spouse by hiring a good financial advisor, but I'm an advisor, of course I am going to say that. And I believe it.)

Steve and Carol like the concept of having this additional guaranteed income. If they decide to proceed with it, the decision is not about which option is the "best" investment. It is about managing risk.

The actual rate of return they will earn using an immediate annuity will depend on how long they live. Using an internal rate of return (IRR) calculation, you can see what equivalent return the immediate annuity is providing.

You use the following data to calculate the IRR:[45]

- *Present Value (PV):* $230,000
- *Payment (PMT):* –$1,031
- *Term (n):* 240 (20 years × 12 payments per year)
- *Future Value (FV):* 0

You then solve for *i*, the interest rate. Using the numbers given, *i* = .0614, which is the monthly return. Multiply by 12 to get .74%, the annualized annuity return for a 20-year life span.

To calculate the IRR over a longer time period, change *n* for a longer life span to 300 for 25 years and 360 for 30 years. Annualized results are then as follows:

- *20-year return:* .74%
- *25-year return:* 2.49%
- *30-year return:* 3.49%

The longer you live, the higher the equivalent rate of return you receive by using an immediate annuity. Regardless of the return, the primary purpose of an immediate annuity is not return; it is risk management.

If Steve and Carol proceed with the immediate annuity purchase, some practical constraints will need to be addressed. They have $284,000 of non-retirement

---

[44]Michael S. Finke, John Howe, and Sandra J. Huston, "Old Age and the Decline in Financial Literacy," Social Science Research Network (August 2011). Available online at http:// papers.ssrn.com/sol3/papers.cfm?abstract_id=1948627.

[45]I do these calculations on an hp12c calculator that I have downloaded as an app on both my iPhone and iPad.

savings outside of their checking account ($226,000 in mutual funds, $48,000 in money market, and $10,000 in savings). Should they use $230,000 of this for an annuity purchase?

A better option may be to split the annuity into two separate purchases, using $115,000 of Steve's IRA (this is called purchasing the annuity with *qualified* money) and $115,000 of non-retirement savings (called purchasing the annuity with *non-qualified* money), or perhaps the entire annuity should be purchased with Steve's IRA money. There are different tax consequences of approaching it one way versus another, which I discuss in Chapter 5. If you do buy an immediate annuity, the tax impact should play a large part in determining which account the annuity should be purchased in.

There is one other option that Steve and Carol may want to evaluate before finalizing their plan: longevity insurance.

Longevity Insurance

An immediate annuity is not the only way to provide guaranteed income. There is something called a *deferred income annuity*, sometimes referred to as longevity insurance, which may be a viable option.

With longevity insurance, you set aside a relatively small sum today that will provide income starting much later (usually at age 85). It is a way of insuring that even if you spend everything else you have, a guaranteed income will be available for you later. If you think in terms of a probability curve, the majority of people will live to about life expectancy, with some living short and some living long. Those who live short and those who live long are said to fall into the tail of the probability curve. Longevity insurance reduces this tail risk of not having enough income if you live long.

If you want to design a retirement income plan that is 100% guaranteed, you could use longevity insurance in combination with a laddered bond strategy. As an example, let's look at a strategy designed to produce $25,000 a year of guaranteed income by combining I Bonds/TIPS with longevity insurance.

First you would set aside $500,000 in I Bonds/TIPS, with $25,000 to be redeemed each year for the next 20 years.[46] You would use I Bonds for your after-tax savings and TIPS in your tax-deferred accounts.

Next you would buy a deferred-income annuity that will provide income starting at your age 85. At a 3% inflation rate, in 20 years it will take about $45,000 of income to buy what $25,000 buys today. You then need to know what it costs to buy $45,000 a year of income starting at age 85.

---

[46]Ideally you would begin to build this bond portfolio when you are 5 to 15 years away from retirement, with bonds placed in each account to mature in the years you need the cash flow from that account.

The cost of a deferred income annuity depends on your age at purchase and what death benefit and survivor options are chosen. Based on quotes I ran in the fall of 2012, I will estimate for a married couple ages 65/61, it costs about $3.93 per $1 of joint and survivor income that will start at the male's age 85 (in this scenario male is the older of the two). That means a price tag of about $176,850 to buy $45,000 a year of income which would begin at age 85 ($3.93 × $45,000).[47]

For a single age 60 today, it costs about $1.98 per $1 of income that would begin at age 85. That means a price tag of about $89,100 to buy $45,000 a year of future income (assuming no death benefit option).

Add this to the $500,000 set aside in I Bonds/TIPS, and you have a total cost of about $590,000 for a single, or $676,000 for a couple, to guarantee life-long income that is inflation-adjusted up until age 85 and then remains fixed.

ESTIMATED PRICING: LONGEVITY INSURANCE QUOTES

Pricing on longevity insurance varies based on interest rates, age at purchase, and age at which the income is to start. To estimate prices, I ran a series of quotes on Steve and Carol.[48] The results reflect a specified income amount, starting at Carol's age 85 for her single life quotes and at Steve's age 85 for their joint life quotes.

- Carol, $34,000 with death benefit: $125,783 ($125,783/$34,000 results in a cost of $3.70 per $1 of future income)

- Carol, $34,000, no death benefit: $67,260[49] ($67,260/$34,000 results in a cost of $1.98 per $1 of future income)

- Steve and Carol, $61,000 joint life: $238,922 ($238,922/$61,000 results in a cost of $3.92 per $1 of future income)

- Steve and Carol, $34,000 joint life: $133,795 ($133,795/$34,000 results in a cost of $3.94 per $1 of future income)

---

[47]This quote was run to maximize income, which means no death benefit option was chosen. That means nothing is paid out if you don't live to age 85. Like most annuities, you can select options that provide a death benefit, or term-certain payout, but that will increase the amount of up-front dollars needed to provide the same income level.

[48]Unless otherwise specified quotes were run November 7, 2012 through www.incomesolutions.com.

[49]This quote was run November 21, 2012 through www.incomesolutions.com.

Let's take a look at how this strategy compares to the other alternatives I have discussed.

Here's a summary of options to provide $25,000 a year of income:

- *Index fund portfolio:* $500,000. Disadvantage: May have to forego inflation raises and outcome is not certain. Advantage: retain access to principal.

- *Noninflation-adjusted annuity:* $453,000 for a 65-year-old couple. (Would be a lower cost for a single.) Disadvantage: no more access to principal and income is fixed with no option for inflation increases.

- *Inflation-adjusted annuity:* $645,000. (Would be a lower cost for singles.) Disadvantage: no more access to principal.

- *I Bonds/TIPS with deferred income annuity:* $676,000. (Perhaps $589,000 if you wanted to insure longevity on only the spouse expected to live the longest.)

The difference in cost in these choices reflects a difference in how much risk you retain. If you want to retain market risk and inflation risk, you may be able to accomplish your retirement income goals with less principal.

If you want to guarantee the outcome, you will need to save more to accomplish your income goals.

A combination of the choices discussed in this section is often the best solution because it helps you hedge against a variety of risks.

Such a combination would involve taking on investment risk with a portion of your portfolio. The reason you would do so is to retain the possibility of earning a higher rate of return than what can be achieved with safe alternatives, and/or the possibility of retaining access to more of your principal.

Index fund portfolios are simply another tool, and like any tool, when used correctly they can be quite effective. The key is making sure you go about building your index fund portfolio correctly using multiple asset classes as shown in prior examples. If you're not going to do it right, you're better off sticking with a low-risk, safe alternative.

▓ **Note**   A guaranteed outcome requires more financial capital to achieve your desired level of retirement income.

Asset Allocation Using Multiple Strategies

When you lay out an allocation plan, the first thing to do is carve out your emergency fund/rainy day money and invest it only in choices that rate a 1 on the 1-5 risk scale. How much should you keep in this category of cash reserves? As with most things, it depends. A standard rule of thumb is six months worth of living expenses. If you want additional security, bump that number up to 12 months.

Steve and Carol spend about $80,000 a year. Between checking, savings, and money market accounts, they have $63,000. They are going to carve out this money as emergency reserves and not consider it part of their "portfolio."

That leaves them with $742,000 (non–retirement account mutual funds of $226,000, and $516,000 in Steve's IRA, ROTH IRA, and Carol's IRA—refer to Figure 2-1). They are going to set aside $230,000 potentially to buy the annuity, leaving them with $512,000 of investable assets.

They then use their timeline to help them figure out how to invest the $512,000. In Figures 4-5 and 4-6, Steve and Carol's last income timeline, you see they anticipate taking about $20,000 a year of withdrawals from 2013 to 2016. Then they will have a surplus for a year that can replenish some of the savings they used. Then they will begin withdrawing about $20,000 a year from 2018 through 2020. After 2020, withdrawals drop to about $15,000 a year for a few years when Carol starts her age 70 Social Security benefit, and then down to about $4,000 a year in 2028 and thereafter, once the mortgage is paid off.

If we add up the first ten years of net withdrawals, we get a total of $152,000. (Add numbers in line C for years one through ten.) Let's assume this money is going to be invested safely and earn the rate of inflation, but no more. They could invest this $152,000 in I Bonds or TIPS (or other safe, risk level 1 and 2 investments) to meet their specific cash flow needs.

Because the first ten years of their cash flow are now secure, they have some flexibility about how their remaining funds are allocated. If they use a traditional asset allocation approach, they might determine they are comfortable with a market-based portfolio of 60% equities and 40% fixed income (bonds).

The 60% in equities will be allocated across index funds that fall in the risk level 4 category. A simple approach would be to use a world index fund or global index fund, such as Vanguard's Total World Stock Index fund (symbol VTWSX) or iShares MSCI ACWI Index Fund (All Country World Index, symbol ACWI) exchange-traded fund.

The 40% in bonds will be allocated across bond funds that fall in the risk level 2 and 3 categories. A simple approach would be to use a total bond market fund such as Vanguard's Total Bond Market Index Fund (symbol VBTLX) or iShares Core Total U.S. Bond Market ETF (symbol AGG).

They could achieve additional diversification by using a more complex approach that would involve choosing specific funds for each asset class, such as large cap, small cap, international, emerging markets and real estate in an allocation similar to that shown in Table 4-3. They could achieve additional specificity by laddering bonds and CDs to meet specific cash flow needs. As a professional, I think additional diversification and specificity have their benefits, and this is the approach I prefer. But for those managing their own investments, a simpler strategy is easier to manage.

After subtracting the amount set aside as their emergency fund, Steve and Carol have $742,000 to work with. Their final allocation across risk management strategies turns out as follows:

- *Immediate annuity:* $230,000 or 31%
- *I Bonds/TIPS:* $152,000 or 21%
- *Bond index funds:* $144,000 or 19%
- *Equity index funds:* $216,000, or 29%

When you use an index fund portfolio or a portfolio of stocks and bonds, one of your challenges is determining which investments to liquidate when you need withdrawals.

Managing Withdrawals

When you are in the withdrawal phase, how you manage withdrawals will depend on how much of your current income is coming from your index fund portfolio.

Here are two common approaches:

- Time segmentation
- Systematic withdrawals

Time Segmentation

In Steve and Carol's situation, you saw that the $152,000 allocation to I Bonds/ TIPS was determined by summing up the withdrawals they would need over the first ten years of their retirement. This process of allocating money according to when you need to take withdrawals is often called *time segmentation*.

A time-segmented approach could have been applied to Steve and Carol's withdrawals beyond year ten as an alternative way of determining the appropriate investment allocation for their index fund portfolio. You can see how this would be done in the calculations at the bottom of Figure 4-6, which are also shown in Table 4-6.

Table 4-6. Time Segmented Approach

Years	Cumulative Withdrawals Needed ($)	Discount Rate Applied[50] (%)	Present Value of Withdrawals Needed ($)
1–10	152,014	0	152,014
11–20	96,160	1	83,623
20–35	57,624	2	33,534

This example reflects an expectation of a 0% real rate of return on the first time segment. That is the $152,000 set aside in I Bonds/TIPS.

For years 11–20 they need to set aside $83,623 that earns a real rate of return of 1% in order to meet their income needs. This segment might get allocated to risk level 2 investments (primarily bonds, CDs, and/or fixed annuities).

For time segment three (years 20–35), they need to set aside $33,534, which earns a real rate of 2%. These funds won't be touched for 20 years, and so can be invested more aggressively.

The present value of these three segments adds up to $269,171 of capital needed. They have $512,000 of capital remaining after the annuity purchase, leaving them with about $243,000 that could be invested more aggressively. Using an immediate annuity with the time-segmented approach in this way results in the following allocation across risk-management strategies:

- *Immediate annuity: $230,000 or 31%*
- *I Bonds/TIPS: $152,000 or 21%*
- *Bonds (or other risk level 2 investments): $84,000 or 11%*
- *Longer maturity fixed-income securities: $33,000 or 4%*
- *Equity index funds: $243,000 or 33%*

Time segments can also be broken up into chunks of five years or seven years or any increment you desire, with investments that are specifically chosen to match each individual time segment.

---

[50]Reflecting the expected real rate of return over that time segment.

If you want to learn more about how you might implement a time-segmented plan, go to the Income for Life Model at www.iflmmovie.com to watch a video presentation that does a fantastic job of explaining the concept.

In my practice I do not use a pure time-segmented approach. Instead, I use the concept of time-segmentation as an educational tool. If you think of your investments in terms of time segments, you realize you will never be in a position where you are forced to sell riskier investments during a market downturn. Thus, even if you have a market-based portfolio, you do not need to be concerned with the daily, weekly, or even monthly gyrations of the stock market. Withdrawals can be taken from safe investments when the equity portion is down. When the equity portion is up, a rebalancing process will force you to sell riskier investments and replenish the safer ones that were used.

Systematic Withdrawals

A systematic withdrawal strategy involves building a portfolio and liquidating investments proportionately from each asset class each year to meet your withdrawal needs. In addition, each year you rebalance to align with your target allocation. Tables 4-3 and 4-4 show the results of using a systematic withdrawal process with rebalancing.

Most mutual fund companies allow you to set up a systematic withdrawal by filling out a minimal amount of paperwork. You tell them what dollar amount of each fund you want liquidated and over what time period. For example, if you have $100,000 in a stock index fund, you might have them liquidate $5,000 a year, but on a monthly basis whereby they send you $416 a month.

If this sounds complicated, you can find a simple solution. Several mutual fund families offer some form of a retirement income fund[51] that builds a balanced portfolio for you and sends you a monthly check. For additional information do research on the following:

- Vanguard Managed Payout Funds
- Fidelity Income Replacement Funds
- Schwab Monthly Income Funds
- John Hancock Retirement Income Funds

[51]For additional details on retirement income funds, see my About.com article at http://moneyover55.about.com/od/investmentincome/tp/retirementincomefunds.htm.

These types of retirement income funds are designed to provide a stable monthly distribution, which means the fund may be paying out both investment income and principal as you go along for the fund to achieve its monthly target payout. The fund's ability to maintain its distribution target depends on market conditions and the underlying investment decisions of the fund's management team.

Systematic withdrawals combined with rebalancing makes for an effective strategy as long as you don't withdraw too much. How much is too much? That is something that must be monitored as you go along. If your investments perform well, you may be able to increase withdrawals. If your investments do not achieve your target rate of return, you may need to reduce withdrawals.

Your Safe Withdrawal Rate

You may read about something called the *safe withdrawal rate*. This is supposed to be the amount you can withdraw each year from savings without running out of money. The truth is, unless they have a working crystal ball, no one can tell you what your safe withdrawal rate is. Each withdrawal plan needs to be designed based on your situation and monitored based on changing market conditions and tax rates.

As you can see from Steve and Carol's situation, your plan may call for more withdrawals in some years than in others. I think it makes sense to secure your near-term cash flow needs and build an index fund portfolio for future needs rather than rely on a rule of thumb that may or may not apply to you.

With improvements in technology, it is getting easier to build an investment plan that is custom designed to match your cash flow needs—something called a *dedicated portfolio*. With a dedicated portfolio, rather than arbitrarily picking an allocation of say 50% stocks and 50% bonds, you ladder out bonds and CDs in each account to meet your first five to ten year's worth of cash flow needs and invest the remainder of your portfolio in growth-oriented equity index funds. A dedicated portfolio uses a combination of many of the tools discussed in this chapter. The merits and historical success of a dedicated portfolio approach are covered in detail in the book *Asset Dedication* by Stephen J. Huxley and J. Brent Burns (McGraw-Hill, 2004).

Wait, I'm Still Accumulating

If you are still in the accumulation phase and are saving money, the first thing you have to decide is whether you want to take investment risk at all. You *can* choose only safe options. There is nothing wrong with that.

If you want to build a traditional market-based portfolio, make sure you diversify. Invest 50–80% of your retirement money in risk level 4 funds (closer to 80% if you are younger, closer to 50% if you are nearing retirement), with the remainder spread across risk levels 2 and 3.

Then turn off the TV, ignore current economic news, and continue to save monthly. Unless you are in the investment industry, do not think about your investments. Focus on whatever it is you do well and figure out how to make more money doing it.

Managing Investments Tax Efficiently

Did you know that many financial advisors are not allowed to offer tax-planning advice? For legal reasons, the companies they work for do not allow it.

Every investment decision you make has a tax consequence. If you make decisions with taxes in mind, you can increase your after-tax returns.

Some companies are starting to catch on to this. LifeYield is a company that builds software that financial institutions can use to help their financial advisors manage investments in a more tax-efficient manner.

An Ernst & Young study[52] took a look at the process that LifeYield uses and concluded that proper tax-smart management of your investments can generate up to 30% more retirement income for a household. Wow!

Properly managing taxes can have a much bigger impact on your end result than spending time analyzing stocks. What does *tax-smart management* mean? You'll learn all about it in Chapter 5.

Alternative Investments

A colleague of mine often says, "If you bet on red and win, did that make it a good investment?"[53] There is a difference between speculating and building a portfolio that needs to produce reliable income for you.

You don't need to own any investments other than a combination of safe choices (like I Bonds, TIPS, and immediate annuities) and index funds to achieve your goals. Why complicate things?

---

[52]Download the study from LifeYield's web site at `www.lifeyield.com/research-paper/`.
[53]David Rosenthal, Wealth Management Solutions, LLC.

If you want to speculate by buying an individual stock or betting on the future price of gold, go right ahead. You might win. But more importantly, you might lose.

Many investment opportunities you'll encounter are designed to appeal to your ego. You may be told they are "exclusive" or previously only available to the super-rich. They may come in the form of a private placement, which is an investment that is not publicly traded. They may be labeled as an "alternative" investment. Unless you have the expertise to thoroughly evaluate these alternatives, or unless you are willing to risk the money you invest, stay away.

From my personal experience, I have seen most alternative strategies result in losses, and the few that delivered positive returns did not deliver returns any higher than what could have been achieved by using a market-based portfolio composed of index funds.

I think most alternative strategies are designed to line someone else's pocket; not yours.

Summary

Your money has a job to do for you. Investing for the purpose of creating life-long income is different than investing with the goal of achieving the highest possible return. It requires looking at risk in a new way.

You can compare choices by using a risk scale of 1–5, by benchmarking against what can be achieved by using a risk-free choice, and by estimating the price tag of producing $1,000 a month of income by choosing a safe strategy versus a riskier one.

An income timeline can help show you how much guaranteed income you have, and when you will need to take withdrawals from savings. You can create alternate income timelines to show you how one strategy compares to another. You can then use your withdrawal schedule to select safe investments for near-term income needs and growth-oriented investments for future income needs.

Taxes matter, and you may be able to improve your results by managing taxes. This is the topic covered in the next chapter.

5

Taxes

Plan—and Pay Less

The conventional view serves to protect us from the painful job of thinking.

—John Kenneth Galbraith

Browsing through an online article on retirement income one day, I came across a paragraph similar to this:

> The other consideration is which accounts to withdraw from first. In general, if you have a taxable investment account, you should withdraw from this account before you touch your retirement accounts. Why? Because the longer the investments in your retirement accounts continue to grow tax deferred, the better.

That paragraph reflects what is called *conventional wisdom*, and many people who follow this particular conventional wisdom are paying far more in taxes than they would be if they took a different approach.

In the case of this article, I knew the journalist, so I sent an e-mail suggesting that the paragraph be replaced with something like this,

> Which accounts should you withdraw from first? It depends on your individual tax situation. Choosing which accounts to withdraw from in a way that matches your tax situation can result in significant savings.

I am happy to say that my e-mail was well received!

I took the time to send the e-mail because incorporating meaningful tax planning with your retirement plan can mean big bucks for you.

■ **Note** My intent with this chapter is not to provide a laundry list of the tax rules. Those are readily available online. Instead, I'd like to focus your attention on the type of tax planning that can save you money.

What matters is not how much income you have; it's how much you have available to spend. If you're expecting $60,000 a year of after-tax retirement income, and proper tax planning can increase it to $63,000 a year, that's a meaningful increase.

A few research papers have begun to quantify the results that can be delivered by incorporating tax planning with investment management.

In a paper titled "Tax Alpha: The Importance of Active Tax Management,"[1] put out by a Canadian wealth management firm, author Tim Cestnick says, "It's possible to reliably and consistently add 200 to 300 basis points annually through attention to taxes." In layman's terms that means it's possible to add the equivalent of an additional return of 2–3% a year by using a strategy to minimize taxes.

An Ernst & Young study[2] commissioned by LifeYield (a company that builds software to help advisors deliver advice that is more tax conscious) says,

> From an historical point of view, Ernst & Young calculated that if each household had been managed over the past 40 years, from 1969 – 2008, the LifeYield ROI methodology versus the Pro Rata approach would have generated up to:
>
> • 44% more retirement income; and
>
> • 39% fewer taxes.

LifeYield's methodology looks at a few key things such as asset location, capital gains management, and tax-managed income distributions. In this chapter, I explain what these things are.

Without knowing your situation, it is impossible to tell you how much increased income-tax planning can deliver, but it can likely make a difference.

Unfortunately, incorporating smart tax planning isn't easy. Putting together a retirement income plan that considers all these pieces is like putting together a complex jigsaw puzzle where each time you decide where to place one piece it instantly changes the shape of some of the other pieces.

---

[1] Available online at www.waterstreet.ca/data/WSG_Tax_Overlay_Management.pdf.
[2] Available online at www.lifeyield.com/research-paper/. Study conducted using 10,000 scenarios on four different hypothetical households of asset levels of $200,000, $400,000, $1 million, and $10 million, covering 40 years, including 15 years prior to retirement and 25 years in retirement.

I break it down into the types of tax planning that apply to three situations:

- While you are still contributing
- When you are taking withdrawals
- How you allocate your investments

While You Are Contributing

Many people get serious about saving as they reach their 50s. This is good! They often begin putting as much away in tax-deferred accounts as possible. This is better than not saving at all, but it might not always be the best strategy based on taxes. To understand why, you have to take a look at the tax brackets.

Table 5-1 shows the U.S. 2013 federal tax brackets. The ranges you see refer to the amount of taxable income you have.[3] Taxable income is calculated after taking all applicable personal exemptions and standard or itemized deductions.

Table 5-1. U.S. Tax Code Brackets

Single	Married	Applicable Marginal Tax Rate (%)	Long Term Capital Gains Rate[4] (%)
Taxable income that falls in this range:			
Up to $8,925	Up to: $17,850	10	0
$8,926 – $36,250	$17,851 – $72,500	15	0
$36,251 – $87,850	$72,501 – $146,500	25	15
$87,851 – $183,250	$146,501 – $223,050	28	15
$183,251 – $398,350	$223,051 – $398,350	33	15
$398,351 – $400,000	$398,351 – $450,000	35	15
$400,001 +	$450,001 +	39.6	20

[3]You can find taxable income on the second page of your 1040 tax form on line 43. If you want to get the most out of this chapter, grab your last tax return and look up the line items as I reference them.

[4]This rate also applies to qualified dividends. These rates are not tiered in exactly the same way the marginal rates are. For a detailed explanation, see the January 4, 2013 *Forbes* article "Capital Gains And The Fiscal Cliff Deal: How Does It Work?" available online at www.forbes.com/sites/anthonynitti/2013/01/04/capital-gains-and-the-fiscal-cliff-deal-how-does-it-work/2/.

Here is what you must know about how tax brackets work: Only the next dollar that falls into a range is taxed at that marginal rate. For example, if you are single and have $36,251 of taxable income, the first $8,925 is taxed at 10%, the next $27,325 is taxed at 15%, and the next $1 is taxed at 25%.

In 2013, each person gets a personal exemption of $3,900 and a standard deduction of $6,100.

- This means in 2013 a single filer will have at least $10,000 of income (their personal exemption plus their standard deduction) that will not be taxed.

- A married couple can have at least $20,000 of income that will not be taxed.[5]

If you itemize deductions[6] (you can see the amount of itemized deductions on page 2 of the 1040 on line 40), you may have additional income that is not subject to taxation. For example, if you are married and have $30,000 of itemized deductions, this amount will replace your $12,200 of standard deductions. Add $30,000 to your combined $7,800 of personal exemptions and you can have up to $37,800 of income that will not be taxed.

You can use your tax rates and an estimate of your taxable income to determine the most advantageous types of retirement accounts to contribute to.

To simplify things, let's break your choices into two options:

- Traditional IRA or 401(k) contributions

- Roth IRA or designated Roth account contributions

I will refer to these choices as traditional or Roth.

With traditional contributions, money goes in on a tax-deductible basis,[7] grows tax-deferred, and you pay taxes at your ordinary income tax rate when you withdraw it.

---

[5]Those 65 and older get an additional standard deduction of $1,500 if single and $1,200 if married. This means a couple who are both 65 or older can have $22,400 of income that will not be taxed, even if they do not itemize deductions (based on 2013 deduction/exemption amounts).

[6]Itemized deductions take the place of standard deductions. Normally you would only use itemized deductions if they were greater than your standard deduction, but there are cases where for someone covered by the AMT (Alternative Minimum Tax), it made sense to intentionally use itemized deductions, even when they were lower than the standard deduction.

[7]If you contribute $1,000 on a tax-deductible basis, you will report $1,000 less of taxable income. If that $1,000 fell in the 25% marginal rate, that $1,000 contribution would reduce your current year taxes owed by $250.

With Roth contributions, money goes in after-tax, grows tax-free (if you follow the rules[8]), and withdrawals are tax-free when you take them.[9]

Using these rules, let's look at an example. Suppose you are a single tax filer and you do not itemize deductions. You make $55,000 a year. You have downsized your lifestyle so you can save as much as possible and you plan on contributing $15,000 a year to your 401(k) plan.

■ **Note**   2013 401(k) Salary Deferral Limits: The 2013 401(k) contribution limits are $17,500 plus an additional $5,500 of allowable contributions for those age 50 or older.

The first $10,000 of your income is not taxed (due to your personal exemption and standard deduction), so you have $45,000 of taxable income. By looking up your taxable income and tax brackets in Table 5-1, you see that of the $15,000 that goes into your 401(k) plan, the first $8,750 of it saves you taxes at the 25% tax rate. The next $6,250 saves you taxes at the 15% rate.

Maybe it would make more sense to put the money that is only saving you taxes at the 15% rate into a Roth (or designated Roth account if your 401(k) plan offers this option). You'll learn why this might make sense throughout this chapter as you see how Roth distributions are treated when you take withdrawals.

Unless you are expecting to be in a significantly higher tax bracket in retirement, it is likely the Roth will be a better long-term solution for you. But to know for sure, you need a multiple-year tax projection that incorporates your future sources of income (such as Social Security and pension income) as well as asset values.

Asset values are necessary because traditional IRA accounts, and other retirement accounts in which the money went in tax-deferred, require you to start taking withdrawals at age 70 1/2. These withdrawals are taxed as ordinary income in the year they occur. In many cases, these additional withdrawals, which are required each year after you reach 70 1/2, also end up making more of your Social Security benefits subject to taxation.

---

[8]I provide more details on Roth IRA withdrawal rules in my About.com article "When Roth IRA Withdrawals are Tax Free and When They Are Not," available online at http://moneyover55.about.com/od/iras/a/rothirawithdrawal.htm.

[9]With both traditional retirement account withdrawals and Roth retirement account withdrawals, a 10% early withdrawal penalty may apply on withdrawals taken before you reach age 59 1/2.

Roth accounts do not require withdrawals at any age, and when you do take withdrawals, they are tax-free. In addition, Roth IRA withdrawals are not included in the formula that determines how much of your Social Security benefits will be subject to taxation.

When you put all this together in a comprehensive plan, it means that a smart strategy during your savings years may result in substantial tax savings throughout your retirement years.

Tax Planning Triggers

If your income and deductions stay fairly consistent from year to year, you can figure out your best strategy and stick with it until something major changes.

When you have a year in which your income or deductions change, you want to pay special attention to your tax planning that year. Here are some triggering events that should cause you to do additional tax planning in the year these events occur:

- Change in amount of mortgage interest you pay (maybe you paid off a mortgage, refinanced, or took on a mortgage)
- Variations in income because you work on commissions, have varied bonuses, or your income varies from year to year. (For one real estate agent I work with, in low-income years we have her fund Roth accounts, and in high-income years we have her make deductible 401(k) contributions.)
- Loss or change of job
- Year of retirement
- A year with a lot of health expenses and/or charitable contributions that may increase your itemized deductions
- Change in number of dependents you claim
- Move to a different state with a different state tax structure

Excellent tax-planning opportunities exist during low-income/high-deduction years. I am going to talk about two of them that are relevant to those nearing retirement: Roth conversions and IRA withdrawals.

■ **Tip** Excellent retirement tax-planning opportunities exist during low-income/high-deduction years.

Roth Conversions

As mentioned, with traditional retirement accounts you put the money in pre-tax. It grows tax-deferred (meaning you don't get a 1099 tax form each year showing you the amount of interest, dividends and capital gains to report—because you don't report them). When you withdraw from these accounts, you pay tax at your ordinary income tax rate, only on the amounts you withdraw, in the year you withdraw it. Your tax rate is determined by all your combined sources of income.

With a Roth IRA, you put the money in after-tax. It grows tax-free (meaning if you follow the rules you never pay tax on the interest, dividends, and capital gains that are earned in the Roth). When you withdraw the money, you pay no tax on withdrawals.

You can convert money in traditional retirement accounts to a Roth. You pay tax on the amount that you convert (but no penalty taxes for early withdrawals) in the year you do the conversion. After that, the money is in the Roth, and Roth tax rules apply.

During the 2008–2009 Great Recession, I had several high-income clients who found themselves out of work. They had deductions because they still had a mortgage and all their other expenses. They had savings to use to pay their expenses, so they didn't need to worry about day-to-day living money.

When we looked at their tax projection, we realized they would have about $40,000–$50,000 of negative taxable income. What does that mean? It means they had more deductions[10] than income. If they had $40,000 of deductions, we could realize $40,000 of income and they would pay no tax. We used up their deductions by converting IRA money to a Roth IRA.

In addition to converting an amount sufficient to offset deductions, it may make sense to "fill up" the 10% or 15% tax brackets if projections show you are likely to pay taxes at a higher rate later on. Also, Roth-conversion strategies make the most sense if you have the money outside of retirement accounts that you can use to pay the additional taxes owed.

The Roth IRA is such a powerful planning tool, it deserves a few more words.

Roth IRAs: The Superhero of Retirement Accounts

I consider a Roth IRA the superhero of the retirement account world. It has some amazing features, and I think it is currently underutilized as a planning tool.

---

[10]The word *deductions* here really means a combination of deductions and exemptions.

First of all, who can contribute to a Roth IRA?

- Single filers who have less than $112,000[11] of adjusted gross income

- Married filers who have less than $178,000 of adjusted gross income

- Employees whose employers offers a designated Roth account as part of the company retirement plan offering, regardless of income level

- Self-employed persons who establish a 401(k) that offers a designated Roth account, regardless of their income level

What makes Roth IRAs so great? Roth IRAs have several features that give them superhero status:

- First of all, you can always withdraw your original contributions[12] from your own Roth IRA without tax or penalties. This gives you liquidity that other retirement account options don't have.

- Interest and dividends earned are tax-free.

- Roth IRA withdrawals do not count in the formula that determines the amount of your Social Security benefits subject to taxation.

- Roth IRA withdrawals do not count in the formula that determines how much your Medicare Part B premiums will be.

- With a Roth, there are no required minimum distributions at age 70 1/2.

For 2013, the maximum amount you can contribute to a Roth IRA is $5,500, plus an additional $1,000 for those age 50 and older.[13]

If your 401(k) plan offers a designated Roth account option, the maximum 401(k) contribution limits apply.

---

[11]Roth contribution limits begin to phase out for single filers with adjusted gross income in the $112,000–$127,000 range and for married filers in the $178,000–$188,000 range. This means if your AGI falls in that range, you may be able to contribute some money to a Roth—just not the maximum allowable amount (2013 limits quoted).

[12]There are limitations on withdrawing amounts converted to a Roth and on withdrawals from designated Roth accounts.

[13]Limits are indexed to inflation in $500 increments.

▓ **Note**   Spousal IRA contributions: To make either a traditional or Roth IRA contribution, you must have earned income in an amount equal to or exceeding the amount of your IRA contribution. If you have a sufficient amount of earned income, you may also make a spousal IRA contribution for a non-working spouse (either traditional[14] or Roth, depending on which is most advantageous for you). You do not have to have earned income to convert IRA assets to a Roth.

IRA Withdrawals Before Official "Retirement"

Between the ages of 55 and 70, you may find yourself temporarily unemployed or forced into retirement earlier than you had planned. Conventional wisdom would suggest you should not take IRA or 401(k) withdrawals for income in such a situation. This isn't always true.

If you find yourself in this predicament, it may pay to look at your tax situation before making any decisions. You may be able to take money out of your tax-deferred retirement accounts and pay no tax.

It makes sense to create enough taxable income (in the form of retirement account withdrawals if you have no other sources of taxable income) to at least offset the amount of your deductions.[15]

Let's look at an example. Suppose you are married, age 60, and find yourself unemployed. You have mortgage interest, charitable contributions, state taxes, and other items that add up to about $34,000 of itemized deductions. In addition, you have your personal exemption of $3,900 for each of you. Now let's say you were laid off at the beginning of the year. You have almost no income and $41,800 of deductions.

You decide to run a tax projection and realize that if you withdraw $50,000 from your IRA, the first $41,800 will be tax-free because of your deductions, and the next $8,200 of your withdrawal will only be taxed at the 10% rate. As a matter of fact, you realize the 10% bracket goes up to $17,850 for a married couple. If you wanted to fill up the 10% tax bracket, you could take a total IRA withdrawal of $59,650. You take the withdrawal, and pay $1,785 of income taxes on a $59,650 IRA withdrawal (a 3% effective rate).

---

[14]If you are an active participant in a company retirement plan, and your income exceeds $178,000, you may not be able to fully deduct a traditional IRA contribution made for a non-working spouse.

[15]For additional information on the most efficient way to withdraw IRA money, see Alan R. Sumutka, CPA; Andrew M. Sumutka, Ph.D.; and Lewis W. Coopersmith, Ph.D., "Tax-Efficient Retirement Withdrawal Planning Using a Comprehensive Tax Model," *Journal of Financial Planning*, available online at www.fpanet.org/journal/TaxEfficientRetirementWithdrawalPlanning/.

Because you had a long-term plan in place, you know if you had waited to take that IRA withdrawal later—when you had other sources of income, like Social Security—you would have paid taxes at the 15% rate at a minimum. That would be $8,947 in taxes.

This strategy thus permanently saved you about $7,000 in taxes.

This is not a manufactured example for the sake of writing a book. I have encountered these planning opportunities several times within a small sample of about 100 people. The key to recognizing the opportunity is that you must do a tax projection before the end of the year.

A similar situation may exist for someone who is laid off after 55 but before 59 1/2. It has to do with the age-related rules on 401(k) withdrawals.[16] One of those rules may allow you to take withdrawals from your 401(k) between ages 55 and 59 1/2, and not have to pay the 10% early-withdrawal penalty. This rule only applies if you left the company after you reached the age of 55.

Rather than remembering all the rules, what you want to remember is that if you have a change of job or a year where your income and deductions change, that is also the year you want to put together an accurate tax projection before the end of the year so you can see if any tax savings opportunities exist.

▓ **Tip**   To take advantage of tax opportunities when you have a life-changing event (like losing your job or buying a new house), you have to do some projections before year's end. It is well worth your time.

When You Are Taking Withdrawals

Prior to retirement, you should create what I call a *withdrawal strategy*. A withdrawal strategy helps you strategically decide which accounts to withdraw from and how to coordinate that with your other sources of income (such as part-time work, Social Security, or pensions) in a way that improves your outcome.

The simplest way to look at it is to realize that all sources of retirement income are not equal when viewed on an after-tax basis.

For example, for each dollar you withdraw from a Roth IRA, you get to spend the entire dollar. No taxes are owed on Roth IRA withdrawals. For each dollar of a traditional IRA or 401(k) withdrawal, a portion will be owed to Uncle Sam. Maybe you only get to keep 60 to 90 cents, depending on your tax bracket (maybe even less after factoring in state taxes).

---

[16]I cover these in Chapter 7.

Then you have Social Security. Depending on how much other income you have, you may get to keep all your Social Security benefits or you may owe taxes on them. Taking extra money out of a traditional IRA can have a double whammy effect by suddenly making more of your Social Security subject to taxation. As a matter of fact, if your income and Social Security fall into certain ranges, you can find yourself paying about 46 cents of every extra dollar of IRA withdrawals in taxes.[17]

Figuring Taxes on Social Security Benefits

To understand how it works, you have to look at the formula that determines how much of your Social Security benefits is subject to taxation. The formula starts by determining something called *combined income.*[18]

For tax purposes, combined income is calculated as the total of your adjusted gross income[19] (page 1 of the 1040 tax form line 37), plus non-taxable interest, plus one half of your total Social Security benefits.

If your combined income is less than the threshold amounts in Table 5-2, you will not pay income tax on any of your Social Security benefits. If your combined income is over the lower threshold amount, then a formula is used to determine how much of your Social Security is subject to taxation.

The formula applied is a three-part test that determines the amount of your Social Security benefits subject to taxation. You pay taxes on the lower of:

- 85% of your Social Security benefits

- 50% of the benefits plus 85% of the amount of combined income over the second threshold amount

- 50% of the amount of combined income over the first threshold amount, plus 35% of the amount of combined income over the second threshold amount

These threshold amounts in the formula are shown in Table 5-2.

Table 5-2. Combined Income Thresholds for Social Security Taxation Formula

	First Threshold ($)	Second Threshold ($)
Single filers	25,000	34,000
Married filers	32,000	44,000

[17]For an example of when this 46% rate may apply, see The Bogleheads article "Taxation of Social Security benefits," available online at www.bogleheads.org/wiki/ Taxation_of_Social_Security_benefits.
[18]You will also see this called *provisional income.*
[19]As calculated, without including the taxable portion of your Social Security.

How would this work for a single woman, age 66, who has $25,000 of Social Security income and $25,000 of IRA withdrawals? Her combined income would be her IRA withdrawals plus half her Social Security, which comes to $37,500. Using these numbers in the three-part test provides these results:

- 85% of her benefits would be $21,250.

- $12,500 (which is 50% of her Social Security benefits) + $2,975 (85% of the amount over the second threshold of $34,000) equals $15,475.

- $6,250 (which is 50% of the amount of combined income she has in excess of the $25,000 first threshold) + $1,225 (35% of the amount of combined income in excess of the second $34,000 threshold amount) equals $7,475.

The lower of the three amounts is subject to taxation, so $7,475 of her Social Security benefits (or about 30% of the benefits) are taxed. This $7,475 then goes into line 20b on the 1040 tax form under the taxable amount of Social Security benefits. When you then calculate your taxable income and tax liability, the results are:

- Taxable income: $20,975 (after applicable deductions and exemptions)

- Tax liability: $2,700[20]

Now, what happens if she takes an extra $25,000 out of her IRA? You would think at most her tax liability would double, right? Not in this case. Her combined income now comes to $62,500 because of her additional IRA withdrawals. Using this combined income amount, the three-part test is applied to determine how much of her Social Security is subject to taxation. With the new, higher combined income amount, the results look like this:

- 85% of her benefits would still be: $21,250

- The final two tests result in a number larger than 85% of her benefits, and the maximum amount of Social Security benefits subject to taxation is 85%, so 85% of her benefits become taxable.

---

[20]These numbers were calculated using 2013 tax rates and verified using BNA Tax Planner. You can verify these numbers by using the "How much of my Social Security benefit may be taxed?" calculator at www.calcxml.com/do/inc08. Take the result and plug it into DinkyTown's 1040 Tax Calculator at www.dinkytown.net/java/Tax1040.html. But at the time of writing, the 2013 tax calculator was not yet available, so using 2012 tax rates gives a slightly different answer: $21,275 of taxable income and $2,756 of total tax.

This $21,250 then goes into line 20b on the 1040 tax form and is used to calculate taxable income and tax liability. With the additional IRA withdrawal, the results are:

- *Taxable income*: $59,750
- *Tax liability*: $10,866[21]

Now if you go back to Figure 5-1, with taxable income of $59,800, she should be in the 25% marginal rate. Yet she paid an additional $8,171 of taxes on her additional $25,000 IRA withdrawal—an effective rate of 32.7%. Her additional IRA withdrawal meant that an additional $13,775 of her Social Security became included as taxable income.

When you look at how all this works, it shows that you can design a withdrawal strategy that can save money. The most comprehensive analysis of this interaction between Social Security, taxes, and retirement account withdrawals that I have found is a chapter called "Rethinking Social Security Claiming in a 401(k) World" from the book *Recalibrating Retirement Spending and Saving* by James I. Mahaney and Peter C. Carlson (Pension Research Council, 2008).[22] In this chapter, the authors provide detailed examples and conclude:

> When considering the after-tax dollars actually available for the retirement lifestyle, the break-even age for comparing early Social Security versus delayed Social Security is often lowered to somewhere between 75 and 76 years old. The actual age varies depending on the tax situation of the individual. It is important to note that the tax advantages created by delaying Social Security may be even more advantageous for a married couple after the death of the primary worker.

When you use this research to take a close look at your claiming options on an after-tax basis, and you account for the fact that after the death of the first spouse filing status will change from married to single (and thus the lower combined income threshold amounts will apply to determine how much of a surviving spouse's Social Security is subject to taxation), for many singles and couples it meaningfully affects when you should begin taking your Social Security benefits.

---

[21]Calculated using 2013 rates. Using 2012 rates, taxable income would be $60,050, and total tax would be $11,043.

[22]Chapter available online at www.pensionresearchcouncil.org/publications/0-19-954910-8.php.

Prudential has a great piece[23] which provides consumer-friendly information on this topic. The author makes it clear that this type of tax planning, which takes a detailed look at the interaction of your Social Security benefits with your other sources of income, is beneficial for those with expected after-tax retirement income of around $90,000 or less.

Here are the key takeaways when looking into a withdrawal plan that minimizes taxes:

- Marrieds have a higher combined income amount than singles. While married you may pay little tax on your Social Security benefits, but a surviving spouse who becomes a single tax filer may suddenly see his or her income reduced by taxes because the lower threshold amounts now apply.

- Roth IRA withdrawals do not count in the Social Security taxation formula, but traditional IRA withdrawals do. With traditional IRAs, you must take required minimum distributions starting at age 70 1/2. Each year thereafter, you are required to take a slightly larger withdrawal.

- You have the option to convert traditional IRA assets to a Roth IRA. By doing so, you reduce your required minimum distributions later, and you can now take Roth IRA withdrawals at any time without affecting the amount of Social Security benefits subject to taxation.

- When doing your planning, if you expect your after-tax retirement income to be $100,000 a year or less, evaluate the potential benefits of a strategy that involves starting your Social Security benefits later and converting traditional IRA assets to a Roth over multiple tax years before you start Social Security.

For many (like Steve and Carol, whose situation we will look at in a few pages) a tax-conscious strategy will result in lowering the cumulative amount of taxes paid over their retirement years by a meaningful amount.

Another factor that plays into withdrawals in retirement is the required minimum distribution rules.

---

[23]James Mahaney, "Innovative Strategies to Help Maximize Social Security Benefits," 2012 edition available online at http://research.prudential.com/documents/rp/ InnovativeSocialSecurityNov2012.pdf?doc=innovativestrategiesLP1112&bu= SI&ref=website&cid=1.

Required Minimum Distributions

Once you reach age 59 1/2, you may take distributions from an IRA without being subject to the 10% early-withdrawal penalty tax. Once you reach age 70 1/2, you *have* to begin taking withdrawals from IRAs and other qualified retirement accounts. These withdrawals are called *required minimum distributions* (RMDs).

The amount of your required distribution is based on two things:

- Your prior year's December 31st account balance

- An IRS table that provides a divisor based on your age

There are three separate IRS tables; a description of each follows. The appropriate one to use depends on your situation:

- *Uniform Lifetime Table:* This table is used for singles and marrieds whose spouse is within ten years of their own age.

- *Joint and Last Survivor Table:* This table is used if you have a spouse who is younger than you by ten years or more.

- *Single Life Expectancy Table:* This table is used if you are taking distributions from an IRA you inherited as a non-spouse beneficiary.

At age 70, using the Uniform Lifetime Table, the divisor is 27.4. Assuming a prior year end account balance of $200,000, you take $200,000 divided by 27.4, and the RMD at age 70 is $7,299.27. RMDs cannot be rolled over into another retirement account, although you can reinvest them in an after-tax savings or investment account.

Note You can find the full tables detailing required distributions in IRS Publication 590 at www.irs.gov/publications/p590/ar02.html.

Each year, you are required to take a larger portion of your remaining retirement accounts as a required minimum distribution. For those with large retirement account balances who don't need the larger withdrawals for income purposes, this can have the effect of steadily increasing their taxable income in retirement. This is one of the reasons strategic planning—and potentially taking IRA withdrawals earlier than you might think—might lower your cumulative tax bill in retirement.

If you miss an RMD, a 50% penalty tax applies to the amount that should have been—but wasn't—withdrawn. This is one of several reasons I think it makes sense to consolidate retirement accounts near retirement. If you have numerous accounts, it can be easy to miss a required withdrawal or overlook important notices or paperwork that may have been mailed to you.

EXACTLY WHEN MUST THE RMD BEGIN?

Your first required minimum distribution must occur by April 1st of the year after you reach age 70 1/2.

Example: Tom's birthday is in March, and he will turn 70 1/2 in September. His first distribution must occur by April 1st of the following year, although he could take his first distribution in the current year. If Tom waits until April 1st of the year following the year he turns 70½, he will have to take an RMD for both years.

His decision whether to wait and take two distributions in the second year or take his first distribution in the year he turns 70 1/2 would be made based primarily on his tax situation. Depending on the amount of his required distributions, two distributions in a single year may cause Tom to pay taxes on a portion of the distribution at a higher rate than if he took the first distribution in the year he turned 70 1/2.

What types of retirement plans require minimum distributions?[24]

- The RMD rules apply to all employer-sponsored retirement plans, including profit-sharing plans, 401(k) plans, 403(b) plans, and 457(b) plans. The RMD rules also apply to traditional IRAs and IRA-based plans such as SEPs, SARSEPs, and SIMPLE IRAs.

- The RMD rules also apply to Roth 401(k) accounts. However, the RMD rules do not apply to Roth IRAs while the owner is alive. And remember, you can roll your Roth 401(k) into a Roth IRA after retirement.

Steve and Carol

Let's put some of these tax rules together and see how they impact Steve and Carol's plan.

Take a moment to look at Steve and Carol's plan, in Chapter 2, Figures 2-10 and 2-11 (as well as the continued examples in Figures 3-1 and 3-2). If you recall, we did not apply an inflation rate to Social Security benefits or to their living expenses. Instead, we left sources of income flat and calculated the present

[24]From the IRS web site: www.irs.gov/Retirement-Plans/Retirement-Plans-FAQs-regarding-Required-Minimum-Distributions#2

value of the amount of savings and investment they would need to meet their anticipated withdrawals, assuming their collective savings and investments earned a 2% real rate of return.

This calculation is sufficient for getting a general idea of whether your current savings and investments are likely to meet your retirement income needs. However, to accurately create a withdrawal strategy, you must get far more detailed.

Some sources of income, like Social Security, are tied to inflation, so they go up each year. Some sources of taxable income, like RMDs, can begin later and cause you to have additional taxable income at age 70 1/2 and beyond. Some deductions, like mortgage interest, go away if you pay your mortgage off part-way into retirement.

Tax rates are tied to inflation, but some components of the tax code—such as the combined income thresholds used in the formula that determines how much of your Social Security is taxable—are not tied to inflation.

To accurately tie all this together, you must create a projection that inflates the things that inflate, that has an estimate of your RMDs based on the projected future balances of your IRA accounts, and that accurately taxes things depending on the tax characteristics of the income they generate. I use Excel spreadsheets and professional tax-planning software[25] to do this type of planning.

For Steve and Carol, I have shown you two possible scenarios. Figures 5-1 through 5-3 are more detailed versions of Figures 2-10 and 2-11. They show the results of Steve and Carol following a conventional strategy. They each take their own Social Security benefits early and delay their IRA withdrawals until they are required to take them.

Figures 5-4 through 5-6 are more detailed versions of Figures 3-1 and 3-2. They show the outcome of an alternate plan. In this plan, they delay the start of Social Security and determine which accounts to draw from based on their long-term tax projection. Their alternate plan involves the use of Roth conversions, which has the effect of lowering their future RMDs.

---

[25]See BNA Income Tax Planner: www.bnasoftware.com/Products/BNA_Income_Tax_Planner/Index.asp

Steve & Carol, Income Timeline – Taking Social Security Now - No IRA Withdrawals Until Required Minimum
As of: Beginning of Year 2013

# of Years	1	2	3	4	5	6	7	8	9	10
Calendar Year	2013	2014	2015	2016	2017	2018	2019	2020	2021	2022
Sources of Income										
Steve (age)	66	67	68	69	70	71	72	73	74	75
Earnings	$48,000	$48,000	$48,000	$48,000	$48,000	0	0	0	0	0
Social Security	$17,616	$27,217	$28,034	$28,875	$29,741	$30,633	$31,552	$32,499	$33,473	$34,478
IRA RMDs	0	0	0	0	$19,741	$20,687	$21,677	$22,712	$23,796	$24,928
Carol (age)	62	63	64	65	66	67	68	69	70	71
Social Security	$9,185	$10,320	$10,932	$11,260	$11,598	$11,946	$12,304	$12,673	$13,053	$13,445
IRA RMDs	0	0	0	0	0	0	0	0	$2,211	$2,317
Joint Account Withdrawals										
Withdrawals from savings*	$6,302	($1,293)	($696)	($15)	($14,491)	$22,377	$22,406	$22,421	$20,704	$20,662
ROTH IRA Withdrawals	0	0	0	0	0	0	0	0	0	0
Gross Income	**$81,103**	**$84,244**	**$86,269**	**$88,120**	**$94,589**	**$85,643**	**$87,939**	**$90,306**	**$93,237**	**$95,829**
Taxes										
Taxable Social Security	$22,781	$31,906	$33,121	$34,114	$35,138	$16,926	$17,991	$19,095	$22,117	$23,465
ROTH Conversions	0	0	0	0	0	0	0	0	0	0
Taxable Income	$60,881	$69,620	$70,822	$70,474	$91,146	$26,522	$27,424	$28,365	$33,440	$34,824
Fed Taxes Owed	$7,104	$8,363	$8,451	$8,306	$12,719	$1,655	$1,771	$1,891	$2,509	$2,718
Available After Taxes	**$73,999**	**$75,881**	**$77,818**	**$79,814**	**$81,870**	**$83,987**	**$86,168**	**$88,414**	**$90,728**	**$93,111**
Account Balances										
His IRA Balance	$467,250	$490,613	$515,143	$540,900	$548,204	$554,928	$560,997	$566,335	$570,856	$574,470
Her IRA Balance	$43,050	$45,203	$47,463	$49,836	$52,328	$54,944	$57,691	$60,576	$61,394	$62,147
His ROTH	$30,000	$31,500	$33,075	$34,729	$36,465	$38,288	$40,203	$42,213	$44,324	$46,540
Joint Account	$230,998	$243,841	$256,729	$269,580	$297,550	$290,051	$282,148	$273,834	$266,821	$259,500
Terminal Value **	**$643,723**	**$677,202**	**$711,759**	**$747,361**	**$784,414**	**$785,743**	**$786,367**	**$786,229**	**$785,332**	**$783,503**

* Negative number is a deposit.

**Net of 25% tax on Traditional IRA Assets

Cumulative Spending Net of Taxes:		Cumulative Taxes:	
85/81	$1,854,357	85/81	$95,690
90/86	$2,455,657	90/86	$132,512
Her 90	$3,004,953	Her 90	$168,983

Figure 5-1. Page 1 of Steve and Carol's income timeline showing tax, account withdrawal, and account balance details without following a Social Security plan or a withdrawal plan designed to minimize cumulative taxes

# of Years	11	12	13	14	15	16	17	18	19	20
Calendar Year	2023	2024	2025	2026	2027	2028	2029	2030	2031	2032
Sources of Income										
Steve (age)	76	77	78	79	80	81	82	83	84	85
Earnings	0	0	0	0	0	0	0	0	0	0
Social Security	$35,512	$36,577	$37,675	$38,805	$39,969	$41,168	$42,403	$43,675	$44,986	$46,335
IRA RMDs	$26,112	$27,221	$28,508	$29,700	$30,930	$32,201	$33,509	$34,856	$36,239	$37,402
Carol (age)	72	73	74	75	76	77	78	79	80	81
Social Security	$13,848	$14,264	$14,692	$15,132	$15,586	$16,054	$16,536	$17,032	$17,543	$18,069
IRA RMDs	$2,428	$2,544	$2,665	$2,792	$2,924	$3,048	$3,193	$3,326	$3,464	$3,606
Joint Account Withdrawals										
Withdrawals from savings*	$20,603	$20,622	$20,532	$20,536	$20,533	$9,245	$9,335	$9,439	$9,548	$9,848
ROTH IRA Withdrawals	0	0	0	0	0	0	0	0	0	0
Gross Income	$98,504	$101,227	$104,072	$106,964	$109,944	$101,717	$104,976	$108,328	$111,779	$115,260
Taxes										
Taxable Social Security	$24,866	$26,212	$27,716	$29,150	$30,624	$32,127	$34,161	$36,239	$38,374	$40,348
ROTH Conversions	0	0	0	0	0	0	0	0	0	0
Taxable Income	$36,277	$37,563	$39,144	$40,521	$41,934	$43,355	$45,876	$48,437	$51,062	$53,276
Fed Taxes Owed	$2,938	$3,133	$3,374	$3,584	$3,801	$4,020	$4,348	$4,681	$5,022	$5,301
Available After Taxes	$95,566	$98,094	$100,698	$103,380	$106,143	$97,697	$100,628	$103,647	$106,756	$109,959
Account Balances										
His IRA Balance	$577,082	$578,715	$579,142	$578,400	$576,389	$573,008	$568,150	$561,701	$553,548	$543,823
Her IRA Balance	$62,826	$63,424	$63,930	$64,335	$64,628	$64,811	$64,858	$64,775	$64,550	$64,171
His ROTH	$48,867	$51,310	$53,876	$56,569	$59,398	$62,368	$65,486	$68,761	$72,199	$75,809
Joint Account	$251,872	$243,844	$235,504	$226,743	$217,547	$219,179	$220,803	$222,405	$223,977	$225,328
Terminal Value**	$780,670	$776,758	$771,684	$765,364	$757,708	$759,911	$761,046	$761,023	$759,749	$757,133

Figure 5-2. Page 2 of Steve and Carol's income timeline showing tax, account withdrawal, and account balance details without following a Social Security plan or a withdrawal plan designed to minimize cumulative taxes

# of Years	21	22	23	24	25	26	27	28	29
Calendar Year	2033	2034	2035	2036	2037	2038	2039	2040	2041
Sources of Income									
Steve (age)	86	87	88	89	90	91	92	93	94
Earnings	0	0	0	0	0	0	0	0	0
Social Security	0	0	0	0	0	0	0	0	0
IRA RMDs	0	0	0	0	0	0	0	0	0
Carol (age)	82	83	84	85	86	87	88	89	90
Social Security	$47,725	$49,157	$50,632	$52,151	$53,715	$55,327	$56,986	$58,696	$60,457
IRA RMDs	$31,803	$37,214	$38,691	$39,933	$41,179	$42,423	$50,000	$50,000	$50,000
Joint Account Withdrawals									
Withdrawals from savings*	$40,010	$37,786	$38,469	$39,364	$40,296	$21,270	$7,888	$157	$23,187
ROTH IRA Withdrawals	0	0	0	0	0	$20,000	$30,000	$40,000	$19,376
Gross Income	$119,538	$124,157	$127,791	$131,447	$135,190	$139,020	$144,874	$148,853	$153,020
Taxes									
Taxable Social Security	$32,492	$36,479	$37,172	$37,597	$37,942	$38,198	$44,591	$45,096	$45,940
ROTH Conversions	0	0	0	0	0	0	0	0	0
Taxable Income	$54,790	$62,129	$62,259	$61,763	$61,052	$60,101	$72,463	$71,963	$72,154
Fed Taxes Owed	$6,280	$7,501	$7,636	$7,687	$7,717	$7,723	$9,638	$9,561	$9,548
Available After Taxes	$113,258	$116,655	$120,155	$123,760	$127,472	$131,297	$135,236	$139,293	$143,471
Account Balances									
His IRA Balance	0	0	0	0	0	0	0	0	0
Her IRA Balance	$606,592	$599,707	$591,002	$580,619	$568,472	$554,472	$532,195	$508,805	$484,245
His ROTH	$79,599	$83,579	$87,758	$92,146	$96,753	$101,591	$85,670	$58,454	$19,376
Joint Account	$196,585	$168,628	$138,591	$106,156	$71,168	$53,457	$48,242	$50,496	$29,835
Terminal Value**	$731,127	$701,987	$669,600	$633,766	$594,275	$570,901	$533,059	$490,554	$412,395

Figure 5-3. Page 3 of Steve and Carol's income timeline showing tax, account withdrawal, and account balance details without following a Social Security plan or a withdrawal plan designed to minimize cumulative taxes

Steve & Carol, Income Timeline – Taking Social Security According to a Plan, Customized Withdrawals and ROTH
As of: Beginning of Year 2013

# of Years	1	2	3	4	5	6	7	8	9	10
Calendar Year	2013	2014	2015	2016	2017	2018	2019	2020	2021	2022
Sources of Income										
Steve (age)	66	67	68	69	70	71	72	73	74	75
Earnings	$48,000	$48,000	$48,000	$48,000	$48,000	0	0	0	0	0
Social Security	0	0	0	0	$26,168	$40,428	$41,641	$42,890	$44,177	$45,502
IRA RMDs	0	0	0	0	$13,262	$13,898	$14,172	$14,850	$15,558	$16,298
Carol (age)	62	63	64	65	66	67	68	69	70	71
Social Security	0	0	0	0	$13,629	$15,312	$15,771	$16,245	$21,876	$23,014
IRA RMDs	0	0	0	0	0	0	0	0	0	0
Other Account Withdrawals										
Withdrawals from savings*	$50,887	$37,490	$39,089	$39,182	($3,479)	$16,042	$14,583	$14,430	$9,296	$8,590
ROTH IRA Withdrawals	0	0	0	0	0	0	0	0	0	0
Gross Income	$98,887	$85,490	$87,089	$87,182	$91,560	$85,680	$86,168	$88,414	$90,897	$93,404
Taxes										
Taxable Social Security	0	0	0	0	$33,827	$17,211	$9,204	$10,099	$13,215	$14,663
ROTH Conversions	$97,050	$39,000	$40,000	$30,000	0	$10,000	0	0	0	0
Taxable Income	$135,150	$74,485	$73,421	$59,876	$74,590	$20,563	$1,520	$1,805	$4,302	$5,370
Fed Taxes Owed	$24,888	$9,610	$9,271	$7,368	$9,710	$1,693	0	0	$169	$293
Available After Taxes	$73,999	$75,881	$77,818	$79,814	$81,870	$83,987	$86,168	$88,414	$90,728	$93,111
Account Balances										
His IRA Balance	$413,250	$394,913	$374,658	$363,391	$368,298	$362,815	$366,783	$370,273	$373,229	$375,592
Her IRA Balance	0	0	0	0	0	0	0	0	0	0
His ROTH	$30,000	$88,200	$133,560	$182,238	$222,850	$233,992	$256,192	$269,002	$282,452	$296,574
Her ROTH	0	$45,203	$47,463	$49,836	$52,328	$54,944	$57,691	$60,576	$63,604	$66,785
Joint Account	$186,413	$158,243	$127,066	$94,237	$108,429	$97,808	$88,115	$78,091	$72,709	$67,754
Terminal Value**	$526,350	$567,830	$589,082	$598,854	$659,830	$658,855	$677,086	$685,373	$698,687	$712,807

Cumulative Spending Net of Taxes:
85/81 $1,854,357
90/86 $2,455,657
Her 90 $3,004,953

Cumulative Taxes:
$73,156
$88,079
$103,118

* Negative number is a deposit.
** Net of 25% tax on Traditional IRA Assets

Figure 5-4. Page 1 of Steve and Carol's income timeline showing tax, account withdrawal, and account balance details after they have followed a Social Security plan and a withdrawal plan designed to minimize cumulative taxes

# of Years	11	12	13	14	15	16	17	18	19	20
Calendar Year	2023	2024	2025	2026	2027	2028	2029	2030	2031	2032
Sources of Income										
Steve (age)	76	77	78	79	80	81	82	83	84	85
Earnings	0	0	0	0	0	0	0	0	0	0
Social Security	$46,967	$48,273	$49,721	$51,213	$52,749	$54,332	$55,962	$57,641	$59,370	$61,151
IRA RMDs	$17,072	$17,797	$18,639	$19,418	$20,223	$21,053	$21,909	$22,789	$23,693	$24,454
Carol (age)	72	73	74	75	76	77	78	79	80	81
Social Security	$23,704	$24,416	$25,148	$25,902	$26,680	$27,480	$28,304	$29,153	$30,028	$30,929
IRA RMDs	0	0	0	0	0	0	0	0	0	0
Other Account Withdrawals										
Withdrawals from savings*	$8,329	$8,120	$7,827	$7,599	$7,363	($4,172)	($4,356)	($4,543)	($4,731)	($4,784)
ROTH IRA Withdrawals	0	0	0	0	0	0	0	0	0	0
Gross Income	**$95,973**	**$98,605**	**$101,336**	**$104,132**	**$107,014**	**$98,693**	**$101,819**	**$105,040**	**$108,360**	**$111,749**
Taxes										
Taxable Social Security	$15,984	$17,290	$18,720	$20,127	$21,584	$23,092	$25,131	$27,243	$29,431	$31,553
ROTH Conversions	0	0	0	0	0	0	0	0	0	0
Taxable Income	$6,340	$7,221	$8,314	$9,295	$10,322	$11,395	$13,559	$15,814	$18,163	$20,297
Fed Taxes Owed	$407	$512	$638	$752	$872	$996	$1,191	$1,393	$1,604	$1,791
Available After Taxes	**$95,566**	**$98,094**	**$100,698**	**$103,380**	**$106,143**	**$97,697**	**$100,628**	**$103,647**	**$106,756**	**$109,959**
Account Balances										
His IRA Balance	$377,299	$378,367	$378,647	$378,161	$376,847	$374,636	$371,460	$367,244	$361,913	$355,555
Her IRA Balance	0	0	0	0	0	0	0	0	0	0
His ROTH	$311,403	$326,973	$343,322	$360,488	$378,512	$397,438	$417,310	$438,175	$460,084	$483,088
Her ROTH	$70,124	$73,630	$77,312	$81,177	$85,236	$89,498	$93,973	$98,671	$103,605	$108,785
Joint Account	$62,813	$57,834	$52,899	$47,944	$42,979	$49,300	$56,121	$63,470	$71,374	$79,727
Terminal Value**	**$727,315**	**$742,213**	**$757,517**	**$773,231**	**$789,362**	**$817,213**	**$845,998**	**$875,749**	**$906,498**	**$938,267**

Figure 5-5. Page 2 of Steve and Carol's income timeline showing tax, account withdrawal, and account balance details after they have followed a Social Security plan and a withdrawal plan designed to minimize cumulative taxes

# of Years	21	22	23	24	25	26	27	28	29
Calendar Year	2033	2034	2035	2036	2037	2038	2039	2040	2041
Sources of Income									
Steve (age)	86	87	88	89	90	91	92	93	94
Earnings	0	0	0	0	0	0	0	0	0
Social Security	0	0	0	0	0	0	0	0	0
IRA RMDs	0	0	0	0	0	0	0	0	0
Carol (age)	82	83	84	85	86	87	88	89	90
Social Security	$62,986	$64,875	$66,821	$68,826	$70,891	$73,017	$75,208	$77,464	$79,788
IRA RMDs	$20,793	$21,628	$22,486	$23,208	$23,932	$24,656	$25,374	$26,082	$26,540
Other Account Withdrawals									
Withdrawals from savings*	$32,389	$33,045	$3,711	$4,769	$5,863	($3,005)	($11,741)	($10,339)	($8,709)
ROTH IRA Withdrawals	0	0	$30,000	$30,000	$30,000	$40,000	$50,000	$50,000	$50,000
Gross Income	$116,167	$119,548	$123,019	$126,803	$130,686	$134,668	$138,841	$143,207	$147,619
Taxes									
Taxable Social Security	$23,431	$23,737	$23,998	$25,350	$26,679	$27,979	$29,668	$31,755	$33,624
ROTH Conversions	0	0	0	0	0	0	0	0	0
Taxable Income	$27,440	$26,538	$25,492	$26,771	$27,950	$29,015	$30,873	$33,543	$35,683
Fed Taxes Owed	$2,909	$2,893	$2,864	$3,044	$3,213	$3,372	$3,605	$3,915	$4,148
Available After Taxes	$113,258	$116,655	$120,155	$123,760	$127,472	$131,297	$135,236	$139,293	$143,471
Account Balances									
His IRA Balance	0	0	0	0	0	0	0	0	0
Her IRA Balance	$352,540	$348,539	$343,479	$337,445	$330,385	$322,249	$312,987	$302,554	$291,142
His ROTH	$507,243	$532,605	$559,235	$555,697	$551,982	$548,081	$533,485	$507,659	$480,542
Her ROTH	$114,224	$119,936	$125,932	$132,229	$138,841	$145,783	$153,072	$160,725	$168,762
Joint Account	$51,325	$20,846	$18,177	$14,317	$9,170	$12,633	$25,006	$36,596	$47,134
Terminal Value**	$937,197	$934,791	$960,954	$955,327	$947,781	$948,183	$946,303	$931,896	$914,795

Figure 5-6. Page 3 of Steve and Carol's income timeline showing tax, account withdrawal, and account balance details after they have followed a Social Security plan and a withdrawal plan designed to minimize cumulative taxes

Scenario Assumptions

Here are the assumptions used in the withdrawal planning (for Figures 5-1 through 5-9):

- Taxable accounts earn a 5% return (net of all investment fees). Of this 5%, 33% is taxed as interest income, with the remaining 67% taxed as long-term capital gains and qualified dividends (at a lower tax rate). Additional planning involving investment allocations may be able to further lower the amount of taxable income this account generates each year.

- IRA accounts earn a 5% return (net of all investment fees).

- Living expenses, not including their mortgage payment, increase by 3% a year.

- In the spreadsheet I use to run these scenarios, tax bracket and deduction amounts are indexed to inflation. However, this indexing does not follow the rounding rules the IRS uses in the official indexing formula. I tested the first 20 years of tax calculations using BNA Income Tax Planner Web; the differences were attributed to the rounding rules and were insignificant to the outcomes.

- In general, I designed withdrawals from accounts so their taxable savings and investment account never went below $10,000, but I did not use an exact formula to determine this.

- In these scenarios, Steve passes away at age 85.

- These scenarios assume Steve and Carol do not itemize deductions.

Things to Notice in the Scenarios

There are several things to note about Steve and Carol's two potential scenarios.

As you study the required minimum distribution for Steve and Carol (listed in the IRA RMDs rows), you see that it is lower in their alternate plan, shown in Figures 5-4 through 5-6. That is because in this scenario, they convert a large portion of their IRA accounts to Roth IRA accounts in years 2013 through 2016. In Figure 5-7 and 5-8, you can see how this changes their expected tax liability in the short term (annual taxes paid comparison) and in the long term (cumulative taxes paid comparison).

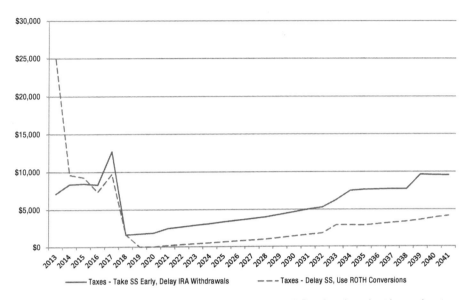

Figure 5-7. Comparison of annual taxes paid by Steve and Carol with and without planning

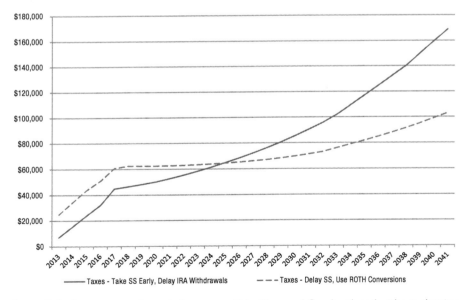

Figure 5-8. Comparison of cumulative taxes paid by Steve and Carol with and without planning

Figure 5-7 shows the comparison of the annual tax liability of their conventional scenario versus their alternate scenario. Figure 5-8 shows the difference in the cumulative tax liability of the two scenarios. If they use the Roth, they pay more taxes up front, but they break even in year 2025, at their respective ages 78 and 74 (meaning from that point forward, their alternate scenario has reduced the cumulative amount of taxes they pay). If they want a strategy that has a break-even point that occurs sooner, we might convert less to a Roth up front.

The next thing to note is that, after taxes, Steve and Carol have the exact same amount to spend if they follow the conventional plan or the alternate plan. You can see their cumulative spending calculated in the bottom left of figures 5-1 and 5-4.

Choosing a delayed start date for their Social Security and using Roth conversions did not lower their standard of living at all. But the alternate plan did result in a higher terminal value. I use the term *terminal value* as a rough approximation of the financial assets they have left if both pass away at year end. To calculate terminal value, I assume that 25% of any IRA assets are taxed, and that Roth and joint account assets are not taxed.

You can see this expressed in the account balances and terminal value rows at the bottom of both Figures 5-1 through 5-3 and 5-4 through 5-6.

Figure 5-9 is a graph that compares the terminal values of one scenario to another. I ran these scenarios to Carol's age 90. Obviously, if she lives longer, the scenario with the higher terminal value at her age 90 will leave her in a more secure situation if she should live even longer.

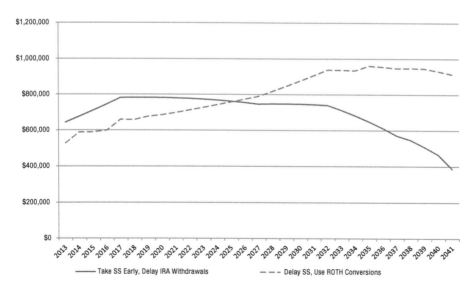

Figure 5-9. Comparison of Steve and Carol's year-end financial account values net of taxes with and without planning

In another scenario that is not shown, I took their alternate plan scenario and figured out how much more they could spend each year that would leave them with a $500,000 terminal value at Carol's age 90. The answer was about $4,850 of additional spending per year than what the conventional strategy would deliver. In other words, if they spent the extra $4,850 using the conventional scenario, they would run out of money right around Carol's age 90.

Using this planning methodology, you could calculate how much you could spend that would result in a zero terminal value, but you would be leaving no margin for error for variables like increased inflation, poor returns, unexpected expenses, or continued longevity.

Smart Planning Delivers Positive Results

The bottom line is that smart planning can deliver measurable results. You can measure the results in terms of the values that are most important to you: higher terminal values if you want to leave more to heirs or increased spending along the way if you want to leave less to heirs. Either way, smart planning provides longevity protection (better outcome if you are long-lived).

Once Steve and Carol decide on a withdrawal strategy, they can begin to allocate their investments in a way that matches up with their plan.

For example, if they follow a conventional plan, in the first ten years they will withdraw $133,541 from Steve's IRA, $4,528 from Carol's IRA (her RMDs in years 2021 and 2033), and $98,377 net[26] from their joint account.

If they follow the alternate plan, in the first ten years they will withdraw $88,038 from Steve's IRA and $220,101 net from their joint account assets.

Once you know which accounts you will draw from, you can match investments in terms of tax efficiency and risk tolerance to the point in time in which they will be needed.

The scenarios shown for Steve and Carol reflect results independent of any investment or allocation changes.[27] Additional attention to building a portfolio that reduces taxable investment income on their non-IRA assets may be able to deliver further improvement.

---

[26]Years with a negative number represent those in which they make a deposit back into their joint account.

[27]Some advisors and/or online planning tools imply that by changing your asset allocation, you can increase your return, and your situation looks more secure. I have often seen this approach used in what I consider to be a completely inappropriate way. You need to isolate all the planning decisions that can improve your outcome and then make investment decisions based on cash flow needs and comfort level with risk.

Asset Allocation and Location Decisions

Regardless of whether you are accumulating or withdrawing, if you have savings and investments in both after-tax and tax-deferred accounts, you want to look at how to position those assets to reduce the annual tax impact. The technical term for this process is *asset location*.

■ **Note**   Asset location is different than asset *allocation*. Asset allocation is the process of determining how much of your money should be in asset classes like stocks, bonds, or cash. Asset allocation can be applied at a household level or on an account-by-account basis. Asset *location* is the process of strategically deciding which asset belongs in which type of account to make the overall outcome more tax-efficient. To apply asset location, you must look at your asset allocation from a household view rather than on an account-by-account basis.

Asset location makes a difference, because not all investment income is taxed at the same rate. Interest income and non-qualified dividends are taxed at your applicable marginal tax rate, whereas long-term capital gains and qualified dividends[28] are taxed at a lower rate. This differential in tax rates provides some opportunities for you.

To understand this, keep three things in mind:

- Your IRA withdrawals are taxed at your marginal tax rate, regardless of the characteristics of the investment income inside the IRA.

- Your Roth IRA withdrawals are tax-free, regardless of the characteristics of the investment income inside the Roth IRA.

- Mutual funds, stocks, bonds, and other investments owned in a regular account (not a designated retirement account of any kind) generate interest, dividends, and capital gains that will be reported to you each year on a form 1099.

Suppose you have two accounts, a traditional IRA and a non-IRA mutual fund. In your IRA, you own a stock index fund that pays a dividend yield of about 2% and accumulates a long-term gain of about 4% a year. Your non-IRA mutual fund is a corporate bond fund that yields about 4% (or it could just as easily be a brokerage account that owns individual corporate bonds).

---

[28]A dividend is qualified if it was paid by a U.S. or qualified foreign corporation, and you held the investment for "more than 60 days during the 121-day period that begins 60 days before the ex-dividend date," per IRS web site: www.irs.gov/publications/p17/ch08.html#en_US_2011_publink1000171584. The 1099-DIV form you receive each year should show you what amount of dividends are qualified versus non-qualified.

For the sake of simplicity, let's say you own $100,000 of each fund.

In your IRA, all interest is tax-deferred. But someday, when you take withdrawals, it will be taxable to you. You have $2,000 a year of dividend income in your IRA, and $4,000 a year of gain accumulating. Let's assume it will be taxed at the 25% marginal rate when it is withdrawn, which means when you take $6,000 of withdrawals you will receive $4,500 net of tax.

In your non-IRA account, you have $4,000 of interest income that is being taxed at the 25% marginal rate each year, so you keep $3,000 after taxes.

On an after-tax basis, you accumulated $7,500 over both accounts for the year.

If you flip-flopped the two investments (meaning you own the bond fund in your IRA and the stock index fund in your non-IRA), what would happen?

Now you would have $4,000 of interest income in your IRA that someday would be taxed as ordinary income. On an after-tax basis you would receive $3,000; same as the first scenario.

In your non-IRA account you would have $2,000 of income that is taxed at the qualified dividend rate of 15% and $4,000 of long-term gain realized when you sell shares, which is also taxed at 15% (assuming you are in the 25% tax bracket). On an after-tax basis, you keep $5,100.

Combined, and on an after-tax basis, you have accumulated $8,100; $600 more than the initial allocation choice delivered.

Now maybe an extra $600 doesn't seem like much to you, but when you add up the tax savings that can be achieved by compounding this result over many years, it can quickly turn into thousands.

In addition, in the second scenario, where you own the bonds funds in your IRA and the stock funds in your non IRA account, say you have a year with less taxable income (perhaps a job transition or larger itemized deductions because of medical expenses). If you end up in the 10% or 15% tax brackets, your long-term capital gains could end up being taxed at zero (see the long-term capital gains rates in Table 5-1).

While you are in accumulation mode, once you set your emergency fund aside, I think it makes sense to design an allocation that is as tax-efficient as possible. And for those in higher tax rates, asset location can have a larger impact than in the example here.

As you near retirement, you may need to forsake some tax-efficiency in your allocation in order to most appropriately align the investments in each account (according to risk) with the withdrawals you will need to take from that account.

■ **Tip** You have numerous opportunities to save on taxes by allocating assets in specific ways. But you need to run some projections to identify the allocation that will save you the most in the long run.

Capital Gains Management

Capital gains management is another area where paying attention to taxes can make a difference.

To illustrate how it works, let's make a few assumptions. Let's assume you use an index-fund investing philosophy. You have allocated your growth-oriented stock index funds to your non-retirement accounts based on the asset location guidelines we just discussed.

Now, you are a savvy investor, and so you clearly recognize that the market will not go up in a straight line. You expect that in some years you will have a negative return. Suppose you look at your statement near year end and you realize that you have invested $50,000 in one of your stock index funds, but it is currently worth $45,000. You exchange it for a similar stock index fund on the same day, so your overall allocation does not change at all. Yet by exchanging it you realize a $5,000 capital loss. This loss flows through to your tax return. First, it is used to offset capital gains. Then $3,000 of it can be used to offset ordinary income, and you are able to carry forward any remaining loss to offset capital gains and ordinary income in the future.[29]

Your ordinary income rate is higher than your capital gains rate—anywhere from 10% to 19.6% higher, depending on your tax rate. That means that tax loss, if used against ordinary income, is worth anywhere from $300 to $588 in reduced taxes. Once again, that may not sound like much to you, but when such strategies are used consistently, the savings can add up.

When it comes to your allocation plan, tax savings can be realized as follows:

- Looking at your investment allocation on a household basis rather than by allocating each account on its own

- Intentionally harvesting capital losses when appropriate

The smart way to do this, as always, depends on your individual situation. It also depends on when you will need to use your money. Your allocation needs to match your risk tolerance, be designed to be tax-efficient, and match your future withdrawal needs. Particularly for couples with age differences, this can lead to some interesting allocation designs.

---

[29]Capital losses and capital-loss carryforward amounts offset long-term capital gains first, and then short-term capital gains. Any remaining losses up to $3,000 can be used against ordinary income.

Let's take Mark and Holly as an example. They were about seven years away from retirement. When we ran their projections, in their case it made sense to follow conventional wisdom (yes, sometimes that does make sense) and defer traditional retirement account withdrawals until they were each required to take them at 70 1/2. Mark is ten years older than Holly. They also had substantial assets outside of retirement accounts. In their allocation plan, we decided to allocate all of Holly's retirement accounts to growth investments, because there would be no withdrawals for 17 years. We placed their taxable bond funds in Mark's retirement accounts, as well as some stock index funds. Then, in their non-retirement account, we used tax-exempt municipal bonds as well as additional stock index funds. When viewed as a household, their allocation was about 45% stock index funds and 55% bonds, CDs, and bond funds. This allocation was appropriate for their risk tolerance, it was tax-efficient, and it matched up with their future withdrawal needs.

Special Considerations for High-Income Tax Filers

There are a few tax rules that high-income tax filers should be aware of. Some of them are new; some have been around for awhile. This section discusses a few I want to draw your attention to.

3.8% Medicare Surtax on Investment Income

If your adjusted gross income (AGI) is in excess of $200,000 for singles and $250,000 for marrieds, a 3.8% Medicare surtax may apply to some of your investment income.[30] Proper asset location can help reduce the effects of this new tax.

Phaseout of Exemptions and Deductions

If you are single with AGI of $250,000 a year, or a married couple filing jointly with AGI of $300,000 or more, you may not be able to use all your deductions and exemptions. A phaseout of the deductions and exemptions begins to apply at these income levels.

The Alternative Minimum Tax

The alternative minimum tax (AMT) is a calculation that runs parallel to the regular tax calculation. If the result of the AMT tax calculation says you owe more tax than the regular tax calculation, then you must pay the difference. AMT is most likely to affect singles with incomes of about $200,000–$350,000 and married couples with incomes in the $250,000 to $475,000 range.

---

[30] I provide additional details and examples about this tax in my About.com article "Medicare 3.8% Tax — What Is It and How Will It Affect You, available online at http://moneyover55.about.com/od/taxtips/a/Medicare-3-8-Tax-What-Is-It-And-How-Will-It-Affect-You.htm.

(You may be more likely to have to pay AMT tax if you have a large family with many dependents, pay high state taxes or high property taxes, or have large miscellaneous itemized deductions.)

When you take a look at the highest tax bracket, add on the Medicare surtax as well as any state and local taxes, and factor in the potential loss of deductions, a high-income tax filer may be paying taxes at a marginal rate of 50% or more.

If you are a high-income tax filer, you'll therefore want to spend more time finding appropriate ways to use tax-deferred products. You'll also want to look at your savings and investments in terms of their after-tax yield.

After-Tax Yield

Assume you own a CD (certificate of deposit) or bond fund, which pays annual interest of 3%.

If you are at the 39.6% tax rate, pay the 3.8% Medicare surtax, and pay state taxes of 5%, for every dollar of taxable interest you earn, 48.4 cents goes to taxes.

Your after-tax yield is 1.55% (Calculated by: 3% × (1−.484).

You might consider investing in tax-exempt municipal bonds issued by your state as an alternative. Interest paid is not subject to federal or state taxes—but it may be subject to AMT. Although yields are low in today's interest-rate environment, on an after-tax basis a municipal bond yielding 3% is paying you nearly double what you may be getting in something that pays taxable interest income.

Another option would be to use a flat-fee variable annuity and tuck your taxable bond investments inside of it. I discuss this in Chapter 8.

There is one additional item that affects high-income tax filers in retirement, and many of them are not aware of it. It is the means-testing that applies to Medicare Part B and Part D premiums.

Medicare Part B and D Premiums

Many people who fall in the high-income category are caught off-guard when the reach age 65 by something that is not technically categorized as a tax, although I would certainly call it a tax.

It has to do with how Medicare Part B premiums are calculated. In Chapter 10, I provide an overview of how Medicare works and what Medicare Part B premiums are. For now, accept that when you turn 65 you will enroll in Medicare and pay a premium for what is called Medicare Part B.

The amount you pay is means-tested, meaning the more income you have, the higher your premiums. Table 5-3 shows you the monthly premium you pay depending on your modified adjusted gross income.

Table 5-3. Medicare Part B & D Premiums Based on Modified Adjusted Gross Income

Single ($)	Married ($)	Monthly Medicare Part B Premium ($)	Monthly Medicare Part D Premium ($)
Based on Modified Adjusted Gross Income (MAGI) as follows:			
Up to $85,000	Up to 170,000	104.90	Your plan premium[31]
85,001–107,000	170,001–214,000	146.90	11.60 + your plan premium
107,001–160,000	214,001–320,000	209.80	29.90 + your plan premium
160,001–214,000	320,001–428,000	272.70	48.30 + your plan premium
214,001+	428,001+	335.70	66.60 + your plan premium

You use tax returns from two years prior to determine your income for assessing the Medicare premium. So if your income exceeds one of the threshold amounts in 2013, then in 2015 you would begin paying the next higher premium amount. Note that those in the highest range are paying $3,568 more per year ($297 more a month) for their combined Medicare Part B and D premiums than those in the lowest range.

Medicare premiums are determined based on your modified adjusted gross income (MAGI). Roth IRA withdrawals are not included in MAGI. By planning ahead, you may be able to avoid paying the higher Medicare premiums in retirement.

So far, I have covered what I call tax-planning strategies. I have discussed various concepts and looked at specific examples to see how tax planning can make a difference. Before I wrap up this chapter, I'd like to discuss a few other miscellaneous tax-related items that didn't quite fit in anywhere else.

Taxation of Annuities

Many years ago in Colorado, I was out with a small group of friends, and one of my girlfriends brought along a date, someone we hadn't met before. I'll call him Evan. As she introduced us, she told us we were in the same line of work, financial planning.

---

[31]Your plan premium will depend on the type of coverage you select in retirement. Additional details are provided in Chapter 10.

As he and I started chatting, he said he worked with seniors on their estate planning. I asked if he was an attorney. He said, no, but they had an attorney in their office, and once the attorney had a list of the senior's account and asset information, he would suggest they set an appointment with Evan.

Evan would then show them how they could save money on taxes by repositioning their taxable investments into annuities. I asked Evan how long he'd been doing this. He said about a year. I asked Evan to estimate the average age of his clients. He said about 70.

I said to Evan, "Well I suppose you inform them that with annuities, heirs will not get a step up in cost basis upon their death, and as a matter of fact will have to pay taxes at their ordinary income tax rate on any accumulated gains in the annuity?"

I got a blank stare.

I went on. "And I suppose you inform them that if they invest after-tax money in a variable or fixed annuity (not the immediate annuity) and take withdrawals, all gain will be taxed as ordinary income at their current tax rate? Whereas it might be taxed at a lower capital gains or qualified dividend tax rate, or possibly even be tax-free[32] if they built a portfolio of investments that were not in the annuity?"

Another blank stare.

I went on. "And I suppose you provide a thorough estimate of the tax consequences of selling any of their existing investments in order to move them into the annuity so they aren't surprised come April 15th?"

At this point Evan decided not to talk to me anymore.

Unfortunately, there are far too many people like Evan selling investment and insurance products—well-intentioned yet perhaps uninformed.

I have no problem with annuities when they are used properly and placed thoughtfully. For example, Chapter 4 discusses the use of an immediate annuity for Steve and Carol. The purpose of this was to hedge against longevity risk. Based on their tax situation, and using a scenario analysis similar to the examples in this chapter, if they buy the immediate annuity it will be to their benefit to buy it with Steve's IRA money. If they buy it with their joint account assets, it will be a less tax-efficient solution.

What I do have a problem with is people selling these products without doing an objective analysis to show someone how it affects their situation in terms of taxes, terminal value, or various types of risk. If you buy a product, it should offer an improvement to your situation, and that improvement needs to be shown in quantifiable terms.

---

[32] If they invested in municipal bonds.

Mortgages

Many people have an inflated view of the value of their mortgage interest deduction. You either claim your standard deductions or itemized deductions. If you and your spouse are both 65 or older, in 2013 your combined standard deduction amount would be $14,600.

A mortgage of $375,000 at a 4% interest rate would generate $15,000 a year of deductible mortgage interest—only $400 more than your standard deduction. But say you have other itemized deductions, like charitable contributions, state taxes or sales taxes, real estate and personal property taxes, health care expenses (only to the extent that they exceed 10%[33] of your adjusted gross income), and miscellaneous deductions (like tax preparation and investment management fees) that already add up to $14,600. In that case, the full value of the $15,000 of mortgage interest paid would be deductible (assuming your income is not high enough to be subject to the phaseout of deductions rule). If you're beginning to think our tax code is overly complex, I agree.

If you want to compare the "return" of paying off your mortgage to that of other investments, you can calculate your mortgage cost on an after-tax basis, but because the full extent of your mortgage interest may not be deductible, it may not be as simple as taking your mortgage rate multiplied by one minus your tax bracket.

Once retired, when you factor in additional tax intricacies, like the necessity of taking additional IRA withdrawals to continue making mortgage payments, it gets even more complicated.

For example, conventional wisdom would tell you it doesn't make sense to take a large, lump sum IRA withdrawal to pay off a remaining mortgage. In some cases conventional wisdom is wrong.

One case I ran for a retired client—who was already taking Social Security—showed that taking about $100,000 out of his IRA to pay off a $75,000 remaining mortgage, allowed him to lower his future IRA withdrawals. That also lowered the amount of his Social Security benefits subject to taxation. The end result was an estimated cumulative federal tax savings of about $45,000 over a 20-year period.

---

[33]Up from 7.5% in 2012.

Cumulative tax savings aren't the only thing to look at. In this tax-planning scenario, as well as with Roth conversions, you are paying a chunk of taxes up front, so the other consideration is the break-even point. In the situation where the mortgage was paid off with a large IRA withdrawal, the break-even point was about nine years out. This was acceptable based on the person's age and health status.

■ **Note**   State taxes: Thirty-six states don't tax Social Security benefits. Some don't tax pension income either, and some have no state income taxes. Property taxes also vary widely from state to state. If you're considering relocating, maybe taxes should play a part in your decision. Use Kiplinger's Retiree Tax Map to find out the tax-friendliest states for retirees: www.kiplinger.com/tools/retiree_map/.

Health Savings Accounts

If Roth IRAs are the superheroes of retirement accounts, health savings accounts (HSAs) are their sidekicks. Together, they make up a dynamic duo.

The basic premise behind the HSA is that you lower your insurance premiums by choosing a health insurance plan that has a higher deductible. Then you contribute the premium savings on a tax-deductible basis to a health savings account.

An HSA is not to be confused with an FSA (flexible savings account):

- With an FSA (usually offered through an employer) it's a "use it or lose it" proposition. Money not used during the year is forfeited.

- With an HSA, even if you don't use it, the money stays in the account and continues to grow tax-deferred.

To establish a health savings account, you must have an HSA-qualified high-deductible plan. Any health insurance provider can provide you with details on such a plan, and I provide additional information in Chapter 10.

As with an IRA, there is a maximum allowable contribution to an HSA. In 2013, the maximum contribution per single plan is $3,250 (plus an additional $1,000 catch-up for those age 55 and older). The maximum contribution for a family plan is $6,450.

As with an IRA, HSA money goes in on a tax-deductible basis and grows tax-deferred (no need to report the annual investment income earned). Unlike an IRA, you can use the funds any time for eligible medical expenses on a tax-free basis.

Even if you spend the full amount of your HSA contribution each year, you still save a fair amount of money in taxes. For example, if you contributed the $3,250 and used it all the next year, doing so saved you $812 at the 25% tax bracket.

One key difference between HSAs and IRAs is the early-withdrawal penalty. With an HSA, a 20% penalty tax applies for early withdrawals not used for medical reasons. For HSAs, an early withdrawal is one that occurs before age 65. For IRAs it is a 10% penalty tax for early withdrawals, and an early withdrawal is one that occurs before 59 1/2.

I have an HSA myself and think they are a great option for those eligible for them.

The Value of Advice

Ellen heard me speak at a women's event and called the next day to set up an appointment. She was 82, and her husband had passed away about nine months earlier. She was trying to sort out the finances. Her husband was an engineer and had left his 401(k) plan with his employer throughout his retirement. He had about $300,000 of company stock in his plan.

I knew there was a way to distribute this stock that would potentially result in $20,000 or more of tax savings for Ellen and her heirs, but some analysis needed to be done to make sure it was the right strategy for her. The strategy is the use of something called *net unrealized appreciation*.

Net unrealized appreciation allows you to distribute stock from a company retirement plan and pay ordinary income taxes on its cost basis. (You have to get the cost basis from the company, which, if you have worked for the company for a long time, is often significantly lower than the market value of the stock.) Then, as you sell the stock,[34] you pay taxes on the gain at capital gains tax rates. Or, if you are 82, after you distribute the stock, perhaps you hang on to it and then upon your death your heirs get a step up in cost basis,[35] so taxes on gain are avoided altogether. If you leave the stock in the retirement plan, this type of tax treatment does not apply. When heirs inherit retirement plan assets, no step up in basis applies.[36]

---

[34]You must hold the stock one year after distribution to be eligible for long-term capital gains treatment.

[35]A step up in cost basis means the value of the asset upon your date of death becomes the heir's value—or basis—for tax purposes. For example if you bought a stock for $10,000 and it is worth $20,000 upon your death, for tax purposes the $20,000 value becomes the cost basis for your heirs. If they sell it for $20,000 no capital gains taxes are owed on the gain.

[36]In this scenario, I am referring to federal income tax, not estate taxes. With the 2013 tax changes, a single person can pass along $5 million that is exempt from estate taxes ($10 million for marrieds). However, an heir—spouse or non-spouse—must still pay income taxes on withdrawals from inherited traditional retirement plan accounts. (Roth IRAs are tax-free, so heirs do not pay tax on withdrawals from inherited Roth accounts.)

Ellen did not want to pay for advice, because her husband had never paid for advice. She wanted to keep things simple: call up a mutual fund company and roll over the 401(k) plan to her IRA. We called her mutual fund company together, and this particular tax strategy came up in the conversation. The mutual fund company representative told her that they could not offer tax advice and recommended she consult with someone about the tax implications before making a decision.

Despite this, Ellen decided she did not want to pay me—nor anyone else—to do the analysis.

Paying for advice is a personal choice. Perhaps in the long run, you'll pay just as much to professionals who can show you how to save in taxes as you would pay in taxes if you simply did no planning. I don't think so, but I do understand that is how some people look at it.

Personally, I'd rather pay for professional advice and be sure that I was taking advantage of all the legal tax strategies available to me. Even if I knew it was a break-even proposition, it would then be a matter of where I'd rather see my money go.

Summary

You can't control tax rates. You *can* manage taxes. Managing taxes can result in a measurable improvement to your bottom line.

When you are saving, managing taxes means strategically deciding which accounts to fund based on your tax rates now and your projected tax rates in retirement. It also means paying attention to how you locate investments between after-tax and tax-deferred accounts as well as managing your capital gains and losses.

As you near retirement, managing taxes means creating a withdrawal strategy that lowers your cumulative tax bill. By projecting your tax rates and account withdrawals over your future life expectancy, and designing a plan that is tax-efficient, your savings and investments can deliver more cumulative income. Tax planning results in savings that you actually can take to the bank.

Insurance, Life, and Disability

Shifting Risk

Not everything that is faced can be changed. But nothing can be changed until it is faced.

—James Baldwin

Insurance, like any other financial instrument discussed in this book, is a tool.

The primary purpose of the insurance tool is to shift risk. To determine if you need insurance of any kind, follow a four-step process:

1. Identify the probability of the risk.
2. Quantify the risk.
3. Evaluate the needed insurance purchase to shift the risk.
4. Decide to shift risk or retain risk.

This process can be applied to any type of insurance purchase—life insurance, disability, property and casualty, long-term care, and so on. Acquiring the proper types and amounts of insurance represents an investment in your family's financial well-being.

Identify and Quantify Risk

Not all risks are equal. Take the common example of your home burning down. Although unlikely to happen, if it does burn down, the consequences are severe. Therefore, if you own a home, you carry homeowner's insurance. You choose to pay a reasonable premium to minimize the financial severity of such an event.

Contrast that with death. There is no argument that death is a high-probability event, and the probability goes up as we age. The severity of the event, however, depends on where in your life cycle it occurs and who is financially dependent on you at the time.

If you are young, have many high-earning years ahead of you, and have a non-working spouse or dependent children, the financial consequences of your death are likely to be severe for your family. The probability and severity of a death might fall in quadrant 4 in Figure 6-1.

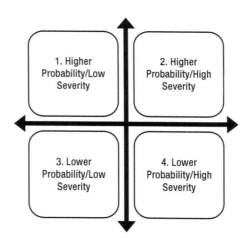

Figure 6-1. Assessing risk for insurance needs

If you are retired, and your spouse will have the same amount of income and resources available regardless of your death, the financial consequences may be minimal. Your situation may fall in quadrant 1 on Figure 6-1.

In the first scenario, you have a need for life insurance. In the second scenario, you don't.

The need for disability insurance might follow a slightly different pattern. The probability of disability is higher than the probability of death when you are younger.

A 50-year-old male is 33% more likely to become disabled than die before age 65, and a 50-year-female is 94% more likely.[1] If you are a working woman between 50 and 60, and you haven't insured your earning power, it's time to give it some thought.

The probability and severity of a disability is likely to start in quadrant 2 in Figure 6-1 and then gravitate toward quadrant 3 the closer you get to retirement.

As you near retirement, all your resources need to work together toward a common goal, including your insurance portfolio. Like other aspects of your financial life, insurance policies need to be reviewed and changed in light of changing exposure to risks.

It can be easy to collect various insurance policies along the way and keep them without giving much thought about whether they are needed or not. It can also be easy to overlook gaps in your coverage.

In this chapter, I provide examples of how I analyze life insurance and disability insurance needs and show how the use of such tools may change as you near retirement.

Life Insurance in and near Retirement

With life insurance, first and foremost, it is important to establish its purpose. We are, after all, rather attached to our own lives, and sometimes this can make us view life insurance rather emotionally.

I have come across some people who don't like the idea of someone benefiting financially upon their death. It makes them uncomfortable. Others are more than willing to spend money on insurance premiums so that a significant amount of wealth can be passed along. Some are spending far more than they realize on insurance that is no longer necessary.

The primary purpose of life insurance is to provide for someone who is financially dependent on you by replacing income or assets that will become unavailable to them upon your death.

Once retired, you are often in a situation in which children are grown, and if you are married, income remains stable for your spouse. In many cases, there is no more financial dependency. At that point, life insurance policies need to be reviewed. You may not need them anymore.[2]

---

[1]www.disabilityquotes.com/disability-insurance/death-disability-odds.cfm
[2]With current estate tax laws (2013), you can pass along an estate of up to $5 million, and it would be exempt from federal estate taxes. A married couple could have a $10 million estate that would be exempt from federal estate taxes. Life insurance for estate planning purposes is applicable for those who expect their estates to exceed these limits.

Let's look at three case studies and see how their existing life insurance holdings were evaluated.

TYPES OF LIFE INSURANCE

Life insurance can be broken out into two main categories:

- Term life

- Permanent life

Term life has only an insurance component. Much like car insurance, you pay a premium, and if an accident happens, it pays. There is no cash value accumulating. If you don't need the insurance any more, you stop paying the premium, and the policy expires.

Permanent life involves a policy that has two components; an insurance component and a cash value component. There are many variations of permanent life policies, such as whole life, universal life, and variable universal life.

If you own some form of a permanent life policy, quite a bit of analysis needs to be done before you decide what to do with it. You should look at a few specific things when analyzing an existing permanent policy:

Is the policy at risk? Many permanent policies were issued when interest rates were higher. Your premium was determined based on the expectation of these higher interest rates, which would result in a higher cash value. If the policy has not performed as initially expected, that premium may no longer be sufficient to keep the policy in force. Such situations can be anticipated by requesting something called an *in-force illustration.*

What are the tax consequences of termination? If you terminate a permanent policy while there is cash value, you may have tax consequences that need to be considered before making decisions.

What other options are available? With a permanent policy, you may be able to lower the death benefit, exchange the policy for an annuity, or change the dividend option to use it to either buy more insurance or to reduce the premium you owe. You should consider all options before deciding what to do with an existing policy.

Single Mom

Patricia walked in with seven whole-life insurance policies. Her dad had been a life insurance agent; he kept selling them, and she kept buying them. Now, here she was at 58, trying to decide what to do with them.

The total death benefit on all of her policies was $379,000. Patricia had a 15-year-old son, Mark, whose dad had passed away several years prior. Patricia planned to work until 70 to get Mark through college. If she were to pass in the midst of her earning years, the financial severity on Mark would be high. Considering Mark's financial dependency on her and the severity of the situation should she die, Patricia most certainly had a need for life insurance.

The first thing I do in such a situation is create a schedule like Figure 6-2. This helps organize the information to see at a glance what we have to work with.

Next, for any policies that have cash value, I request an in-force illustration on the policy based on current interest rate and premium assumptions. This helps determine how the policy is expected to perform if you leave it alone.

For example, many permanent policies were issued with the expectation that the cash value would grow at a much higher rate of return than has actually occurred. In such cases, the policy owner may receive a notice that they either have to pay additional premiums or their policy will lapse. An in-force illustration helps identify many years in advance which policies may have this problem.

Patricia's in-force illustrations showed that all of her policies were in good shape, meaning none were at risk of lapsing. The particular type of policies that Patricia owned had participated in dividends from the company, and the company had done well.

Policies that pay dividends offer you options on what you do with your dividends. Initially, Patricia's dividends were set to purchase additional paid-up insurance; however, Patricia's biggest concern was not her need for more insurance, it was reducing her expenses.

By exploring options with the insurance company, we decided to change her dividend option so that dividends would be used reduce her annual premiums rather than buy more insurance. In Patricia's case, she was able to keep all of the policies but reduce her cash outflow. Patricia started off paying about $3,771 a year in premiums, which you see in Figure 6-2 totaled at the end of the row labeled Premium. With the change in dividend option, her out-of-pocket costs were reduced to about $792 a year, which you see in Figure 6-2 totaled at the end of the row labeled Out of Pocket Premium. This change saved her almost $3,000 a year while enabling her to retain the insurance coverage she needed.

Patricia's Life Insurance Policy Schedule
As of March 20xx

	Patricia	Patricia	Patricia	Patricia	Patricia	Patricia	Patricia	Totals
Client	Patricia	Patricia	Patricia	Patricia	Patricia	Patricia	Patricia	
Policy #	xx-xxx-xxx	xx-xxx-xxx	xx-xxx-xxx	xx-xxx-xxx	xx-xxx-xxx	xx-xxx-xxx	xx-xxx-xxx	
Company	x	x	x	x	x	x	x	
Date Issued	1998	1992	1988	1981	1979	1974	1973	
Type of insurance	Whole	Whole	Whole w/adj term	Whole	Whole	Whole	Whole	
Owner	Patricia	Patricia	Patricia	Patricia	Patricia	Patricia	Patricia	
Insured	Patricia	Patricia	Patricia	Patricia	Patricia	Patricia	Patricia	
Beneficiary 1	Trust for Mark	Trust for Mark	Trust for Mark	Trust for Mark	Trust for Mark	Trust for Mark	Trust for Mark	
Beneficiary 2								
Death Benefit Amount	$ 50,098	$ 56,133	$ 100,000	$ 36,227	$ 99,995	$ 19,309	$ 17,450	$ 379,212
Net Death Benefit	$ 50,098	$ 56,133	$ 100,000	$ 36,227	$ 99,995	$ 19,309	$ 17,450	$ 379,212
A or B Death Benefit								
Premium	$ 1,101	$ 919	$ 558	$ 291	$ 492	$ 209	$ 202	$ 3,771
Premium frequency	annual	annual	annual	annual	annual	annual	annual	
Last Dividend	$ 605	$ 660	$ 924	$ 863	$ 455	$ 342	$ 322	
Out of Pocket Premium	$ 496	$ 259	$ -	$ -	$ 37	$ -	$ -	$ 792
Cost basis	$ 11,051	$ 11,400	$ 12,782	$ 5,122	$ 7,232	$ 2,458	$ 1,480	
- as of date:	xxxx	xxxx	xxxx	xxxx	xxxx	xxxx	xxxx	
or taxable inc. on surr.	$ -	$ 6,176	$ 5,819	$ 12,915	$ 5,318	$ 7,291	$ 7,083	$ 44,602
Cash Value	$ 10,418	$ 17,576	$ 18,601	$ 18,037	$ 12,550	$ 9,749	$ 8,563	
Surrender Value	$ 10,418	$ 17,576	$ 18,601	$ 18,037	$ 12,550	$ 9,749	$ 8,563	
Avail to loan at 80%	$ 8,334	$ 14,061	$ 14,881	$ 14,430	$ 10,040	$ 7,799	$ 6,850	$ 76,395
Outstanding loans:	$ -	$ -	$ -	$ -	$ -	$ -	$ -	$ -
Loan Rate	8%	8%	8%	8%	8%	6%	6%	
Other Expenses 1								
Other Expenses 2								
Div Option	Reduce Premium	Reduce Premium	Reduce Premium	Reduce Premium	Reduce Premium	Reduce Premium	Reduce Premium	
Last in-force illustration	2011	2011	2011	2011	2011	2011	2011	

Figure 6-2. Sample life insurance schedule

We also have a future plan for these policies. When Mark is established, and Patricia's need for life insurance is gone, we will look at using these policies for guaranteed income by converting them to an immediate annuity.

Older Husband/Younger Wife

Matt was a successful surgeon who married a beautiful woman 28 years younger than he. He was 56 when he and his wife Tina came in to see me. They had a three-year-old daughter.

They owned several properties and loved to travel and spend money. When we ran their retirement projections, it was sobering. Normally, retirement assets need to provide for a 20- to 35-year life span. In their case, the combined retirement time-horizon was potentially 50 to 60 years. Yikes.

We discussed a combination of all of the following:

- Matt extending his career to 70 or beyond
- Tina building and developing a sustainable career once their daughter reached school age
- Spending less and saving more now
- Using life insurance as a leverage tool

Matt owned three term policies and three permanent insurance policies. Some of his term policies would expire in a few years, and one had what was called an *annual renewable term*, which means the premium goes up each year. He was paying $15,000 a year for a combined $1.4 million of life insurance, with the expectation that to keep this amount of insurance the costs would soon go up.

Just as I do with any insurance situation, I started with a life insurance schedule and requested in-force illustrations on the permanent insurance policies.

Like many high-wage earners, Matt had bought his life insurance in a haphazard manner over the years. No one had taken the time to structure his insurance properly.

By working with an agent to restructure his insurance, for the same out-of-pocket premium we were able to secure $1.8 million of permanent insurance on Matt with a fixed cost. We used a 1035 tax-free exchange (see sidebar) to transfer his existing permanent policies into a new policy without any tax consequences. Without costing the couple a penny more, we made a significant improvement to their plan both in the amount of insurance and in capping the projected future cost of maintaining this important part of their plan.

THE 1035 TAX-FREE EXCHANGE

Life-insurance policies that have a cash value can be exchanged, or transferred into a new life insurance policy, with no tax consequences, through a 1035 exchange. A 1035 exchange can also be used to transfer cash value in life insurance into an annuity. Before cancelling a life-insurance policy that has cash value, evaluate your exchange options.

What made insurance such an attractive option for Matt and Tina is the leverage it provided. You can compare owning the insurance to trying to save the equivalent amount of money by calculating the rate of return the insurance provides depending on how long Matt lives.

You use the following data to calculate it.[3]

- *Present Value (PV):* –$61,000 (amount of net cash value in the existing policies they would receive if they cashed them in)

- *Payment (PMT):* –$15,000 (amount of annual premium)

- *Term (n):* 25, 30, 35 (years remaining to Matt's respective ages of 86, 91, and 96)

- *Future Value (FV):* $1,800,000 (death benefit guaranteed to be paid)

You solve for *i*, the interest rate.

Annualized results are tabulated here:

- *25-year return:* 9.01%

- *30-year return:* 6.78%

- *35-year return:* 5.26%

If Matt lives 25 years to his age 86, slightly longer than the average male life expectancy, the insurance has provided a guaranteed return of 9%.

In Matt and Tina's case, we also had conversations about the risk of spending this much on life insurance. In Matt's case, the risk is that he and Tina should separate or Tina should pass first. In either case, Matt would have a few options. The death benefit on the policies could be reduced, and the beneficiary redirected to a trust for their daughter, or the cash accumulated inside the policies could be used for his own retirement income.

---

[3] I do these calculations on an hp12c calculator that I have downloaded as an app on both my iPhone and iPad.

▨ **Note**   Normally, term policies for a high wage earner make sense; they are a form of low-cost temporary insurance that will replace earnings in the event of death in the midst of a worker's highest-earning years. In Matt and Tina's case, due to the age difference, they have a need for insurance that will extend far past Matt's working years. We needed to know that a death benefit was in place long after the term policies were set to expire. Permanent insurance was therefore a better solution for them.

I'm Retired—What Do I Do With These Policies?

Marvin was 62, and his wife Beth was about to turn 66 when we began working together. Both were still working part-time. Initially Marvin just wanted to pay me hourly to answer some specific questions. One of his first questions for me was what to do with his life-insurance policies. My initial response was:

> The first thing to consider when evaluating life insurance is the need for life insurance. Inside every policy, even those with a cash value, there is a cost to the insurance component of the policy.[4] If there is a financial dependency, then this cost becomes worth the benefit. If retirement income and assets are sufficient that either surviving spouse will be financially sound, than the need for life insurance diminishes greatly. This is why it is more difficult to make life-insurance recommendations prior to running a retirement income plan.

Financial decisions should not be viewed in isolation, and you ought to be skeptical of anyone who tries to advise you on one piece without having a thorough understanding of your entire financial situation.

Marvin understood the interaction of the variables. We began working together on a more comprehensive basis and happily discovered that he and Beth had sufficient savings for their retirement income goals, no matter who should be the longest-lived. Marvin had no need for life insurance. There was no financial dependency.

The question of whether to keep the policies or not now became a question of values. They didn't need the cash value in the policies to support their retirement goals and they could afford the premiums. Paying premiums for life insurance because you want to provide an additional benefit for loved ones is a perfectly acceptable use of cash. Marvin and Betty decided they wanted to keep the policies until they both had stopped working and then re-evaluate.

---

[4]Even with a "paid-up" life insurance policy, there is a still in essence a premium being paid. But this cost is being paid internally with the cash you have accumulated in the policy rather than from a check you write for the premium. If you don't need the insurance, cash might be better used invested elsewhere than inside the insurance policy.

I had another couple in a similar situation who viewed the cash in their policies as an unexpected windfall, and cashed in their policies to buy a motorhome. Once you know the policies are not needed, it frees you up to make whatever choices suit you.

Blended Families

Some of the most complex situations I encounter are when I work with a couple who is on their second or third marriage and have children from those previous marriages.

Assets need to be used to provide income for the current couple; yet each often has accounts they accumulated before they married, and they want those accounts to go to their respective children.

Life insurance can be a good solution in many of these complex situations. You can use it to make sure a specified amount is left to your children regardless of how you and your current spouse choose to spend the rest. Or you can choose to buy life insurance to provide for your current spouse. The right solution depends on your individual situation.

Life Insurance Reviews

To my dismay, I have met very few life-insurance agents who offer unbiased and comprehensive reviews of their client's insurance policies. It seems too many agents contact their clients only to sell them more insurance. Many clients I work with have not heard from their agents in over a decade. The insurance industry does not yet seem to be well designed to incentivize agents to provide such reviews.

I have found that a new type of advisor is cropping up to meet the demand for objective advice: the fee-only life-insurance advisor. Many of these advisors are former actuaries or insurance agents who now offer unbiased advice on existing life-insurance policies for an hourly rate. The hourly rate may seem steep. But for business owners or executives looking at a large life-insurance purchase, it can be smart to get an objective analysis before making a decision.

In addition, those with large policies that may or may not still be necessary may want an objective opinion in deciding what to do. You can search your favorite search engine for "fee-only life insurance advisor" to find such a person.

Many fee-only financial advisors also offer analysis and advice on life-insurance policies. Some have more knowledge than others. I used to carry insurance licenses and sold both term and permanent life insurance. Although I have prior experience, I would certainly not consider myself an expert.

When making important life-insurance decisions, I seek advice from people who know life insurance inside and out—I rely on the counsel of experienced agents. A knowledgeable agent brings valuable expertise to the table, and when an agent works as a team with an advisor who is looking at your entire financial picture, I think you get solid advice.

Whether it is a review or a new purchase, look for advisors or agents who

- *View insurance in light of your entire financial situation.*

- *Have experience.* Yes, new agents have to get started somewhere, but as you near retirement, you cannot afford to make mistakes. Work with people who have been in the industry for quite some time.

- *Are objective.* Someone should be willing to tell you when you no longer need a policy, even if they are the person who sold it to you.

Disability Insurance

I figure that unless I sustain brain damage, I can pretty much do what I do for a living. I could lose a limb, an eye, or become paralyzed, and still I would be able to write and think and help people sort through complex financial decisions.

Despite the fact that I consider the odds that a disability would seriously impair my income to be rather small, I still carry disability insurance. God forbid something should happen; I do not want to become a burden to my family or a ward of the state.

It's a good thing I carry disability insurance, because my own view of my odds of a chronic disability is naïve. To calculate the odds that a disability would affect you, you can use an online calculator[5] called the Personal Disability Quotient at www.whatsmypdq.org.

When I put my information in, it tells me that my odds of being injured or becoming ill and unable to work for three months or longer are 14%. It also tells me if I do fall into the 14%, there is a 40% chance my disability could last for five years or longer. These odds are much higher than I would have guessed.

---

[5]This calculator is sponsored by a nonprofit called Council For Disability Awareness. It appears most of the members of this nonprofit are large insurance companies. Of course, they have an incentive to sell more insurance. Regardless of what the incentive may be, I find the calculator useful, and the information they provide at www.disabilitycanhappen.org is quite informative.

The first step in any insurance decision is getting a realistic idea of the probability the event will occur. Most people, like me, underestimate the risk of a disability:

- Prior to age 60, you have a higher probability of disability than death.

- Women are at greater risk for disability than men.

- Risk varies by occupation.

- The severity of a long disability is high. You can lose years of income.

- The cost to cover such a loss might be lower than you would guess. Once you estimate costs, you decide whether you want to retain the risk or pay the insurance company a premium and shift the risk to them.

You can typically insure somewhere between 50–70% of your gross income with a policy that would provide income through your age 65. You can also purchase policies that will provide income replacement for a specific time period, such as five or ten years, which could make sense if you are in your peak earning years and expect that you will retire in five to ten years at an early age—say 55 or 60.

ADDITIONAL RESOURCES FROM THE COUNCIL OF DISABILITY AWARENESS

Disability statistics: www.disabilitycanhappen.org/chances_disability/disability_stats.asp

Disability awareness quiz: www.disabilitycanhappen.org/chances_disability/quiz.asp

Personal disability quotient calculator: www.disabilitycanhappen.org/chances_disability/pdq.asp

---

Purchasing Disability Insurance

If you still have many earning years ahead of you, you have several ways to go about protecting your earning power:

- Rely on Social Security disability

- Explore all benefits offered by your employer

- Evaluate buying your own coverage from an independent agent

Social Security Disability

It is beyond the scope of this book to go into details about Social Security disability. I will simply say that if you are taking the time to read this book, and you are getting serious about your retirement planning, Social Security disability is unlikely to provide benefits in an amount sufficient for what you will need.

Just as Social Security retirement benefits were not designed to provide anything more than a basic amount of income in retirement, Social Security disability benefits are not designed to do anything other than provide a bare-bones amount of income should something unfortunate happen. If you make a decent living, you should look into coverage that provides benefits in addition to any provided by Social Security disability.

Employer Plans and Individual Policies

If your employer offers disability insurance, that is likely going to be the most cost-efficient way for you to secure coverage. But beware: many employers offer only short-term disability coverage. If you're 50, what you need is coverage that would pay benefits until you reach age 65.

Small business owners and professionals such as CPAs, attorneys, and doctors need to look at purchasing their own policies. Great coverage is often available through professional associations, such as the AICPA (American Institute of CPAs) for CPAs, the AMA (American Medical Association) for doctors, and the ADA (American Dental Association) for dentists.

In my case, I obtained coverage in a group policy offered through the Financial Planning Association. If you are a member of a professional group or trade association, start there to see what group benefits are offered.

If you need to find an agent to assist you, start with the National Association of Health Underwriters and use their online find-an-agent tool at www.nahu.org/consumer/findagent2.cfm.

MORE ON WHAT TO LOOK FOR WHEN BUYING A DISABILITY POLICY

Both of the following articles provide additional details about what you need to look for in a disability policy.

"Do You Need Disability Insurance?" (AARP): www.aarp.org/health/health-insurance/info-08-2012/disability-insurance-do-you-need-it.1.html.

"The Disability Insurance Maze: How to Select and Purchase a Policy" (Get Rich Slowly): www.getrichslowly.org/blog/2008/02/27/the-disability-insurance-maze-how-to-select-and-purchase-a-policy/

Reviewing Existing Coverage

When reviewing disability policies, I rely on agents who specialize in disability. They are skilled at determining which policies, benefits, and riders are best for which professions.

Interestingly enough, with disability insurance, I have yet to encounter a single case where an existing policy needed to be replaced.

Instead, if additional coverage is needed, we buy a new policy to stack on top of the old one, or we exercise options within the client's existing policy to purchase additional benefits.

Because most of the clients I work with are only a few years away from retirement, the situation I frequently encounter is determining when disability policies should be terminated.

For example, some policies pay benefits only to age 65. The policy may have a 90- or 180-day waiting period before benefits begin. If you're 64, does it make sense to keep a policy that might, at most, pay out six months of benefits? Perhaps not.

You may be phasing into retirement. If a disability forced you from part-time work to full retirement a few years earlier than anticipated, it may not result in a severe financial hardship. Missing a few years of part-time income is not going to have the impact that missing ten years of your highest-earning years will have.

I went back into the Personal Disability Quotient and put in figures for a 62-year-old, relatively healthy male making $85,000 a year:

- The odds of being injured or becoming ill and unable to work before retirement at age 66 were 3%.

- Assuming 3% raises, the amount of income at risk is $355,608.

- The odds for the same male at age 50 are 10%, and it jumps to 16% factoring in an unhealthy lifestyle and any chronic conditions such as diabetes, high blood pressure, back pain, anxiety or depression, frequent alcohol consumption, or substance abuse.

- At 50, the amount of income at risk is $1,713,335.

For a female age 62 with the same income and health status:

- The odds of disability before an age 66 retirement are also 3%.

- For that same female at age 50, the odds of disability are 12%, and jump to 18% with the presence of an unhealthy lifestyle and any of the chronic issues named earlier.

Ladies, if you are working woman as I am, make sure you look into disability insurance.

As you near retirement, both the probability and financial severity of a disability go down. The closer you get to retirement, the more important it is to review your existing coverage and make sure it is still needed.

If you are near retirement and have limited cash flow, disability premiums may need to be repositioned to purchase long-term care insurance. I discuss long-term care insurance in Chapter 10.

Summary

Insurance, like any financial instrument, is a tool. It ought to be used when appropriate by determining the probability and severity of a given risk. Then you determine whether you want to retain the risk or shift it to an insurance company.

Life and disability insurance needs should be evaluated within the scope of your entire financial situation. Look at how these products can protect you and your family against risks that can derail your retirement security.

All insurance should be reviewed on a periodic basis in light of changing risks and changing financial circumstances.

Using Your Company Benefits

401(k)s, Pensions, and Rollovers, Oh My

Our lives bear almost no resemblance, in hardship, pain, or danger, to the lives of our grandparents.

—Jacob Ward, Editor in Chief, *Popular Science*

Company benefits used to be rather simple. Our grandparents, and in some cases our parents, worked for the same company for 25 or 30 years and retired with a gold watch and a pension.

They did not have to manage their company benefits. They did not have to decide how to invest their 401(k) money, when to make their deferred compensation elections, whether they should participate in the voluntary group universal life policy offered, or when to exercise their incentive stock options.

As the quote that begins the chapter says, the hardship, pain, and danger we are exposed to are significantly less cumbersome than that of our grandparents; nevertheless, the company benefits decisions that must be made are infinitely more complex.

Although I would like to, it is impossible for me to delve into the nuances of all the different types of benefit plans you may encounter, so I will stick with the basics: 401(k) plans and pensions. Let's discuss the most important aspects of these plans and the decisions you need to make as you near retirement.

Your 401(k)

Not all 401(k) plans are created equal. Some have only three or four investment options. Others have so many choices, trying to sort through them all is overwhelming. Some employers offer matching contributions. Others don't. Some 401(k) plans allow loans. Others don't.

Despite their differences, all 401(k) plans do have several rules in common.

Creditor Protection

Your 401(k) assets are creditor protected, even in the event of bankruptcy. I can't tell you how many people get themselves in financial trouble and cash in a 401(k) plan because they think that is their best option. I hope you are reading this book because you are not anywhere near that kind of financial trouble. But trouble is bound to find a few of you.

Maybe you have a great business idea. You decide to use 401(k) money to get your business started rather than take out a bank loan. Bad idea. If your business doesn't work out, your 401(k) money is gone. If you use a bank loan instead to fund your business, and your business doesn't work out, the worst case is that you file for bankruptcy—your 401(k) assets are protected and still available for your retirement.

In recent years, many people faced with a job loss have used 401(k) money to try to keep their homes. Making objective decisions about one's home can be difficult, but as difficult as it may be, you need to look at the long-term consequences of any financial decision. You may spend a substantial amount of retirement money trying to keep a home that you end up losing anyway. One lady I spoke with said, "The stupidest thing I ever did was cash out my 401(k) plan to try to keep that house." The quality of such decisions often becomes clear only in hindsight.

Your 401(k) money is for retirement. That's it. I don't advise you use it for any other purpose—particularly if you are in financial trouble. I think using your 401(k) money before retirement voids a valuable form of protection available to you.

IRA CREDITOR PROTECTION

You will likely end up rolling 401(k) money to an IRA. IRA money is also creditor protected in several ways:

- Up to $1 million of IRA assets are protected from bankruptcy under federal law if you contributed directly to the account (meaning this protection may not be extended to an inherited IRA account).

- The entire IRA account balance is protected if the money was rolled over into an IRA from a company plan.

- State laws determine whether IRA assets are sheltered from creditor claims other than bankruptcy, and laws vary widely from state to state.

Age-Related 401(k) Rules

401(k) plans have some interesting age-related rules that differ from IRA accounts. You should know these rules before you decide whether to move money out of a 401(k) plan into an IRA.

Age 55

If you withdraw IRA money prior to age 59 1/2, your withdrawals are subject to a 10% early-withdrawal penalty tax in addition to ordinary income taxes. 401(k) plans have a rule that may allow you to access funds a few years earlier—at age 55 instead of 59 1/2.

This early access to funds applies if you

- Terminate employment no earlier than the year in which you turn age 55, but before age 59 1/2.

- Leave your funds in the 401(k) plan to access them penalty-free.

If your employment terminates between 55 and 59 1/2, therefore, think twice before you roll your 401(k) plan into an IRA because if you do so, you'll have to wait until 59 1/2 to have penalty-free access to your funds.

Tip If you have a job that ends when you're between 55 and 59 1/2, think twice before you roll your retirement funds into an IRA or your new employer's 401(k) because if you do, you can't access the money without paying a penalty until you're 59 1/2. If you don't, you can access the money now.

Age 59 1/2

You can access funds from an old 401(k) plan once you reach age 59 1/2 (*old 401(k)* here means you no longer work for that company). But if you want access to 401(k) money at a company you are still working for, you may not be able to get your hands on it, even if you are 59 1/2.

If you are still working and have a 401(k) plan with your current employer, you will have to check with your 401(k) plan administrator to see whether your plan allows what is called an *in-service* withdrawal at age 59 1/2. Some 401(k) plans allow this, and others do not.

Age 70 1/2

Employer plans as well as IRAs require you to start taking withdrawals at age 70 1/2.

If you are still working at age 70 1/2, and you are not a 5% owner of the company, you may be able to delay your required minimum distributions from your current employer plan until April 1 of the year after you retire. Check with your plan to see whether you may do this. (In such a situation you would still be required to take distributions from other retirement plans, just not the one from your current employer.)

In general, plan on starting your required minimum distributions from any and all retirement accounts by age 70 1/2.[1]

Aligning Your 401(k) with Your Retirement Goals

Something happens as people near retirement. They wake up one day and look at this collection of accounts they have and think "Now what do I do?" That's usually when I hear from them. The sooner you ask yourself that question, the better off you will be.

With a 401(k), you need to answer several questions before you can appropriately decide how to invest it.

For example, do you invest it as if it were in isolation, or do you invest it after seeing how it fits in with other investments you have? Will you need to begin to use the money at 55 because it will be more tax-efficient for you to do so, or does your plan work best if you don't touch the funds until age 70?

---

[1] With the exception of Roth IRAs. There are no required minimum distributions from Roth IRA accounts.

If you only have a single 401(k) and no other accounts, the answer is relatively easy. You thoughtfully decide how to allocate your money across the funds in your plan by investing according to risk and choosing the funds with the lowest fees in each risk category. If you don't need to touch the funds until 70, you might choose a more aggressive allocation than if you start withdrawing at 55.

It might even be easier than that. Most 401(k)s offer *model portfolios* that are already built for you, or something called a *target date fund*. Pick the model that fits your comfort level with investment risk, or the target date fund that is the closest match to your expected year of retirement, and you are done.

If you have multiple accounts outside your 401(k), and/or your spouse also has a 401(k), there might be a better way than allocating each account as if it were its own isolated entity. In this case you look at your investments as a household rather than on an individual account basis.

Investing as a Household

Most people collect investment accounts over time without aligning them toward a common goal. Although it takes work to view investments across a household, this work can pay off. Sometimes the household view can increase your after-tax return. You saw an example of how this works in Chapter 5 with the concept of asset location. Sometimes a household view can be used to lower the total investment fees you pay. The second situation was the case for John and Mary.

John and Mary

John is an architect, and Mary is a nurse at a large hospital. Both had 401(k) plans with about $300,000 each. After discussing investment risk, John and Mary determined that they wanted their investment allocation to be approximately 50% fixed income (bond funds and other low-risk options) and 50% equities, which were to be divided equally among U.S. and international equities.

Mary's 401(k) plan had hundreds of mutual funds as well as a "fixed account" option[2] that was currently paying a 5% fixed rate. The mutual fund choices were actively managed and had internal expenses that ranged from about .55% on the U.S. equity funds to 1.23% on the international funds.

John's 401(k) plan offered eight equity index mutual funds and four bond index funds. The internal expenses on the equity funds in John's plan ranged from about .15% on the U.S. funds to about .35% on the international funds.

---

[2] These fixed account options are sometimes called guaranteed interest, investment, or insurance contracts (GICs). A GIC is typically a contract issued by an insurance company to a qualified retirement plan.

We chose to allocate John's account 50% to U.S. large-cap equity and 50% to international because these fund choices had substantially lower fees than the equivalent choices in Mary's account.

We allocated Mary's entire 401(k) to the fixed account, because this was a unique option that did not have the volatility that bond funds have, and something equivalent was not offered in John's 401(k) plan.

By allocating their accounts this way, we were able to reduce their investment expenses by over $1,500 a year—and as you have learned, the best consistent predictor of future fund performance has proven to be lower expenses.

Viewed independently, when equity markets are down, Mary's 401(k) will look great. When equity markets are going up, John's 401(k) will look great. When viewed together, John and Mary have an appropriately allocated investment plan.

When allocating across a household, you cannot compare one account's performance to another. They are designed to work in unison. In John and Mary's case, they were about the same age, so this allocation plan worked for them. If one of them had been substantially younger, we might have taken a different approach.

In many cases, I recommend intentionally planning to draw on an older spouse's retirement accounts first, leaving the younger spouse's accounts to accumulate until required distributions start at their age 70.

In these situations, it sometimes makes sense to allocate the younger spouse's accounts more aggressively. If the younger spouse is 50, and the account will not be tapped until 70, there is no need to worry about the day-to-day or even year-to-year fluctuations in account values. In such cases, you want to design an investment approach to maximize the account value 20 years from now, not one that protects the account's value 1 year from now.

■ **Tip**   It's usually best to view your retirement investments across your household. Doing so offers more choices and more ways to reduce risk.

To Roll Over, or Not to Roll Over

I regularly meet people who have the mistaken belief that any time they move funds out of their company plan they will have to pay taxes. That isn't true.

Once you terminate employment with an employer, you are permitted to move funds that were in the company retirement plan into your own IRA through a process called a *rollover*. As long as you do it correctly, a rollover is not a taxable transaction.

If you take the money out of the company plan and spend it, put it in an account other than your IRA, or fail to deposit the funds in your IRA within the allotted 60 days, than the rollover rules do not apply, and the money withdrawn is considered taxable.

In most cases, if you left an employer prior to reaching age 55[3] and have an old 401(k) plan still hanging out there, I think you are best off rolling your company retirement accounts to an IRA account for the following reasons:

- *Ease of administration*: Your employer may change 401(k) providers at any time. Each time it does so, the investments offered change, and you have to take a fresh look at the fund choices and fees. In addition, you need to remember to update your old 401(k) plans with changes to your address or beneficiary designations.

- *Wider array of investment choices*: In an IRA, you can build a great portfolio using low-fee index funds. Such choices may not be available in your 401(k) plan.

- *Better beneficiary options*: 401(k) plans differ in their distribution requirements. They may offer all the options allowed under current law, but they don't have to. Some plans offer a limited set of distribution options to a beneficiary, in which case your beneficiary would have more options with an IRA.

- *Easier-to-handle required minimum distributions*: Once you are required to take distributions, it is going to be easier to manage the process if you have consolidated retirement accounts.

Rollover Rules to Take Note Of

Watch out for mandatory tax withholding. If an eligible rollover distribution is paid directly to your new IRA or 401(k) custodian, no tax withholding is required. If the check is payable to you, your employer-sponsored plan must withhold 20% of the rollover amount for mandatory federal tax withholding. They send this tax withholding directly to the IRS on your behalf.

In such a case, you have 60 days to get the full amount of the distribution into your IRA. This means you have to come up with cash to contribute to your IRA to replace the 20% that was withheld for taxes. If you do so, the full

---

[3]If you left after 55, leaving your money there will allow you penalty-free access. If you left prior to age 55, even if you are now older than 55, that rule does not apply.

amount of the distribution would be considered to be rolled over, and no taxes would be owed. When you file your tax return, you get a refund for any excess taxes that were automatically withheld and were now owed back to you.

You can avoid tax withholding by choosing a direct rollover option, where the check is payable directly to your new IRA trustee or custodian. This is highly advisable.

IRA rollovers are not an all-or-nothing proposition. You can use an IRA rollover to move a portion of your company retirement account to an IRA. I can think of two reasons you might do this:

- If you left your employer after 55 but before 59 1/2 and wanted to leave some funds in your 401(k) plan for potential penalty-free access.

- You may want to allocate a portion of your account to a particular investment choice offered in your company plan, but allocate the remainder among a broader array of investment choices that aren't available in the plan.

INHERITED 401(K)S

If you inherit an IRA or 401(k) plan from a spouse, you can roll the funds into your own IRA, and it isn't a taxable event. But that isn't always the best choice. You may want to structure the account as an inherited IRA, which is subject to slightly different required minimum distribution rules than if you roll the funds into your own IRA. I have written two online articles that go into greater depth on the choices available when you inherit an IRA or 401(k):

- "I Inherited an IRA—Now What?" http://moneyover55.about. com/od/iras/a/I-Inherited-An-Ira-Now-What.htm

- "401k Beneficiary—Inherited 401(k)s—When and How You Can Take Money Out" http://moneyover55.about. com/od/RetirementAccountWithdrawals/a/401(k)- Beneficiary-Inherited-401k-When-And-How-You-Can- Take-Money-Out.htm

IRA rollovers are reported on your tax return as a non-taxable transaction. Even if you correctly execute an IRA rollover, on occasion your plan trustee or custodian will report it incorrectly on the tax form 1099-R it issues to you and to the IRS.

Typically, people hand off tax forms like a 1099-R to their tax preparer without looking too closely. Not to worry—the return can be amended if the error is caught, but not incurring the error in the first place is best.

Be sure to carefully explain any IRA rollover or transfer transactions to your tax preparer or double-check all documentation if you prepare your own return.

When a Rollover May Not Be the Best Idea

If you left your employer after you turned 55 but before age 59 1/2, moving your 401(k) plan before age 59 1/2 will void your ability to access your funds penalty-free between ages 55 and 59 1/2. If you won't need the money during that time, this won't be relevant. But if there's a chance you might need to take withdrawals, you may want to wait until age 59 1/2 before you proceed with the rollover.

If your 401(k) plan offers a unique fixed income or guaranteed account option, that might warrant keeping funds in the plan. For example, some plans offer something called a *guaranteed insurance contract* (GIC) that pays an attractive fixed rate of return. Other plans, such as TIAA-CREF, offer a fixed account that usually pays a competitive rate. This type of investment option is not easily replicated outside of the plan.

Pension Choices

When it comes to your pension, you have important, irrevocable decisions to make. Single or married, your decisions today will have a big impact on the 82-year-old you. If you're married, your decision affects your spouse.

Your pension decision can be grouped into three main categories:

- Whether to take a lump sum or annuity
- When to start your pension
- What survivor option to choose

Let's look at two case studies to see how these pension options can be analyzed. The first case is Helen, a single woman about to turn 55.

Helen: Lump Sum or Annuity

Helen was just finalizing her plans to leave corporate America at the age of 55. She had the option of taking her pension plan as a lump sum distribution and rolling it over to an IRA account—with no taxes due at the time of the rollover—or taking a lifetime annuity payment of $28,322 a year.

The simple spreadsheet in Figure 7-1 illustrates how long Helen's lump sum money would last if she withdrew the same amount each year that the annuity was guaranteed to provide her.

	Single Life					
Age	Year	Annuity @ 55	Lump Sum @ 4%	Lump Sum @ 5%	Lump Sum @ 6%	Lump Sum @ 7%
			$ 341,000	$ 341,000	$ 341,000	$ 341,000
55	1	28,322	326,318	329,728	333,138	336,548
56	2	28,322	311,049	317,892	324,804	331,784
57	3	28,322	295,169	305,465	315,971	326,687
58	4	28,322	278,653	292,416	306,607	321,233
59	5	28,322	261,478	278,715	296,681	315,398
60	6	28,322	243,615	264,329	286,160	309,154
61	7	28,322	225,037	249,223	275,008	302,472
62	8	28,322	205,717	233,362	263,186	295,323
63	9	28,322	185,623	216,709	250,655	287,674
64	10	28,322	164,726	199,222	237,373	279,489
65	11	28,322	142,993	180,861	223,293	270,731
66	12	28,322	120,391	161,582	208,369	261,361
67	13	28,322	96,885	141,339	192,549	251,334
68	14	28,322	72,438	120,084	175,780	240,605
69	15	28,322	47,014	97,766	158,004	229,126
70	16	28,322	20,572	74,333	139,163	216,842
71	17	28,322	(6,927)	49,727	119,190	203,699
72	18	28,322	(35,526)	23,892	98,020	189,636
73	19	28,322	(65,269)	(3,236)	75,579	174,589
74	20	28,322	(96,202)	(31,719)	51,792	158,488
75	21	28,322	(128,372)	(61,627)	26,577	141,260
76	22	28,322	(161,829)	(93,031)	(150)	122,826
77	23	28,322	(196,624)	(126,004)	(28,481)	103,102
78	24	28,322	(232,811)	(160,627)	(58,512)	81,997
79	25	28,322	(270,445)	(196,980)	(90,345)	59,415
80	26	28,322	(309,585)	(235,151)	(124,087)	35,252
81	27	28,322	(350,290)	(275,230)	(159,855)	9,398
82	28	28,322	(392,624)	(317,314)	(197,768)	(18,266)
83	29	28,322	(436,651)	(361,502)	(237,956)	(47,867)
84	30	28,322	(482,439)	(407,899)	(280,555)	(79,539)
85	31	28,322	(530,059)	(456,616)	(325,711)	(113,429)
86	32	28,322	(579,583)	(507,768)	(373,575)	(149,691)
87	33	28,322	(631,088)	(561,479)	(424,312)	(188,492)
88	34	28,322	(684,654)	(617,875)	(478,093)	(230,008)
89	35	28,322	(740,362)	(677,091)	(535,100)	(274,431)
90	36	28,322	(798,298)	(739,267)	(595,528)	(321,963)
91	37	28,322	(858,552)	(804,552)	(659,582)	(372,822)
92	38	28,322	(921,216)	(873,102)	(727,479)	(427,242)
93	39	28,322	(986,387)	(945,079)	(799,450)	(485,471)
94	40	28,322	(1,054,165)	(1,020,655)	(875,739)	(547,776)
95	41	28,322	(1,124,653)	(1,100,010)	(956,605)	(614,442)
96	42	28,322	(1,197,961)	(1,183,332)	(1,042,323)	(685,775)

Figure 7-1. Helen's Pension: Annuity vs. Lump Sum

If she could be assured of earning a 6% rate of return (net of all fees), the lump sum would provide the equivalent income as the annuity until about age 76. At a 7% rate of return, it would last until about age 81. Contrast that with the annuity payments, which are guaranteed to pay out for Helen's entire life. I advised that Helen take the annuity option, which she did.

If Helen had any health concerns that would lead her to believe she might have a shortened life expectancy, the recommendation may have been different.

Eric: When to Start Pension Benefits

Eric was retiring at 60. His pension plan did not offer a lump sum distribution option, but it did offer numerous choices regarding when he could take his pension.

He and his wife Julie had a substantial amount of savings in IRAs and company retirement plans. Although he was retiring at 60, if it was more beneficial for him to wait until 65 to begin his pension, he could use other savings to supplement his income for those five years.

He needed help deciding when to begin his pension and whether he should choose an option that provided ongoing income to Julie if he died first. With a single life option, his pension payments would stop upon his death. With a 100% joint and survivor pension option, he would receive less annual income, but the payments were guaranteed to continue for Julie's life span as well as his own.

Here is a summary of four of Eric's pension choices:

- *Single life at age 60:* $19,536 a year
- *Joint and survivor at age 60:* $15,888
- *Single life at age 65:* $34,128
- *Joint and survivor at age 65:* $26,568

First let's discuss the single life choices versus the 100% joint and survivor choice. If Eric chooses the single life and dies a year later, the benefits end. Julie misses out on $15,888 a year for potentially 30 years or more—what she would have received had he chosen the 100% joint and survivor option. The present value of $15,888 a year, for 30 years and assuming a 4% return, is about $275,000.

The annual difference between the two choices is $3,648 at Eric's age 60 and $7,560 at age 65. He and Julie are the same age.

So, at age 60, the question is: can Eric buy $275,000 of life insurance that has an annual premium of less than $3,648 a year? If so, he might choose the single life option and buy a life insurance policy. The advantage to this option is if Julie were to die first, the life insurance policy could be dropped. The disadvantage to this option is that as people age, they can become forgetful. I have seen older couples inadvertently miss insurance premium payments, causing policies to lapse.

■ **Tip**   One problem with buying life insurance to protect family income in the case of your demise is that you could become forgetful as you age. You may miss payments and lose the policy. It's better to lock in guaranteed income that will continue no matter your state of your mind.

If Eric waits until age 65, the present value of 25 remaining years of $26,568 in income for Julie would be $415,000 (again at 4%). Would he be able to buy $415,000 of life insurance for less than $7,560 a year? Perhaps, depending on his health situation.

In Eric's situation, some health conditions ruled out life insurance as an option. He and Julie both agreed that the joint and survivor option was best for them.

The next question was when to start the pension—at age 60 or 65? Figure 7-2 shows a comparison of the two pension options.

To understand Figure 7-2, assume that Eric and Julie are going to spend $26,568 a year whether they start Eric's pension at his age 60 or at 65. If they start the pension at 60, they will receive $15,888 from the pension and will need to withdraw $10,680 a year from savings and investments every year to have the $25,568 of income. You see this withdrawal in column A. If they wait and start the pension at his age 65, they will need to withdraw the full $25,568 for five years and nothing thereafter. You see this withdrawal in column B.

Assume they have $150,000 in savings earning 4% they can make these withdrawals from. In column C, you see that if they take the $10,680 annual withdrawal, they run out of money at Eric's age 81. In column D, you see that if they take the $25,568 withdrawal for five years and then nothing thereafter, it leaves them with more assets. They could use these assets to generate additional income or to pass along more to heirs. The break-even age on this decision is Eric's age 74.

If he or Julie lives longer than 74, the delayed start date will end up providing more—by age 90, $234,000 more (shown in column D), assuming their spending in both scenarios is the same. In lieu of accumulating more assets, they could choose to spend more along the way.

		Joint Life		A	B	C	D	D
		Annuity	Annuity	Withdrawals needed		$150,000 invested at 4% after respective withdrawals in columns A and B		
Age	Year	@ 60	@ 65	to have $26,568				Difference
60	1	15,888		10,680	26,568	145,320	129,432	(15,888)
61	2	15,888	-	10,680	26,568	140,453	108,041	(32,412)
62	3	15,888	-	10,680	26,568	135,391	85,795	(49,596)
63	4	15,888	-	10,680	26,568	130,127	62,659	(67,468)
64	5	15,888	-	10,680	26,568	124,652	38,597	(86,055)
65	6	15,888	26,568	10,680	-	118,958	40,141	(78,817)
66	7	15,888	26,568	10,680	-	113,036	41,747	(71,289)
67	8	15,888	26,568	10,680	-	106,877	43,416	(63,461)
68	9	15,888	26,568	10,680	-	100,473	45,153	(55,319)
69	10	15,888	26,568	10,680	-	93,811	46,959	(46,852)
70	11	15,888	26,568	10,680	-	86,884	48,838	(38,046)
71	12	15,888	26,568	10,680	-	79,679	50,791	(28,888)
72	13	15,888	26,568	10,680	-	72,186	52,823	(19,364)
73	14	15,888	26,568	10,680	-	64,394	54,936	(9,458)
74	15	15,888	26,568	10,680	-	56,290	57,133	843
75	16	15,888	26,568	10,680	-	47,861	59,418	11,557
76	17	15,888	26,568	10,680	-	39,096	61,795	22,700
77	18	15,888	26,568	10,680	-	29,979	64,267	34,288
78	19	15,888	26,568	10,680	-	20,499	66,838	46,339
79	20	15,888	26,568	10,680	-	10,639	69,511	58,873
80	21	15,888	26,568	10,680	-	384	72,292	71,907
81	22	15,888	26,568	10,680	-	(10,280)	75,183	85,464
82	23	15,888	26,568	10,680	-	(21,372)	78,191	99,562
83	24	15,888	26,568	10,680	-	(32,907)	81,318	114,225
84	25	15,888	26,568	10,680	-	(44,903)	84,571	129,474
85	26	15,888	26,568	10,680	-	(57,379)	87,954	145,333
86	27	15,888	26,568	10,680	-	(70,354)	91,472	161,826
87	28	15,888	26,568	10,680	-	(83,848)	95,131	178,979
88	29	15,888	26,568	10,680	-	(97,882)	98,936	196,818
89	30	15,888	26,568	10,680	-	(112,478)	102,893	215,371
90	31	15,888	26,568	10,680	-	(127,657)	107,009	234,666
91	32	15,888	26,568	10,680	-	(143,443)	111,290	254,732
92	33	15,888	26,568	10,680	-	(159,861)	115,741	275,602
93	34	15,888	26,568	10,680	-	(176,935)	120,371	297,306
94	35	15,888	26,568	10,680	-	(194,692)	125,186	319,878
95	36	15,888	26,568	10,680	-	(213,160)	130,193	343,353
96	37	15,888	26,568	10,680	-	(232,367)	135,401	367,767
97	38	15,888	26,568	10,680	-	(252,341)	140,817	393,158
98	39	15,888	26,568	10,680	-	(273,115)	146,450	419,564
99	40	15,888	26,568	10,680	-	(294,719)	152,308	447,027

Figure 7-2. Comparing pension distribution options

WHAT RATE OF RETURN TO USE

When running an analysis on how a lump sum compares to an annuity, or which age it might be best to start the annuity, what rate of return should you use? You need to use something that at least has somewhat of an equivalent risk level as the pension. The pension is guaranteed. The investment portfolio most likely is not. It's great if you think you can earn 8% a year in your investments (net of fees), but know you are not comparing apples to apples. Although interest rates are currently quite low, I think 4% is an appropriate proxy for what you might get in long-term guaranteed choices like CDs and fixed annuities. That's why I use 4% as a starting place when doing a pension analysis.

Pension Choice Mistakes

The single biggest mistake I see people make with their pension is assuming that they can secure a better outcome by taking a lump sum and investing the funds themselves. If you could be assured of an 8% return or higher (net of fees), the lump sum option will usually look more attractive. Even in a good market, achieving an 8% return would require a high allocation to equities, and the sequence of returns can have a serious impact on the outcome. I do not think such returns are something you can be assured of.

Pension annuities provide a floor of guaranteed income and can be a valuable benefit to offset longevity risk. Don't be too quick to make choices about your benefits without doing a thorough analysis.

IS YOUR PENSION SAFE?

Pension plan benefits are insured by an organization called the Pension Benefit Guarantee Corporation (PBGC). If your company participates in the PBGC, it is likely that at least a portion of your pension benefit is insured.

The amount of your pension benefits that is insured depends on your age and is subject to a cap.

In 2013, for a pension recipient age 65, the maximum monthly insured benefit is as follows:

- $4,310 per month for a joint life payout with 50% that would be paid to a survivor

- $4,789 per month for a single life payout

Important: The maximum monthly insured amount of pension benefits is reduced if you are not yet age 65.

Employee Stock

I worked as a team with a few CPA firms throughout the Phoenix area. Intel has a location in Chandler, Arizona, and so we did a fair amount of work with Intel execs and employees. In August of 2000, Intel stock was at $73 a share. In August 2001, when I moved to the area, it was about $31 a share. Today, it is about $21 a share.

I was reading through a client file, preparing for an upcoming meeting with an Intel executive who owned 150,000 shares of stock. At $73 a share, that stock had been worth nearly $11 million. He needed to diversify, but the CPA had not been successful at getting him to do so. At the time of our meeting, his shares were worth about $4.5 million. He was convinced the stock would come back, and I also was unsuccessful at convincing him to diversify. I suppose today at $21 a share his stock is now worth just over $3 million. Had his stock been sold and invested in a conservative, diversified portfolio of index funds, his portfolio would be worth somewhere in the $7–8 million range today. Diversification would have served him well, but he refused.

If you are an employee of any kind, I hope you are proud of the company you work for and I hope you wholeheartedly believe in the products and services you produce. But don't confuse that pride with making prudent personal financial decisions.

Remember   Don't pile up company stock in your portfolio. Even if it's an excellent company. Even excellent companies can get in legal trouble, and the stock price can quickly go tumbling down.

Many people mistakenly think that if they part with company stock it reflects a lack of faith in the success of the company. The success of the company is dependent on numerous factors outside of your control. Your personal financial success is dependent on factors within your control.

You can and should take great pride in your work and at the same time be able to make prudent decisions about diversifying financial risks that you and your family are exposed to. Having a large portion of your financial assets, as well as your income and benefits, tied to a single company represents a large financial risk. Do what you can to reduce this risk by setting up a systematic plan to reduce your holding of company stock as it accumulates.

Employee stock accumulates in numerous ways:

- *Employee stock purchase plan (ESPP)*: With this type of plan, employees can purchase company stock at a discount from its fair market value.

- *Employee stock ownership plan (ESOP)*: With this type of plan, employees are given an ownership interest in the company. Shares are held in trust and sold when the employee leaves the company or retires.

- *Incentive stock option (ISO)*: This type of option grants the employee the right to buy shares at a specified price and has preferential tax treatment.

- *Non-qualified stock option (NQ)*: This type of option grants the employee the right to buy shares at a specified price but has no preferential tax treatment.

- *Restricted stock unit (RSU)*: This type of compensation is typically in the form of stock grants given to executives with restrictions on when the stock can be sold or transferred.

The tax implications of selling the stock vary widely from plan to plan. In some cases you may be able to minimize tax consequences by selling stock over 13 months but across three calendar years by selling some in December, some in January, and some the following January. In this way you can diversify rapidly and yet spread the taxes out over three filing years. Taxes should be considered when selling stock, but they shouldn't be the only consideration. Minimizing risk should be the primary objective.

Consolidating Retirement Assets

Most tax-deferred retirement accounts that belong to the same individual can be combined into one IRA account for that individual. (Spouses cannot combine retirement accounts.)

The following is a list of all the types of retirement accounts that can be consolidated into one IRA at or near retirement:

- SEP IRAs

- SIMPLE IRAs

- Traditional IRAs

- Non-deductible IRAs (but you need to keep track of the amount of any non-deductible contributions)

- 401(k)s

- 403(b)s

- 457(b)s

- Profit-sharing accounts

- Money purchase

- Defined benefit plans (if the plan allows you to take a lump sum distribution option)

- Other qualified plans. Your employer may offer a plan that uses a different name but is still considered a qualified plan. If it is a qualified plan with pre-tax dollars in it, you can roll the funds into an IRA.

If your employer offers a designated Roth account, it cannot be rolled into a traditional IRA, but it can be rolled into a Roth IRA account.

In an ideal retirement situation, you would consolidate your accounts so you have one IRA, possibly one Roth IRA and one after-tax investment account.

Consolidating accounts can help reduce fees, certainly makes it easier to design and maintain an appropriate investment allocation and manage withdrawals and cash flow. It also reduces the amount of paperwork you have to deal with each month and the number of institutions your beneficiaries will eventually have to deal with.

Once your accounts are consolidated, you can structure how much money should come from each type of account (based on your plan and what is most tax-efficient for you) and set up a direct deposit into your working checking account, essentially replacing your monthly paycheck.

The alternative is dipping into accounts ad hoc as needed. This is not advisable, because it makes it too easy to spend more than is prudent based on your plan.

Setting up regular withdrawals in a system designed to replicate your paycheck makes it easy to monitor, compare results to your plan, and system-atically decide if and when it is appropriate to increase your withdrawals by the rate of inflation.

Consolidating accounts near retirement makes sense. I can think of no meaningful reason not to do so.

Summary

When it comes to company benefits, you need to use them based on your overall plan after viewing your plan at a household level.

With a 401(k) plan, while working you need to take into account when you expect to draw on the funds, how investment options differ from plan to plan, and what the expenses are on the investments inside the plan.

As you near retirement, you want to begin consolidating IRAs and employer plans to make your withdrawal phase easier to manage and more cost efficient.

With pensions, you need to do careful analysis before you determine what pension option to take. Don't be too quick to take a lump sum; people routinely underestimate how long they think they'll live, and it can be difficult to achieve a rate of return required to provide the same income that many pension annuity options provide.

Speaking of annuities, maybe your company doesn't offer any form of pension or annuity option and you're thinking of buying one. Should you? I cover that in Chapter 8.

Should You Buy an Annuity?

Buy Them for the Income

It's paradoxical that the idea of living a long life appeals to everyone, but the idea of getting old doesn't appeal to anyone.

—Andy Rooney

Some people walk into my office with a definite opinion.

"Annuity? Oh no, I don't want one of those."

I reply, "Oh, which kind do you want to avoid? Fixed annuities, variable annuities, immediate annuities, or indexed annuities?"

The same response applies to those who walk in and declare, "I want an annuity." (Yes, people do this.)

"Oh, which kind do you want? A fixed annuity, variable annuity, immediate annuity, or an indexed annuity?"

Most of the time the person is not sure. This is understandable because a considerable amount of conflicting information on annuities is out there, and many articles do not clarify which type of annuity they are talking about. Sometimes I receive a call from someone who is trying to make an urgent decision. A salesperson has shown them a fancy brochure about an annuity product that must be bought by the end of the month. That is not the way to buy an annuity.

As with any investment, buying an annuity should be a thoughtful choice that fits into your plan. To be objective about annuities, you need to know about the many different types. Sometimes people read an article or have a bad experience and conclude that all annuities are bad. All annuities are not alike and certainly all annuities are not bad, so before forming a conclusion, you have to specify what you are talking about. I think many planning objectives can be accomplished without the use of annuities, yet, like any tool, they ought to be considered and used when appropriate.

Let's take a look at the four main types of annuities you might encounter—immediate annuities, fixed annuities, indexed annuities, and variable annuities—and see if and when they are appropriate savings or income vehicles.

Immediate Annuities

All annuities are contracts with an insurance company. With an immediate annuity you enter a contract to buy a stream of income. If you buy a ten-year term certain annuity, you are buying a stream of income for ten years.

If you recall the cookie jar analogy from Chapter 4, you'll remember that when you buy a life-only immediate annuity, you are buying income that is guaranteed for as long as you live. You hand over the jar of cookies (a lump sum of money), and in return the insurance company gives you back a cookie each year. If the jar runs empty, they keep providing cookies out of their own jar. If you pass away before the jar is empty, they keep any remaining cookies.

You can buy life annuities that also have a death benefit feature. Death benefit features increase the cost of the annuity. From the insurance company's viewpoint, if they must pay you a life-long income and provide a death benefit to a beneficiary, that represents additional risk than only being obligated to provide life-long income.

You would consider an immediate annuity for two primary reasons:

- It protects against longevity risk (outliving your income)
- It protects against overspending risk

Let's see how an immediate annuity can be used to accomplish your retirement income goals.

As you near retirement, you often have two competing goals. Goal one is having adequate inflation-adjusted spending money for your lifetime. In pursuit of this goal, many come to me and say, "I want to die with a dollar in the bank."

An immediate annuity,[1] also called a *single premium immediate annuity* (SPIA), can help you accomplish this, because it converts your assets into a guaranteed income stream.

Goal two is preserving financial assets for unexpected expenses and to pass along to heirs. A SPIA does not meet this goal.

One of my favorite fellow retirement-income geeks, Wade Pfau, has done quite a bit of research on how you might combine the use of an immediate annuity with a portfolio of stock index funds to meet these two competing goals.

His work shows that rather than the traditional allocation of stocks and bonds, a retiree may consider an allocation of stocks and immediate annuities.

In his paper, "An Efficient Frontier for Retirement Income," he says:

> [T]he evidence suggests that optimal product allocations consist of stocks and fixed SPIAs, and clients need not bother with bonds, inflation-adjusted SPIAs, or VA/GLWBs.[2] Though SPIAs do not offer liquidity, they provide mortality credits and generate bond-like income without any maturity date, and they support a higher stock allocation for remaining financial assets. Altogether, this allows a client to better meet both retirement financial objectives.[3]

Most people I know would not be comfortable with a portfolio that was entirely immediate annuities and stocks, but the research does shed light on the fact that an immediate annuity, when used as part of a plan, can help you achieve the dual goals of maximum current spending along with preservation of assets.

As you saw in Chapter 4, immediate annuities are offered in both inflation-adjusted and noninflation-adjusted versions. They also offer payments that cover a fixed term, a single person's life, or two lives (with payments guaranteed for the longer of the two to live).

---

[1] Immediate annuities and how they work are covered in Chapter 4; here I am expanding upon that introduction.
[2] VA/GLWBs stands for variable annuity/guaranteed living withdrawal benefits, discussed later in this chapter.
[3] Wade D. Pfau, "An Efficient Frontier for Retirement Income," National Graduate Institute for Policy Studies (September 24, 2012).

THOSE WHO REALLY NEED IMMEDIATE ANNUITIES

I strive to offer as objective an opinion as possible, recognizing that we are all different and we all perceive risk differently.

I have run immediate annuity quotes and longevity insurance quotes on many clients and have looked at how such a vehicle might add value to their plans. Most will not buy these products because they do not want to give up control of their assets. These types usually feel confident in their ability to stick with a diversified portfolio and adjust spending down later if needed. It is not that they are ignoring longevity risk; instead, they have a plan in place to manage it.

There are a few, though, who I think need an annuity to protect them from themselves. These clients are either overspenders or are prone to making rather random and irrational investment decisions. Unfortunately, despite my efforts, these are often the ones who won't implement such a strategy.

It seems those who need annuities the most are often those who won't buy them.

Immediate annuities might fit into your plan if

- You or your spouse's family and health history indicates you might live longer than average.

- You have trouble sticking within your spending limits.

- You have trouble sticking with an investment plan and allocation model.

- You have no pension or sources of guaranteed income other than Social Security.

- You understand Wade's research and are comfortable with a dual allocation of stock index funds and immediate annuities.

What to Watch Out For

Immediate annuities often publish what is called their *payout rate*. This is not equivalent to yield or rate of return. If a life-only immediate annuity has a published payout rate of 7%, and you invest $100,000, yes, you get $7,000 a year for as long as you live. If you live 30 years, that would be equivalent to about a 5.75%[4] rate of return. If you live only five years, you received a total of $35,000

---

[4] If you calculate the return as an annual payout instead of monthly, you get 5.65%.

in income, and nothing more gets paid out, so your actual return would be negative. You buy annuities to manage risk, not for the rate of return.

If an immediate annuity fits in with your plan, there are a few strategies to consider.

Stagger Your Purchases

Immediate annuity payouts vary by interest rate and with your age. If an immediate annuity fits into your plan, consider buying your guaranteed income in increments by staggering your purchases over several years.

Staggering your purchases may allow you to lock in a higher payout rate a few years later, because payouts increase with age. Considering today's low interest rates, higher future rates may also increase the payout.

This strategy also allows you to spread your purchases over several different insurance carriers so your benefits fall within state guaranty limits.[5]

Take a Wait-and-See Approach

With immediate annuities, you get more income for single lives than for joint lives. For marrieds, a wait-and-see approach involves implementing an immediate annuity strategy if you become a surviving spouse, or if you reach a particular age.

For example, a couple might allocate a portion of their investments to something that was low on the risk scale, with the intention of annuitizing this at the earlier of the time one became a surviving spouse or when the first reached age 85.

WHAT DOES ANNUITIZE MEAN?

Annuitize is a term that is frequently used with deferred annuities. You may have an annuity that is in the accumulation phase, and you have not yet "turned on" the income phase. You are said to *annuitize* at the point where you trade in a lump sum of money for a guaranteed income stream.

---

[5]For an explanation of state guaranty limits, see the sidebar "How Good Are Insurance Company Guarantees?" later in this chapter.

Fixed Annuities

A fixed annuity is a contract with the insurance company in which they provide you a guaranteed interest rate on your investment. Think of a fixed annuity as a CD in a tax-deferred wrapper. Instead of the bank guaranteeing your interest rate, the insurance company is providing the guarantee. The interest accumulates tax-deferred, as it does in an IRA, until you take withdrawals. Interest withdrawn prior to age 59 1/2 is subject to a 10% early-withdrawal penalty tax as well as ordinary income taxes.

The interest-rate guarantees typically run for about one to ten years, at which point you can continue the annuity at whatever rate is then offered, exchange it for a different type of annuity, or (like a CD) cash it in and decide to invest the funds elsewhere. (If you cash it in, you will owe taxes on the accumulated tax-deferred interest.)

The interest rate might be

- Fixed for the life of the annuity.

- Fixed at a higher rate the first year and then at a lower fixed rate for remaining years.

- Fixed at a higher rate the first year and then at a variable rate for subsequent years with a minimum rate guarantee.

With a fixed annuity, no investment fees are debited out of the account. The fees are embedded in the product, so, as with a CD, the rate you are quoted is the rate you will receive. There are, however, *surrender charges*, and they can be quite hefty. The insurance company can only guarantee you the rate if they know they have your money for the full length of the contract. A surrender penalty is imposed to provide an incentive for you to leave your funds there for the full term. It also functions as a way for the insurance company to recoup its up-front costs if you change your mind and cancel the contract early.

Tip Annuity FYI offers a comparison of current fixed annuity rates at www.annuityfyi.com/fixed-annuities.html.

If you are looking for a safe investment that provides a guaranteed interest rate, you might compare a fixed annuity to CDs and municipal bonds to decide which is most appropriate for you. In some cases fixed annuities pay a higher interest rate than CDs, and the interest is tax-deferred. With a CD you must pay taxes on the interest earned each year (unless you own the CD in an IRA, in which case the interest would be tax-deferred).

What to watch out for: Some fixed annuities lure you in with a high initial year rate, but the blended rate over the life of the contact may end up being quite low.

Example of how a fixed annuity might fit into a plan: Suppose you are 55 and receive an inheritance. You plan on retiring at 65, and your planning shows you are likely to be in either the same or a lower tax bracket in retirement.

Your planning also shows that you need only a 4% rate of return to achieve your goals. You find a ten-year fixed annuity that pays 4%. In this case a fixed annuity would fit nicely into your plan.

AGE 59 1/2 AND FIXED, VARIABLE, AND INDEX ANNUITIES

When you place money in a fixed or variable deferred annuity (*deferred* meaning the income phase is being deferred until later), you do not have to pay taxes on the gain in the annuity until you take withdrawals. Like most retirement vehicles that offer tax deferral, if you take withdrawals prior to age 59 1/2, any gain withdrawn is taxed at your ordinary income tax rate and is subject to a 10% penalty tax. In a non-qualified deferred annuity (one not owned by an IRA, Roth IRA, or other tax-deferred retirement vehicle), gain is considered to be withdrawn first.

Indexed Annuities

An indexed annuity is a type of fixed annuity that is often called a *fixed indexed annuity* (FIA) or an *equity-indexed annuity*. With this type of annuity, the insurance company offers a minimum guaranteed return with the potential for additional returns by using a formula that ties the increases in your investment to a stock market index.

For example, assume you buy a fixed indexed annuity that is tied to the S&P 500 index. It might allow you to participate in 80% of any increases in the stock market index as measured from January 1 to December 31, with a 3% minimum guaranteed interest rate. You might have a 10% cap on the return.

In this situation here are a few possible outcomes:

- The S&P 500 index goes up 10%. Your return is 8% because you participate in 80% of what the index does.
- The S&P 500 goes up 20%. Your return is 10% because the annuity contract has a cap on your maximum return.
- The S&P 500 goes down 10%. Your return is 3% because the contract provides a minimum guaranteed 3% interest rate.

In writing about this product, Scott Stolz, senior vice president, Private Client Group Investment Products at Raymond James Financial, says, "The entire point of an indexed annuity is to get a long-term rate of return that is 1.5–3.0 percent above prevailing CD rates without putting principal at risk."[6]

This is a great description of the purpose of this product. The question is, do they accomplish this goal?

A preliminary analysis of existing equity index contracts suggests that sometimes they do, and sometimes they don't. In an article called "Real-World Index Annuity Returns," the authors analyze existing FIA contracts to determine how well they have performed over various five-year time periods in relation to stock and bond funds. The authors conclude, "Our rather modest conclusion is that some index annuities have produced returns that are competitive with other asset classes, such as equities and equity/T-bill combinations."[7]

I took the returns published in their article and in Table 8-1 compare them to the comparable five-year CD returns for the same time period.

Table 8-1. Fixed Index Annuity Returns vs. CD Returns

5-Year Time Periods	FIA Avg. Return (%)[8]	5-Year Average CD Rates (%)[9]
1997–2002	9.19	6.76
1998–2003	5.46	6.19
1999–2004	4.69	6.36
2000–2005	4.33	7.6
2001–2006	4.36	5.56
2002–2007	6.12	4.99
2003–2008	6.05	3.85
2004–2009	4.19	4.41
2005–2010	3.89	4.96

You can see that in some five-year periods, the FIA outperformed the CD, and in some time periods it did not.

---

[6]Article available online at www.advisorone.com/2010/10/01/do-living-benefits-on-indexed-annuities-make-sense.

[7]Geoffrey Vander Pal, Jack Marrion, and David F. Babbel, Ph.D., "Real-World Index Annuity Returns," *Journal of Financial Planning* (March 2011).

[8]Ibid.

[9]Source: Jumbo CD Investments, at www.jumbocdinvestments.com/historicalcdrates.htm.

What to watch out for: Indexed annuities have complex features such as participation rates and cap rates that spell out the formulas for how your returns are calculated. Compare such features side by side when looking at this type of product. In addition, consider this product as a CD alternative, not as an equity alternative. If someone proposes it to you as an equity alternative, think twice.

Example of how a fixed index annuity might fit into a plan: For a risk- averse investor, a combination of CDs and indexed annuities might be the perfect solution.

■ **Tip**   For comparing annuities and learning more about the different features and riders, I have found Annuity FYI to be a valuable resource. If you're considering any type of annuity, it's a great place to start your search: www.annuityfyi.com.

Variable Annuities

A variable annuity is a contract with an insurance company in which you get to choose how the funds inside the contract are invested. The insurance company provides a list of funds (called *sub-accounts*) to choose from. It is called a *variable* annuity because the returns you earn will vary depending on the underlying investments you choose. Contrast this with the fixed annuity, where the insurance company is contractually providing you with a guaranteed interest rate.

Investments inside a variable annuity grow tax-deferred, so, just as within an IRA account, you can exchange between investments without paying capital gains taxes.

For the variable annuity to qualify as an insurance contract, guarantees must be provided. The standard death benefit guarantee that comes with a variable annuity simply guarantees the greater of the current contract value or the full amount of your contributions (minus any withdrawals) as a death benefit. For example, if you invested $100,000, and the investments went down in value to $90,000, and you passed away at that time, the contract would pay out $100,000 to your named beneficiary. If the investments had gone up in value and were worth $110,000, the contract would pay out $110,000.

Today's variable annuities come with additional death benefit guarantees and living benefit guarantees that make them one of the most complex consumer financial products I have ever seen. From what I can see, most of the representatives who sell these products don't really understand them, so how the heck is the average person supposed to? I'll do my best to simplify this product into its most relevant features.

First, you would consider a variable annuity for one of two reasons:

- Tax deferral
- Income guarantees

Let's take a look at how a variable annuity provides tax deferral and income guarantees.

Tax Deferral

The traditional variable annuity offers a series of mutual-fund like separate accounts inside a tax-deferred wrapper. If you are a taxpayer in a higher tax bracket, the advantage is that inside a variable annuity you can invest in a portfolio of stock and bond accounts and defer the income (interest, dividends, and capital gains) until retirement, when you may be in a lower tax bracket.

When the Bush tax cuts were implemented in 2001, the lower capital gains, qualified dividend, and ordinary income tax rates took effect, and the tax benefits of traditional variable annuities were diminished.

With the 2013 tax rate changes, capital gains and qualified dividend rates remain significantly lower than ordinary income tax rates. For this reason, I do not see a compelling reason to hold traditional stock funds inside a variable annuity. Let me explain why.

Inside the variable annuity, when you take withdrawals, gain is considered to be withdrawn first, and all gain withdrawn is taxed at your ordinary income rate. If you owned stock funds that were not in the variable annuity, the long-term gains and qualified dividends would be taxed at long-term capital gains tax rates, which are lower than ordinary income tax rates. Once you tuck those stock investments into the variable annuity, you lose the preferential tax treatment on long-term gains and dividends.

In addition, when heirs inherit a stock or stock fund, they receive a step up in cost basis. That means the value at your date of death becomes their basis for tax purposes. For example, suppose you own a stock or stock index fund that has a current value of $100,000. You paid $50,000 for it many years ago. This means you have $50,000 of unrealized gains. If your heir inherits this, their basis for tax purposes is "stepped up" to the $100,000 value, and they pay no taxes on the $50,000 of gain. If this same situation occurs inside the variable annuity, the heir would owe tax on the $50,000 gain at their ordinary income tax rate.

When you put all this together, I don't think it makes sense to own stock funds in a variable annuity. But I can see why you might want to own taxable bond funds inside a variable annuity. Bond funds generate interest income that is taxed at your ordinary income tax rate, and they are unlikely to offer significant unrealized gains. By tucking taxable bond funds into a variable annuity, you are gaining tax deferral on the interest income and you are not losing any form of preferential tax treatment.

If tax deferral fits into your plan, there is one variable product worth consid-ering: Jefferson National's Flat Fee Variable Annuity.[10] It charges a flat fee of $20 a month. That's it. There are over 380 investment options to choose from.

Example of how a variable annuity for tax deferral might fit into your plan: I can see two scenarios where a low-cost, variable annuity for tax deferral makes sense:

- *High tax bracket/Lots of after-tax investments:* If you are in a high tax bracket and have a large conservative portfolio that is not inside of any type of retirement account, a flat-fee variable annuity might be an attractive option for you. Rather than buying CDs, you could build a portfolio of bond funds inside the variable annuity. All interest income would be tax-deferred.

- *Existing high-fee annuity:* If you already own a high-fee vari-able annuity with non-IRA money, you could use a 1035 exchange to transfer your high-fee annuity to one with lower fees and continue to defer the taxes on any gains. You would do this if you have a low cost basis in your current annuity, which means if you cashed it in instead of exchanging it, you would have to pay taxes on the gain at your ordinary income tax rate.

IRA-OWNED ANNUITIES

Many people use IRA money to buy an annuity. In such a case, if you no longer want the annuity, you can use an IRA rollover or IRA transfer to move your money out of the annuity and into a regular IRA account where you can buy index funds (or any other type of investment). This kind of transfer is not a taxable event. Of course, you want to inquire about any surrender charges before you cancel any annuity contract.

What to watch out for: One of the concerns I have with variable annuities is the substantial fees they can come with. Many variable annuities are saddled with all of the following expenses:

- *Mortality expenses (M&E).* All annuities are some form of insurance product. With a variable annuity, the mortality and expense fee is charged to provide you with some form of a death benefit. This is often a simple guarantee

---

[10]Product details available online at www.jeffnat.com.

to pay out to your beneficiaries at least the amount of money you contributed. This mortality and expense fee can range from .50–1.5% of the policy value per year.

- *Administrative expenses.* Most variable annuities charge some form of administrative expense, which ranges from .10 to .30% of the policy value per year. Sometimes this expense is included in the mortality and expense fee and sometimes it is separate.

- *Investment expense ratio.* Inside a variable annuity, the underlying stock and bond investment choices, called sub-accounts, have an investment management fee or expense ratio just as mutual funds do. The expense ratios on the underlying sub-accounts typically range from .25–2.00% per year.

- *Surrender charges:* Many investment and insurance products pay an up-front commission to the agent or representative who sells the product to you. The fees inside the product are designed to slowly reimburse the company for their up-front costs. Surrender charges are usually structured on a decreasing scale from about 4 to 15 years, with most broker-sold annuities having a surrender charge schedule of about 7 years. With a typical surrender charge schedule, if you terminate the annuity within one year of purchase, you will be charged 7% of your invested amount, 6% in year two, 5% in year three, and so on.

- *Additional cost of riders:* Variable annuities today come with all kinds of optional guarantees called *riders*. The most common features are guaranteed living benefit riders, guaranteed withdrawal benefit riders, and guaranteed death benefit riders. Each rider can cost anywhere from .40–1.50% of the policy value per year.

When you add up these expenses some variable annuity contracts have fees in excess of 4% a year."

■ **Tip** Never forget—fees matter. A 4% annual charge for investment expenses, over time, takes a big bite. If you are buying an annuity just for tax deferral, look for annuities whose underlying fees are 1% a year or less.

Income Guarantees

Variable annuities offer numerous types of income guarantees which are broadly classified as guaranteed living benefits (GLBs). They are often an optional benefit that you can add on to the policy and are referred to as riders. The income riders all have a similar function: you pay an annual fee to insure the amount of future income you can withdraw from your portfolio.[11] Much like the cookie jar analogy used earlier, with an income rider the insurance company is providing a guarantee that if your cookie jar runs empty, they'll keep providing cookies out of their jar.

Living benefit riders are referred to by various terms such as lifetime withdrawal benefits (LWBs) or guaranteed minimum withdrawal benefits (GMWBs).

The typical income guarantee has two phases: the deferral phase and the income phase.

HOW GOOD ARE INSURANCE COMPANY GUARANTEES?

Insurance company guarantees are only as good as the claims-paying ability of the insurance company that issues the contract. In the event the insurance company fails, limited guarantees are provided by each state's insurance guaranty association.

State insurance guaranty associations protect policyholders (and beneficiaries) of policies issued by a life or health insurance company in the event the insurance company must file bankruptcy. If you want to make sure the full amount of your investment is covered, learn your state's guaranty limits and don't invest more than the maximum coverage amount in any single policy with the same insurer. In addition, each state may have aggregate benefits covered for all lines of insurance and different limits that apply to different types of policies.

Guaranteed coverage amounts typically vary from $100,000–$500,000 in benefits, but you will need to check with your state insurance guaranty association to see what amounts are covered for which types of benefits in your state.

It is currently not clear whether state guaranty associations provide coverage for the income that falls under living benefit riders.

For additional information visit the National Organization of Life & Health Insurance Guaranty Associations at www.nolhga.com/factsandfigures/main.cfm/location/stateinfo.

---

[11] Fixed annuities guarantee the interest rate you earn on your investment. Income riders on variable annuities function more like immediate annuities—they guarantee the amount of monthly income you can withdraw.

Deferral Phase

The deferral phase of an annuity is the time period where you are not draw-ing out income. Many variable annuities with income riders have a five- or ten-year deferral phase, meaning you need to own the product for five or ten years before the income guarantee features can be utilized.

During the deferral phase, there is often a guarantee that creates a hypotheti-cal "income base" that will grow at a specific rate of return, such as 5% (or with older contracts, possibly 6%), and usually for a specific time period, such as ten years, or up until a specific age, such as 80.

With contracts that come with an income base feature, think of it as having two wallets of money. In wallet one is your actual account value, which is going up and down based on whatever the underlying investments are doing. In wallet two is a hypothetical income base based on the contractual guarantees offered.

Wallet one is real money. If you cash in the annuity, that's what you get.

Wallet two is a little different. The amount in wallet two is simply an account-ing entry used to calculate the amount of guaranteed withdrawals you can take when you enter the income phase. Once income begins, the value of wal-let two becomes irrelevant; its only purpose is to calculate the amount of the guaranteed lifetime income. The typical income guarantee allows you to take about 4–6% (the older you are when you start the withdrawals, the higher the percentage) of the wallet two value each year for as long as you live.

INDUSTRY EXPERT COMMENT

After reviewing this chapter Scott Stolz offered this additional comment, which I thought appropriate to include:

"Unfortunately, by insisting on putting a "$" sign before the wallet two value on every client statement, the insurance companies add to the confusion about what wallet two is and what it isn't. The $ sign implies that it is real money. It is not. Always remember that it is only used to calculate your allowable annual income."

Income Phase

When you turn the rider "on" or reach the income phase of the contract, most income riders guarantee that you can withdraw a specific percentage, such as 5%, of the income base for life.

When you take a withdrawal, it reduces the amount in wallet one. This means until wallet one is empty, withdrawals are simply a return of your money.

The advantage is that even if wallet one is emptied out, you continue to receive the guaranteed income amount specified in the calculations based on wallet two.

Many of these income riders offer an additional feature, called a *step-up* in the income base. Such a feature says that if the underlying investments in wallet one perform well and are worth more than the income base, then the value of the income base (wallet two) will be stepped up so it matches the higher value of wallet one. This allows you to lock in a higher income base if markets do well.

I see the primary function of these income riders as protecting you against sequence risk. If markets go down right around the time you retire, or returns are poor during the first ten years of your retirement, these policies ensure that you will at least have a minimum known amount of income and that you'll never run out of it.

What to watch out for: There are three things to watch out for when it comes to variable annuities with income riders:

- *The income base is hypothetical:* Many people who buy these annuities with income riders think the income base is real money. It is not. It is a hypothetical figure used only to calculate the amount of your guaranteed withdrawal. If you cash in the annuity, you get the contract value, not the income base.

- *Not using them for income:* Variable annuities with income riders are often presented as offering the best of both worlds: potential for growth if the underlying investments do well, while providing a lifetime income feature much like an immediate annuity, but with any remaining principal getting passed along at death. When you look under the hood of these products, in many cases the hefty fees will in fact make it almost impossible in any but the best market conditions for the investment portfolio value (wallet one) to ever exceed that of the income base (wallet two). The fee structure may force you to rely on the guarantees the product provides. If you are not going to use the guaranteed income feature in this type of product, don't buy it. If you are going to buy a variable annuity with an income rider, find one with reasonable fees, buy it for the guaranteed income feature, and use it for income.

- *Death benefits:* I have seen these products presented as an attractive way for someone to meet the goal of passing along assets to heirs. I disagree. In one variable annuity case I reviewed, when compared to a similar portfolio of index funds, over 20 years in normal market conditions, the variable annuity was likely to pass along $500,000 less to heirs because of the effect of fees.[12] The more bells and whistles the contract offers, the higher the fees. The higher the fees, the lower the investment performance. Don't buy these products for their death benefits.

Most of the annuities that offer an income rider place some restrictions on how you allocate the funds inside the annuity. Why do they do this? To limit their risk. That should tell you something. They think investing by following a diversified portfolio model means that you're unlikely to ever have to use the guarantees they provide.

Other buying considerations: For tax reasons, under current tax law, I think these products are best owned inside an IRA.

THE ACADEMIC VIEW

One of the big challenges faced by both financial advisors and consumers alike is sorting through all the product choices and figuring out which ones actually add value to your situation and which ones are just smoke and mirrors.

As more people near retirement age, academic interest in analyzing retirement income products has greatly increased, and more and more research is becoming available that offers an objective analysis.

If you want to dig into the academic research on annuities, do a search for articles and research papers written by Moshe Milevsky or Wade Pfau.

How Fees on Income Riders Are Calculated

In variable annuities with living benefit riders, many of the asset-based fees can be charged on the income base rather than on your actual contract value. This means you can be paying fees based on an amount of money that you don't actually have. Strange, but true.

When you add all this up, it is not uncommon to see variable annuities with annual fees in excess of 4% a year.

---

[12]See my analysis in my About.com article "Variable Annuity Compared to Index Funds," available online at http://moneyover55.about.com/od/understandingannuities/a/variableannuitycomparison.htm.

Let's think about these fees with some common sense. Inside the annuity you have the same stuff to invest in as you do outside the annuity: stocks, bonds, and cash.

If you take a typical mix of stock and bond funds, saddle it with a 4% fee, and then fast-forward 20 years and compare it to the same mix of stock and bond index funds with fees of less than 1% a year, which is going to be worth more money?

Fees matter. I describe many of these products as facilitating the slow and smooth transfer of your family's wealth right into the hands of the insurance company.

The key to understanding the fees is to know what value you are getting. If you are paying for an income guarantee that is important to you, just as with any type of insurance, you can look at it as if you are paying a premium to shift risk to the insurance company.

Example of how an income rider *might* fit into a plan: I can think of two specific situations where an income rider might be appropriate.

The first is for someone 5 to 15 years away from their target retirement date. Suppose you have IRA money or an old 401(k) plan that needs to be rolled into an IRA. A contract with an income rider that guarantees a specific growth rate on your income base would allow you to lock in market upside and protect your income against a sudden drop in your portfolio right as you neared your retirement date.

The second situation is someone who is about to retire, needs to take income, and wants to maintain a high equity allocation. A contract with an income rider that guarantees a 5% withdrawal rate would protect your income level.

There is one last point to address about variable annuities: the psychological benefits of having guarantees. When the investment markets go down, emotions can usurp logic, and many people are known to liquidate holdings at an inopportune time. Having a safety net can give you the courage to stay invested during these times. Just remember, you pay for this courage in the form of annual expenses.

STAND-ALONE LIVING BENEFITS

There is one additional solution that is rather new: the standalone living benefit (SALB). You use the SALB to wrap an insurance guarantee around a portfolio of index funds. The benefit terms will be slightly different than what is offered in an annuity, but the premise is the same—you are insuring a floor or baseline of income that will be available to you. With an SALB, the underlying investments maintain their natural tax treatment. Capital gains and dividends are taxed as such. This could make an SALB an appropriate alternative for insuring income from a non-retirement account. For a

detailed analysis of this new insurance solution, read Wade Pfau's thoughts in his
Advisor Perspectives article called "The Next Generation of Income Guarantee Riders:
Part 1—The Deferral Phase."[13]

Existing Variable Annuities

I can't tell you how many times a new client comes in to see me wondering
what to do with an annuity they already own. They don't know whether they
should keep it, when they should take withdrawals, or how it fits into their plan.

There are several things to consider in evaluating an existing contract:

- *Death benefits:* Many current variable annuity contracts
  are underwater—the contract value is less than the
  death benefit.

- For example, Bernard came in to see me with an annuity that has a death benefit of $410,000. But the actual
  contract value, if he cashed it in today, is $280,000. He is
  married and in his mid 70s. He has no need to take withdrawals from the policy. We decided at his current age, it
  makes the most sense for him to keep this policy because
  of the death benefit.

- Although I don't think you should buy a variable annuity for its death benefit features, if you already own one,
  consider the current death benefit it is providing before
  terminating a contract.

- Income guarantees: Many current variable annuity contracts have an income base that is much higher than the
  contract value.

- For example, Kathy came in with an annuity bought in
  2003. She had invested $200,000. The contract value
  was $251,000, the death benefit was $348,000, and the
  income base (wallet two—remember?) was $348,000,
  which would provide a guaranteed withdrawal of $1,570
  a month for her and her husband's joint life.

- Currently Kathy is 63 and getting ready to retire. If she
  cashes in the annuity, she gets $251,000. A $1,570 monthly
  withdrawal ($18,840 a year) would be a 7.5% withdrawal
  rate, which is not sustainable in any but the very best

[13]Available online at http://advisorperspectives.com/newsletters12/The_
Next_Generation_of_Income_Guarantee_Riders.php.

market conditions. If she cashes in the contract, it will be impossible for her to replicate the income stream the annuity will guarantee.

- I recommended that Kathy keep the contact and turn on the income stream. If she lives just 20 years, she'll have received **$376,800** of income. Also, I must note, total fees in Kathy's contract were 3.6% a year. In her case, due to the timing of when she invested and the guarantees provided, high fees or not, the contact is providing a valuable benefit.

- *Fees and taxes:* Other things to consider in evaluating an existing contract are surrender charges, fees, and taxes. Sometimes high-fee contracts can be surrendered or exchanged for lower-fee alternatives. This should not be done without examining all the aspects of the contract.

- *Features you can no longer buy:* You may have an annuity issued several years ago that offers unique features or benefits that are no longer available. For example, fixed annuities used to come with 3% minimum interest rate guarantees, something that is hard to find today. Variable annuities used to offer additional investment flexibility and more attractive death benefit and living benefit calculations than those typically offered today. Someone trying to sell you a new annuity may not be forthright in giving you an objective opinion of your current annuity. Make sure you do a careful analysis before abandoning an existing contract.

Over the years, I have found many opportunities to exit out of an annuity contract altogether, many opportunities to exchange a contract for one with lower fees, and many times where keeping the existing annuity was the right solution. Each situation is unique, and there is no way to provide a one-size-fits-all answer on what to do with an existing annuity.

Summary

An annuity is an insurance product. The first question to ask when considering an annuity is: what are you trying to insure?

Here are the primary reasons you would consider each type of annuity:

- Want to insure you won't outlive your money? Consider an immediate annuity to protect against longevity risk and overspending risk.

- Want to insure safety of principal? Consider a fixed annuity or equity index annuity for safety.

- Want to insure tax deferral on interest income? Consider owning bond funds inside a flat-fee variable annuity.

- Want to insure your retirement income against market fluctuations? Consider a variable annuity with an income rider to protect against sequence risk.

As with any form of insurance, compare outcomes against non-insured alternatives and decide whether you want to retain the risk or shift it. If you want to shift the risk, shop carefully and spend time figuring out whether the product fits into your plan. To do that, look at when the income stream would begin and what account you should own it in based on the most favorable potential tax treatment.

Real Estate and Mortgages

All Part of the Plan

Real estate cannot be lost or stolen, nor can it be carried away. Purchased with common sense, paid for in full, and managed with reasonable care, it is about the safest investment in the world.

—Franklin D. Roosevelt

Several years back, I was having a conversation with a woman who I considered to be successful and intelligent. She was asking me questions about what I do, and in the midst of our conversation she said, "Well, stocks are a much better investment than real estate, right? You're a financial planner, so of course that's what you tell your clients."

I was speechless. She went on. "After all, if you had put all your money in Google when it came out with its IPO, you'd be set now, right?"

I thought, *Absolutely. And if I had put my money in a hundred other stocks I could name off, right now I'd be broke*. I'm not sure why I didn't say this out loud. I should have.

A good planner plans. Planning encompasses all aspects of one's financial life, including real estate and mortgages. It would be irresponsible for a planner to make a statement such as "stocks are better than real estate."

Many of the financially independent people I know achieved their independence through investing in real estate. On the flip side, many people I know have gone through bankruptcy and foreclosure by stretching their real estate investments too far. Real estate can be quite a profitable investment if you know what you are doing, and a disaster if you don't.

When nearing retirement, all aspects of your financial situation need to align toward a common goal: generating a reliable source of income. That means real estate and mortgages need to be evaluated as carefully as anything else. Let's start by taking a look at when investment property might fit into a retirement income plan.

Investment Property

For those looking for a steady source of retirement income, rental real estate may look like the right solution. I've seen people reach 50, 55, or 60 and, after spending a lifetime in whatever their current profession is, they decide the foundation of their retirement plan is going to be a portfolio of rental real estate. With no experience or training, they head out and buy a property. If they're lucky, it works out. Many aren't so lucky. Investing in real estate is a profession in and of itself and it is not to be embarked upon without careful consideration.

Whether it's an apartment building, duplex, residential rental, or commercial property, real estate comes with expenses. Following are some of the expenses you incur with investment property:

- Property taxes
- Repairs and upkeep
- Advertising and marketing (to get tenants)
- Legal costs (if you have to evict someone)
- Insurance

As with any profession, to make money doing it, you have to know what you are doing. You can turn real estate investing into a profession that allows you a lot of free time, but it takes patience, knowledge, and a decent sense of intuition. You need to plan on doing plenty of reading and learning before you head down this path.

Tip   Think twice or three times before you invest in real estate. The field is vast, and there are a lot of sharks in the business.

If you are interested in getting into real estate, where do you start your education? You may see numerous seminars on how to invest in real estate.

Some are decent, and some are just going to cost you thousands of dollars for a lot of pretty binders.

If I were starting out in real estate, I'd skip the seminars and instead I'd get my hands on all of John T. Reed's books on real estate investing. Start with *How to Get Started in Real Estate Investing.* His material is not just full of fluff; it provides you with the nuts and bolts of what it really takes to be successful. You can buy his books through his web site at www.johntreed.com. He has over 20 books on real estate investing as well as a web page where he ranks other real estate "gurus."

Whether you want to invest in real estate or not, the guru rankings make for fascinating reading. There are plenty of people willing to put together some form of a "get rich quick" packet of information, whether it's on stocks, trading options, real state, or network marketing. Apparently, plenty of people are willing to buy this information. Reading these guru rankings will provide you with a healthy dose of skepticism about the next "proven" way to riches that you see advertised.

If your career up until this point has not been related to real estate, please think twice before embarking on a real estate investment. I've watched people lose millions in real estate partnerships they thought were a "sure thing." I've watched people pour thousands into rental income properties that were supposed to generate cash flow and instead turned into giant money pits. In nearly every situation that turned out poorly, the person had no experience and did not go through a rigorous learning curriculum before they dove into their new venture. I'm all for real estate as an investment for those who are going to treat it with the respect that any serious profession deserves.

ADJUSTING YOUR PLAN AROUND YOUR REAL ESTATE

Gary and Susan were about to turn 70 when they first came in to visit me. Gary had just retired from his medical practice. He owned part of the medical building, which produced monthly income. In addition they owned two homes, one in New Mexico and one in California. The New Mexico home was paid off, and the California home still had a mortgage on it.

When I completed their plan, I had to be the bearer of bad news. With their desired level of spending, it was not going to be possible to maintain both homes. I suggested they sell one.

They asked whether they might sell the medical building instead. I had already considered this. However, it didn't make sense. If they sold their share of the medical building and invested what they would receive after taxes, it would not be possible to deliver the same level of income that the building was providing. Selling one of their homes delivered gain that was tax-free; the gain on the medical building was subject to taxes.

Interestingly enough, their solution was for Gary to continue working. He chose to work locum tenens (as a substitute for other physicians) for about two weeks a month, and has continued to do so for years. He enjoys it, and it allows the couple to continue the lifestyle they desire. This was not their only solution, but it was the one that fit their values.

Your Home

Plenty of finance writers insist that your home is not an investment. If I were to plot my thoughts on a scale of one to ten, with one being your home is absolutely not an investment, and ten being you should only buy one if it can be profitable, I would say I'm at a three.

A portion of the value of your home may need to become part of your retirement income plan at some point. Knowing this, it makes sense to put thought into your home purchase, how you finance it, and figure out how that fits into your plan.

■ **Note**   Your home is neither purely an investment nor purely a noninvestment. It may not seem like an investment—until you need its equity or potential income to live to a happy old age.

For example, one way you can protect yourself against inflation is to choose a home that has ample access to public transportation, make your home as energy-efficient as possible, and make sure it has a garden or other area conducive to growing your own food. In addition, you can choose an area that is tax-friendly for retirees. If you're willing to do the research to secure such a location and then move, your home may offer a substantial contribution to stretching your retirement dollars.

Of course, the values side of the decision must also come into play. You may want to be near family or choose a location that fits your hobbies and lifestyle, or you may be in a home that you've been in for years and you have no desire to move.

If your plan shows you have ample assets to support your retirement lifestyle, then think of your home as an asset you use for enjoyment. If your plan shows you are constrained, meaning your assets may leave you short of the retirement income you desire, then spend more time analyzing your home choice and see if making some changes could improve your plan.

I've worked with retirees who choose to downsize so they could travel more. Others prefer that people come visit them, and so they choose to invest in a beautiful living space that facilitates having company. Either choice involves understanding your values and making financial decisions that support those values.

I can't tell you what your values are. I can analyze numbers and show you how the cost of one home choice versus another affects your plan. Both factors, values and the analytical side, also affect the decision about when to pay off a mortgage.

Paying Off the Mortgage: Sometimes an Easy Savings Plan

Jackie and Bob wanted to retire early. Each time they came in to review their plan I would explain to them what they needed to be saving in order to make that happen.

Six months or a year later, they would come back, and their savings had not increased. They had the income to save more, but it just wasn't happening.

Next time they came in, I decided to try a different approach. In their situation, the extra amount they needed to save by retirement was about equivalent to the dollar amount needed to pay off their mortgage. I suggested they make extra payments on their mortgage and told them as soon as their mortgage was paid off they could retire.

Suddenly they began making progress! Seeing the mortgage balance go down was tangible. They could measure their progress toward a goal they wanted to achieve. Accumulating money in their investment accounts, where the value would fluctuate so much from month to month, did not have this same effect for them.

Their case had two sides to the "should we pay down the mortgage?" question. There was the analytical side, which can be determined by running numbers through a spreadsheet, and there was the psychological or values side, which varies from person to person.

Let's take a look at their numbers first.

Jackie and Bob owed $150,000 on their mortgage. The principal and interest portion of their payment was $1,205 a month. Their mortgage rate was 5%. They were in the 25% federal tax bracket and paid about 3% of their income a year in state taxes. They were able to itemize deductions, so their mortgage interest of about $7,500 in the current year was reducing their income taxes owed by about $2,100. With their current payment, their mortgage would be paid off in 15 years.

They had an extra $500 a month available to save. If they applied the extra $500 to the mortgage, it would be paid off in about nine years.

Jackie and Bob were already maxing out their tax-deductible retirement plan contributions, so they could either apply the extra $500 to the mortgage or contribute it to a savings/investment account.

Net of fees, if they could earn the same return on savings and investments as the rate they were paying on their mortgage, at the end of their mortgage term, they would end up in an identical place regardless of how they applied the extra $500 a month.

Even if they earned only 4% on their savings, prepaying the mortgage was to their benefit by only $3,578. At a 6% return, investing over paying extra on the mortgage added only $1,063 to their net worth over 15 years.

If there were a chance of earning a lower return on savings/investments than the cost of the mortgage, they would be in a more secure situation by applying extra savings toward paying down the mortgage.

For Jackie and Bob, the conclusion was they would need to be assured of earning a return higher than 6%,[1] net of all investment fees, to make investing their monthly savings a wise decision.

Even if Jackie and Bob earned a 7% return (net of fees), in 15 years the choice of investing versus paying extra on the mortgage added only about $3,550 to their net worth. From a risk/return standpoint, an additional $3,550 over 15 years ($236 per year) did not add up to sufficient compensation for taking on the additional level of investment risk required in an attempt to earn 7% returns net of investment fees.

If they were not maxing out their retirement plan contributions, there would be a slight advantage to applying their extra savings toward a tax-deferred and/or tax-deductible retirement plan. By my calculations, when factoring in the tax deductibility of the $6,000 annual contribution and assuming they then saved/invested the tax savings, funding a deductible retirement plan over paying excess on the mortgage would result in about a $20,000 increase in their net worth after ten years.[2]

In addition, there was a psychological benefit to Jackie and Bob toward applying savings to pay down their mortgage. They could see the results each and every month, and it motivated them to save even more. The result was that, in many months, they applied more than an extra $500 toward their mortgage.

---

[1] If you want to use after-tax returns, the 5% mortgage rate is costing them 3.6% (5% × (1−.28)) on an after-tax basis, but the available deduction for the mortgage interest will gradually go down as the mortgage is paid off. Because you must pay taxes on investment income, if the 5% investment earnings were all taxed as ordinary income, the after-tax return of the investments would also be 3.6%. If you assume some investments have a long-term gain tax treatment, it changes the analysis only slightly more in favor of investing over paying extra on the mortgage (assuming the same gross rate of return).

[2] SoundMindInvesting.com provides this scenario in great detail. Available online at www.soundmindinvesting.com/visitor/2010/feb/level1.htm.

"PAY OFF THE MORTGAGE OR INVEST" CALCULATORS

There are several online calculators you can use to crunch the numbers for you. Here are a few I like.

Hugh's Investment versus Loan Payoff calculator: I don't know who Hugh is, but I like his mortgage payoff calculators. They aren't fancy, but they are transparent, and he provides a clear explanation of the assumptions used. His "payoff vs. borrow" calculator shows you the results over time of either investing a lump sum or using it to pay off a mortgage. It allows you to specify whether mortgage interest is deductible and whether the lump sum you are using is after-tax or tax-deferred dollars. Find it at www.hughchou.org/calc/payoff_v_borrow.cgi.

Hugh's Prepay vs. Investment calculator: This shows you the effects of contributing an extra monthly amount to your mortgage versus investing it. You can specify whether your mortgage interest is deductible or not, and whether your investments are after-tax or tax-deferred. You cannot specify whether your monthly investment would also be tax deductible, such as if contributed to a 401(k) or deductible IRA. Find it at www.hughchou.org/calc/prepay_v_invest.cgi.

MortgageSum.com Pay Down Mortgage or Invest calculator: This calculator seems to be identical to Hugh's Prepay vs. Investment calculator. It allows you to specify the amount of monthly savings available to apply toward the mortgage or toward an investment. It also allows you to specify whether mortgage interest is deductible and whether savings will go into a tax-deferred account. And it lets you choose various rates of return that your savings may earn; but it does not offer enough low-return choices. For example, at the time I tried this calculator, it showed CDs earning 6%. That would be nice, but it is not realistic in today's economic conditions. Find it at www.mortgagesum.com/mortgagecalculator/mortgage-prepayorinvest.php.

In its brief "Should You Carry a Mortgage into Retirement?", the Center for Retirement Research concludes that most retirees are better off repaying their mortgage. Specifically, it says:

> The . . . analysis indicates that retired households are, in theory, better off repaying their mortgage. In addition to this theoretical conclusion, there is also a very practical argument against borrowing to invest. If a household with a mortgage mismanages its investments, or over-estimates the rate at which it can decumulate those investments, it risks losing the house, its only remaining asset.[3]

---

[3] Anthony Webb, "Should You Carry a Mortgage Into Retirement?" Center for Retirement Research (July 2009) no. 9–16.

The brief "then considers and (for most households) rejects the argument that households should retain their mortgage because they can earn a higher expected return in stocks and other risky assets."

I agree with the general conclusions of the brief. I also think that before making a decision, each family needs to look at its individual circumstances. The right answer for you will depend on all of the following:

- Whether you are in the accumulation phase or already retired

- If accumulating, whether you have already maxed out tax-favored retirement plan contributions

- Your sources of income and expected taxes in retirement (for example, will extra IRA withdrawals needed to make mortgage payments make more of your Social Security income taxable?)

- Available mortgage rates

- Your comfort level with investment risk

- Your desired level of liquidity

MORTGAGE PAYOFF ASSUMPTIONS

In this chapter I assume that you have an adequate emergency fund and that you are not carrying high-interest-rate debt, such as credit card debt. Otherwise, both accumulating an ample emergency fund and paying down high interest rate debt should take precedence over making extra mortgage payments.

As I'm writing this chapter, Bankrate.com says the current average 30-year mortgage rate is 3.45%, and the 15-year is 2.85%.[4] With mortgage rates currently at all-time lows does it still make sense to pay off a mortgage?

---

[4] As of December 2012.

It depends on your individual circumstances and comfort level with invest-ment risk. If any of the following scenarios applies to you, you might think twice before paying down the mortgage:

- You are still accumulating assets and still have room to add savings to tax-favored accounts like IRAs, 401(k)s, or Roth accounts. In particular, if you are not taking full advantage of employer-matching contributions, this is something you should do before applying extra money toward the mortgage.

- You are retired, with all assets in tax-deferred accounts, your other sources of income put you at the point where all Social Security will be taxed at 85% even if you pay off the mortgage and reduce retirement account withdraw-als, and you feel comfortable that over time your retire-ment accounts will earn a return (net of fees) at least equivalent to your mortgage rate.

- You live in a non-recourse state and incur frequent job changes or moves.[5]

- Your have locked in a mortgage rate at current historical lows and are comfortable taking on investment risk with your savings by viewing results over the same duration as your mortgage. This means, if you have a 15-year mort-gage, you're viewing investment results over a 15-year time horizon and not measuring them on a week-to-week, month-to-month, or even year-to-year basis.

Refinancing

With current low interest rates, many people are refinancing to reduce their monthly mortgage payment. Refinancing may or may not be appropriate for you.

For example, suppose you owe $248,671 on your mortgage. You are paying $2,098 a month in principal and interest payments (this does not include real estate taxes and insurance, which may also be part of your monthly payment) and your home will be paid off in about 15 years. You can refinance into a new

---

[5]If you end up in a situation where your home is underwater (home value is less than remaining mortgage balance), in a non-recourse state the lender cannot go after your personal assets for the difference. Such borrowers have the option of pursuing a short sale (lender agrees to sell the home to a third party for an amount less than the remaining mortgage) or letting the home go to foreclosure. Although many homeowners would be reluctant to pursue such options, they are viable financial choices to be considered in such a situation.

30-year mortgage at a 4% rate. You are going to pay $2,500 in closing costs, which you finance into the balance of the new mortgage. Your monthly payment will go down by $898 a month. That sounds good! But over the life of the loan, you will pay $51,471 more in interest.[6] That sounds bad.

So, is it a good or bad decision to refinance? It depends on numerous other factors. If your mortgage payment goes down $898 a month and you were taking IRA withdrawals to cover the mortgage, now you need to take less out of your IRA each month. This might mean less of your Social Security benefits would be subject to income taxes, and it might mean your overall tax rate would be lower. Decisions like this that are made in isolation do not take into account all the factors that affect your long-term outcome.

■ **Tip**   The decision to refinance requires both serious thought and number crunching. Get help doing the analysis, if you need it, before you make a decision based solely on monthly payments.

Home Equity Lines of Credit

Unexpected expenses will come up in retirement, just as they do now while you are working. If you have to take a significant extra withdrawal out of an account, it may mess up your investment and tax plan.

For example, say you have matched up your investments so that bonds or CDs mature in each account to match the amount of your anticipated withdrawals. But now you need an extra $25,000 to help an adult child. Where should the money come from? If the growth portion of your portfolio has done well, you may be able to liquidate some of your long-term holdings to meet your extra cash needs. But what if the market is down?

In addition, what if you only have assets in tax-deferred accounts? An extra withdrawal may be taxed at a higher tax bracket, causing you to pay more tax on your Social Security benefits, or may push you into an income bracket where you pay additional Medicare Part B and D premiums.

A standing home equity line of credit provides liquidity that may come in handy in retirement. It can provide a ready source of cash that buys you time to figure out how to fit unexpected expenses into your plan in a strategic way. In this situation, you could write a check to your child for the $25,000 without it having a major effect on your other plans other than your need to make loan payments until your child can pay you back (anyone who has children knows they may be waiting awhile).

---

[6]Numbers calculated using Realtor.com's mortgage refinance calculator at www.realtor. com/home-finance/financial-calculators/mortgage-refinancing-calculator. aspx?source=web.

Be careful though. A line of credit must not be used to fund extra living expenses. I had one recent retiree who was consistently spending more than we had projected. We discussed the dangers of running out of money if the spending level didn't change. He agreed and we reduced his portfolio withdrawals. Next time we met, he had accumulated a significant amount of debt on his home equity line. "What happened?" I asked. Instead of taking portfolio withdrawals to fund excess spending he had tapped into his home equity line. This was like taking money out of the left pocket instead of the right pocket. We had some more tough discussions and eventually got him on track. Home equity lines are best used as a reserve strategy, not as an extra source of spending money.

Reverse Mortgages

It is amazing how readily people will take out a mortgage, and how adverse they are to the words *reverse mortgage*. A reverse mortgage is a financial tool. There should be no adverse reaction to the words.

Years ago, reverse mortgages got a bad rap, and it hasn't entirely gone away. People seem to cling to false beliefs about this financial instrument. Like a regular mortgage, a reverse mortgage is a tool that allows you to access the equity in your home.

Reverse mortgages are *non-recourse* loans—if the value of the mortgage grows to the point where it exceeds the value of the home, there is only the property as collateral. The bank cannot attach your other assets or those of your heirs.

Reverse mortgage programs are federally mandated through the FHA (Federal Housing Administration). The U.S. Department of Housing and Urban Development provides a thorough overview of reverse mortgages on its web site.[7]

With a reverse mortgage, you own the home at all times, not the bank. Your responsibilities are to pay the taxes and maintain the property, the same responsibilities you have with any mortgage.

Note   Despite what you may have read, a reverse mortgage in the right circumstances can be a very useful retirement planning tool.

---

[7]See "Frequently Asked Questions about HUD's Reverse Mortgages" at http://portal. hud.gov/hudportal/HUD?src=/program_offices/housing/sfh/hecm/rmtopten.

Here are a few key things that make a reverse mortgage attractive in the right situation:

- You can use a reverse mortgage to pay off an existing mortgage.

- Reverse mortgage income is tax-free.

- No minimum credit score is required, and a reverse mortgage does not affect your credit score.

- When you sell your home, just as with any mortgage, the mortgage gets paid off and any additional equity belongs to you or your heirs.

- You own the property at all times.

Let's take a look at how reverse mortgage work, when to use them, and when not to use them.

How They Work

A reverse mortgage allows you to borrow money against the value of your home without entering into a monthly repayment agreement. Instead of making monthly payments to repay the amount borrowed, the bank agrees that the loan will be repaid at some point in the future when the house is sold. Thus the balance owed increases each month as interest accumulates.

To be eligible for a reverse mortgage, you

- Must be age 62.

- Own a home that you live in.

- Have no mortgage or a low mortgage balance that can be paid off at closing with proceeds from the reverse mortgage.

- Agree to participate in a home equity conversion mortgage (HECM) counseling session to learn more about reverse mortgages.

You can receive the proceeds from a reverse mortgage in the following ways:

- Equal monthly payments for a fixed number of months

- In the form of life-long monthly payments

- As a line of credit

- In any combination of the above

The amount you receive depends on the following:

- *Age of the borrower:* The younger you are, the less you can receive

- *Value of the property:* But there's a maximum of $625,500

- *Type:* The type of reverse mortgage program you pick

You can use the online reverse mortgage calculator at the National Reverse Mortgage Lender's Association web site[8] to get an estimate of the amount of income that a reverse mortgage might provide to you.

Using a St. Louis ZIP code of 63017, a couple age 65, and home value of $300,000, the calculator estimated they could receive $961 of monthly income for life.

Another option would be monthly income of $695 with a $50,000 credit line to be used as needed.

With a reverse mortgage, a lender can foreclose on you if you do not pay your property taxes, insurance, and repairs. I frequently see this mentioned as a caution against reverse mortgages. I find this a silly reason to say reverse mortgages are bad. If you own a home outright with no mortgage and don't pay your property taxes, you can lose your home too.

With a reverse mortgage, the lender also has the right to demand repayment if you don't live in your home for 12 straight months or more. This means if you move in with relatives, or into a care facility, you need to make plans to sell the home if you don't think you'll be returning. Upon sale of the home, any equity is yours. If the mortgage balance exceeds the value of the home, you have no risk.

When to Use Them

I can think of multiple situations in which a reverse mortgage might be a good planning solution. Let's take a look at a few of them.

To Allow You to Defer Your Social Security Start Date

Suppose you are out of work in your mid-60s. You have little savings and a paid off home. You think you are going to have to start Social Security early, but you know you will get more if you can wait to begin benefits until age 70. Proceeds from a reverse mortgage might fill in the gap, allowing you to defer the start date of your Social Security and lock in a higher guaranteed income amount for life.

---

[8]Calculator at www.reversemortgage.org/About/ReverseMortgageCalculator.aspx.

To Manage Taxes

You have Social Security and tax-deferred savings, and your income puts you on the border of a marginal tax bracket, meaning each time you take extra money out of your IRA, it is taxed at a higher rate. Because reverse mortgage income is tax-free, it may be the perfect solution either as a credit line to be used when additional money is needed for major purchases or repairs, or as a form of monthly income.

To Manage Sequence Risk

When investing in a traditional portfolio of stocks and bonds, you want to avoid liquidating investments during a market downturn. This is typically managed by some form of time segmentation, such as holding cash reserves and lower-risk investments to meet near-term cash needs. There is an opportunity cost to this strategy: to manage risk you must hold more short-term, low-risk investments that earn lower returns. In an article called "Standby Reverse Mortgages: A Risk Management Tool for Retirement Distributions,"[9] the authors propose using a reverse mortgage to manage this process. Instead of recommending the holding of excess cash reserves, they establish rules that determine when the reverse mortgage should be used for income needs and when portfolio withdrawals should be used. The executive summary concludes: "We find this risk management strategy improves portfolio survival rates by a significant amount."

As Plan B

A reverse mortgage can be a strategy you keep on the shelf only if needed. You might build your plan based on a reasonably conservative set of assumptions about investment returns, longevity, and spending—a plan that works without incorporating the use of your home equity. Then, if investment returns are lower than expected or if it looks like you may outlive your money if you don't implement some changes, you can consider a reverse mortgage as plan B. In several cases where I have recommended a reverse mortgage, it was a combination of overspending and low returns in the first ten years of retirement that put the client's plan in jeopardy. I was happy that a reverse mortgage had not been part of their original plan. If it had been, we would have had no viable Plan B options.

---

[9]John Salter, Ph.D., and Harold Evensky, "Standby Reverse Mortgages: A Risk Management Tool for Retirement Distributions," *Journal of Financial Planning* (August 2012).

When Not to Use Them

Those who seem to think *reverse mortgage* is a bad word frequently cite fees as one reason to avoid them.

If you look at a reverse mortgage as a long-term solution, the fees, when amortized over the life of the loan, are reasonable. The reverse mortgage calculator I used on the St. Louis ZIP code estimates fees. For the scenario I ran, depending on which program you chose, fees ranged from $5,500 to $11,500. To me this seems quite reasonable when you consider this financial instrument is providing you with guaranteed income for life.

Whether you consider the fees reasonable or not, there are situations where a reverse mortgage might not be the right solution. Here are a few of them:

- *Moving soon:* As with any mortgage, it doesn't make sense to pay refinancing costs and fees if you think you may be moving soon. A reverse mortgage is most appropriate for someone who plans on remaining in their home for quite some time.

- *Overspenders:* If you are an overspender, you ought to get a handle on your overspending before you use a reverse mortgage. You may end up not being able to pay the property taxes one day, and the lender can foreclose on you in that situation. Of course if you spend too much, you're going to have a problem no matter what financial tools you use, unless you choose an immediate annuity.

- In all cases where you receive aid based on your income and asset amounts, check all the rules before making any changes to your financial situation.

If you need additional income, and your home has equity, your other alternative to using a reverse mortgage is to move. All options should be explored before you make a final decision.

Summary

Your real estate and mortgage decisions should be viewed, as objectively as possible, as part of your retirement income plan.

When it comes to taking on new real estate investments, you should realize that it is a profession unto itself. Do plenty of homework before diving into real estate as a solution to generating your retirement income.

When it comes to your residence, your home choice can have a significant effect on your income needs. Extreme savers and those with constrained plans can find creative home solutions that reduce their spending needs on transportation and energy. Those with ample room in their plan will make values-based decisions, aligning their home choice with their desired retirement lifestyle.

Mortgages are financial tools. If you have the money to pay down the mortgage, and don't do so, what you are effectively doing is borrowing in order to invest. Whether this makes sense or not depends on your individual circumstances.

Reverse mortgages can provide guaranteed income later in your retirement years, or they can serve as an optional cash reserve bucket to draw from as part of your plan. You may not want to count on using one, but don't rule it out on based on hearsay.

Managing Health Care Costs in Retirement

What? It's Not Free?

Yet this is health: To have a body functioning so perfectly that when its few simple needs are met it never calls attention to its own existence.

—Bertha Stuart Dyment

In recent years, it seems there's hardly a subject more controversial than health care coverage, except maybe gun control.

Regardless of your personal views on a minimum standard of care that should or should not be available to everyone, as with most things in life, the more money you have, the more health care choices are available to you. You have choices about how much you spend, and some choose to spend quite a bit more than others.

The purpose of this chapter is to provide a very broad outline of those choices and to give you a few tools to estimate health care expenses and incorporate them into your retirement income plan.

Total Medical Costs in Retirement

A couple age 65 can expect to spend anywhere from $230,000–$250,000 on health care in retirement.[1] You need to plan for these costs, but I do like to put them in perspective. The cost of raising a child is estimated to be in the same price range, about $230,000.[2] Yet despite this scary price tag, people do find a way to finance the cost of raising their children.

I am not sure what you do when you are ill, but I stay in bed, drink tea, and sip chicken soup. When I am not feeling well, I am not likely to be out shopping, traveling, or eating out. In the latter part of your retirement years, as spending on health care increases, it is often not an additional cost in the budget. It replaces other items.

That doesn't mean you shouldn't take the expense seriously. If there is one item that is nearly always missing from a retirement budget, it is the adequate accounting of health care costs. You want to do your homework and estimate this expense as accurately as possible, but you also want to keep a healthy perspective on it. It is likely that when excess health care expenses come up, they will displace other flexible items in your budget, just as they do now while you are working—with one exception.

The one exception is end-of-life care. Some types of health plans do not cover extended hospital stays, which are those most likely to occur during one's last year of life. Such expenses can cause a serious dent in the amount one leaves to heirs or leave a loved one saddled with debt.

To do your best to account for such costs, you want to gain an understanding of how the system works and develop a basic estimate of how much you can expect to spend on health care. Of course, that depends on numerous factors such as where you live, when you retire, what medications you take, and whether you are self-insured or have an employer that provides retiree medical benefits.

Considering these variables, I break planning for health care expenses into four segments: early retirement (pre-age 65), Medicare-age health care (age 65+), long-term care, and saving for health care.

---

[1] "Planning for Retirement, Don't Forget Health Care Costs," *New York Times* (October 5, 2012). Available online at www.nytimes.com/2012/10/06/your-money/planning-for-retirement-dont-forget-health-care-costs.html?pagewanted=all&_r=0.
[2] www.washingtonpost.com/blogs/wonkblog/post/the-cost-of-raising-kids-in-two-charts/2012/06/18/gJQA35ENlV_blog.html.

Early Retirement and Health Insurance

Doug worked for a construction firm and had planned on working until 65. He was forced into retirement a few years early, at 62, when the economy took a dive. His wife Beth, was about eight years younger, and had no plans to retire in the near future.

With a little rearranging, and through Doug's use of extended unemployment benefits, their plan absorbed the change in Doug's retirement date fairly well. To my surprise, a year later they came in to see if they might find a way for Beth to retire as soon as possible.

Beth explained that her take-home pay was only about $1,450 a month and that if she started her pension at 55 it would be $1,247 per month. "What was the point of her continuing to work?" she asked.

On the surface, her logic made sense, until I explained to them the cost of health insurance. Beth was paying only $54 a month for health coverage; her employer was paying the rest of the premium. Once retired, as neither was yet Medicare age, equivalent health insurance for the two of them would run $1,400 a month. When we factored in benefits, Beth's job was paying her nearly twice what she had thought.

If your employer provides some type of group health plan, it is likely subsidizing the cost, and you may have no idea how expensive it can be if you leave the workforce.

Estimating Health Care Costs pre-65

If you plan on transitioning to self-employment or leaving the work force early (before age 65), you must factor the expense of health care into your plan.

Your potential choices will depend on whether you have pre-existing conditions and the implementation of some of the provisions of the Affordable Health Care Act that are set to go into effect January 2014.

Right now, if you have preexisting conditions, you may find yourself bound to your current employer and its health care plan. You may be afraid to leave and potentially experience a gap in medical coverage.

If you are in this situation, visit Healthcare.gov[3] and choose the Find Insurance Options tab. Walk through the options by answering questions about your situation. You'll come to the Pre-Existing Condition Insurance Plan (PCIP)/High Risk Pool section, which should then lead you to choices available in your state.

---

[3]See www.healthcare.gov/index.html.

If you are a healthy individual out shopping for insurance, you can start your search with a health insurance broker[4] or by visiting one of the large health insurance company web sites that provide online tools to help you find a plan that fits your needs. Here are five health insurer web sites you may want to check out:

- *Aetna*: www.aetna.com
- *Blue Cross Blue Shield*: www.bcbs.com
- *Humana*: www.humana.com
- *United Health Care*: www.uhc.com
- *Cigna*: www.cigna.com

For a healthy individual who is not yet 65, I think one of the most effective ways to compare plans is to look at your maximum out-of-pocket cost, including premiums.

For example, one of the decisions you'll need to make is choosing between a high-deductible plan and a low-deductible plan. Let's walk through an example.

Using the Blue Cross Blue Shield web site, I chose an Arizona ZIP code and examined plans for a female age 62.

The most expensive plan on a monthly premium basis had the following features for in-network services:

- *Deductible*: $250
- *Coinsurance*: 80%
- *Monthly premium*: $979
- *Maximum out-of-pocket*: $2,500
- *Co-pays*: $30 primary care /$50 specialist

If you add up the costs for a year with no doctor visits other than preventative care (which was covered), this woman would spend her monthly premium for a total of $11,748 for the year.

If she had a year with maximum expenses, she would spend her monthly premium plus her maximum out-of-pocket amount, for a total of $14,248.

If she chooses this plan, she will have to count on the $11,748-per-year cost, and she should expect it to increase a bit each year until she reaches age 65 and becomes eligible for Medicare.

---

[4]For assistance finding an agent, visit the National Association of Health Underwriters web site at www.nahu.org and use the Find an Agent tool.

The least expensive plan on a monthly premium basis was an HSA-qualified plan[5] and had the following features:

- *Deductible*: $5,500

- *Coinsurance*: 100%

- *Monthly premium*: $257

- *Maximum out-of-pocket*: $5,500

- *Co-pays*: With these plans you pay all costs up to your deductible, and there is no charge after you meet your deductible.

If you add up the costs for a year with no doctor visits other than preventative care (which was covered) with this plan, she would spend her monthly premiums for a total of $3,084 for the year and use her savings to fund an HSA account to the maximum allowable amount of $4,250 ($3,250 2013's single limit plus $1,000 catch-up contribution amount for those age 55 and older).[6] This would put her annual expense at $7,334, although technically much of that would be savings rather than a current-year expense.

If she had a year with maximum expenses, she would spend her monthly premium plus her maximum out-of-pocket amount for a total of $8,584.

For those who are eligible for HSA plans, I think they are a great choice. Unfortunately, preexisting conditions may prevent you from moving to such a plan—at least until 2014, when insurers must take on all those who can pay the premium.

Of course, the choices online include all kinds of additional plans offered with various combinations of deductibles, premiums, and coinsurance amounts. I picked these two extremes to give you a sense of the diversity of your options.

If you want an early retirement, the key will be to explore your options based on your health situation, geographic location, and plan choices. Then build the estimated expense into your budget.

Your choices and expenses will change once you become eligible for Medicare at age 65.

---

[5] I discussed the tax benefits of Health Savings Accounts in Chapter 5. Additional HSA features are outlined later in the present chapter.
[6] Once you reach 65, you are no longer eligible to fund an HSA.

Age 65: Medicare Basics

When you reach 65, the health insurance landscape changes. You become eligible for Medicare, the U.S. federal health insurance program for people age 65 and older.[7]

You may be years away from 65. What's the point of learning about a health program that may evolve by the time you are eligible?

Although today's rules may not apply to you, they do apply to your parents and other age 65+ loved ones. It has been proven that navigating complex financial decisions gets more difficult as one reaches their late 60s and beyond.

Those who may need it most may not ask for your help. It can be challenging to approach a loved one with the offer to help them navigate through their health care and financial choices. Consider this comment from HealthView Services:

> A recent study conducted by the National Council on Aging (NCOA) and United Healthcare reveals that large numbers of seniors don't understand Medicare and are unaware of recent changes. The findings highlight the need for more education regarding Medicare. This becomes all the more pertinent as over 10,000 people are turning 65 and becoming eligible daily. In the next twenty years, tens of millions will sign up for Medicare, whether or not they know what they are doing.[8]

If you know someone who may need your help, use this chapter as an opportunity to learn. Then ask them questions and offer assistance.

Medicare Gaps

The biggest misconception I see regarding Medicare is the belief that it will cover all your health care expenses. Perhaps this belief is why so many people do not include an expense line for health insurance premiums and other medical costs in their retirement budgets.

According to the Employee Benefit Research Institute, Medicare only covers 51% of health care expenses.[9]

---

[7]It also covers certain young people with disabilities and those with End-Stage Renal Disease. See medicare.gov for details.

[8]"Baby Boomer Confusions About Medicare Soars as Enrollment Date Looms," HealthView Services (December 19, 2012). Available online at www.hvsfinancial.com/2012/12/baby-boomer-confusions-about-medicare-soars-as-enrollment-date-looms-2.

[9]EBRI Issue Brief No. 295 (July 2006).

This means the other 49% will be paid by you or by other insurance coverage that you carry.

According to the Kaiser Family Foundation, health expenses accounted for nearly 15 percent of Medicare (age) household budgets in 2010.[10] If you want to create a very simple estimate of your post-65 health care expenses, take your expected retirement income and multiply it by 15 percent. This can give you a starting place, but the number may be too low.

A 2011 Credit Suisse report puts the number quite a bit higher. It says that health goods and medical services account for 33% of household consumption for those age 60 and over in the United States.[11]

You can use the online tool by HealthView Advisor to come up with your own estimate at `http://apps.hvsfinancial.com/hvadvisor/`.

Using the HealthView Advisor calculator, I did not check off any of the health conditions and said I was a 65-year-old female. It estimated health care expenses in 2013 (age 65) as ranging from $4,485 to $8,117, depending on income level. For a 65-year-old male, the estimate was $4,389 to $8,021.

Yes, this is a broad range, but it gives you a starting place. You need to budget for spending somewhere around $370 to $675 per month on health care starting at age 65. This amount will increase with inflation.

If you want top-notch health care, choice of providers, and long-term care coverage, you'll want to budget more.

Let's take a brief look at what Medicare covers and why additional insurance coverage (and thus additional money) is often needed to cover non-Medicare eligible expenses.

THINGS YOU MUST DO BETWEEN 62 AND 65

Once you hit age 62, it's time to do some Medicare homework to prepare you for reaching age 65. You'll need to do the following:

- Learn Medicare basics.

- Find out how your current plan interacts with Medicare. The earlier you do this the better so that you have ample time to change plans if you need to.

---

[10] Kaiser Family Foundation Medicare Policy. Available online at `www.kff.org/medicare/upload/8171-02.pdf`.
[11] "Longer Lives, Changing Life Cycles: Exploring Consumer and Worker Implications," Credit Suisse (July 20, 2011).

- Explore your new health insurance options, such as Original Medicare combined with Medigap/Supplement policies or through a Medicare Advantage plan.

- Enroll in Medicare when you turn 65.

Medicare: Parts A, B, C, and D

Medicare.gov offers a wealth of information. When you near 65, or if you are assisting someone who is Medicare age, I suggest you spend some time on it.

It offers this concise overview of what Medicare is all about:

> Medicare covers services (like lab tests, surgeries, and doctor visits) and supplies (like wheelchairs and walkers) considered medically necessary to treat a disease or condition.[12]

Of course, it is the definition of *medically necessary* that is so difficult to determine. I'll leave that one alone and instead take a brief look at how Medicare benefits are structured.

Medicare coverage is broken into four parts: Parts A, B, C, and D. The foundation of Medicare is Part A, which is often referred to as *hospital insurance*. If you are eligible for Social Security, you are eligible for Medicare Part A for free.

Medicare Part B, which covers additional services and supplies needed to treat medical conditions as well as some preventative services, is not free. Most benefit recipients pay a monthly premium for Medicare Part B, which is announced annually.

As discussed in Chapter 5, the basic Medicare Part B premium in 2013 is $104.90 per month. Those with modified adjusted gross incomes over $85,000 for single filers or $170,000 for married filers pay more, according to a schedule based on their income; the more income, the higher the premium.[13] Medicare estimates this schedule results in increased premiums for about 5% of the population.

Medicare Parts A and B comprise what is now often referred to as *Original Medicare*. With Original Medicare, as with most other insurance plans, you still have deductibles, co-pays, and coinsurance expenses as well as prescription costs. That's where Medicare Parts C and D come in—offering additional coverage you can purchase.

---

[12]Source: Medicare.gov.
[13]This means-tested premium schedule is provided in Chapter 5.

Medicare Part C is called a Medicare Advantage Plan. It provides coverage in a single plan that includes Medicare Parts A and B as well as prescription drug coverage (Part D). Medicare Advantage plans may also include extra covered services like vision, dental, and hearing, but they do not include coverage for extended hospital stays. The terms and conditions of Medicare Advantage plans are set by private insurers. The intention of allowing these plans was to provide an alternative, and thus competition, to Original Medicare.

Medicare Part D refers to prescription drug coverage that you can add as an a la carte plan to your basic Medicare Part A and B benefits. As with Medicare Part B, high-income recipients pay more for Medicare Part D.

Medigap and Medicare Supplement plans are intended to wrap around Original Medicare. Currently, you must choose between either a Medicare Advantage plan or Original Medicare augmented with Medigap/Medicare Supplement policies.

The right choice for you will depend on your health care needs. Some plans provide a significant advantage over others, depending on the medications, lab work, and other services you may routinely use.

To help you wade through these choices, Medicare.gov offers a feature called Plan Finder at www.medicare.gov/find-a-plan/questions/home.aspx.

QUALIFY FOR MEDICARE

To be eligible for Medicare at no cost, you or your current or former spouse[14] must have

- Entered the United States lawfully.

- Lived in the U.S. for five years.

- Paid Medicare taxes while working in the United States and have 40 or more quarters of Medicare-covered employment, or would be entitled to Social Security benefits based on your spouse's (or divorced spouse's) work record, and that spouse is at least 62.

- Achieved age 65 (except in limited exceptions explained in footnote 7).

---

[14]Rules for eligibility based on a former spouse's work record mirror the rules for eligibility for Social Security based on a former spouse's work record.

If you do not qualify based on these criteria, in some cases you can still purchase Medicare by paying a monthly premium.[15] A situation where this might occur would be with an older spouse who is not eligible for Medicare based on his/her own work record and who is married to a younger spouse who will be eligible for Medicare but is not yet 62. I the following *Consumer Reports* article to be most helpful in reviewing such a situation: http://news.consumerreports.org/health/2011/11/im-65-and-have-been-denied-medicare-because-my-husband-is-five-years-younger-help.html.

I used the Plan Finder feature with a Brooklyn, New York ZIP code to see what it would come up with. It gave me the option to choose the specific medications I was on, the dosage, and to substitute generic versions. It also asked if I bought from a retail pharmacy or via mail order. I chose "none" for the medications, but my understanding is that this tool can be quite useful when you need to find a plan that covers something specific.

The results were categorized as follows:

- *Prescription Drug Plans with Original Medicare*: 28 plans

- *Medicare Health Plans with Drug Coverage*: 34 plans available

- *Medicare Health Plans without Drug Coverage*: 8 plans available

Yikes! How is the average person supposed to wade through all these choices?

Some of the plans listed provided an estimate of annual health and drug costs, which ranged from $1,650–$3,300, but this estimate did not include hearing, vision, or dental, which were included in the estimate using the HealthView Advisor calculator. It also did not include Medicare Part B premiums, which would tack on another $1,258 per year for the average person and as much as $4,020 a year for high-income recipients.[16]

I decided I needed help understanding some of the key differentiators between these plan choices. I called Dan McGrath, whom I had met several times through the Retirement Income Industry Association (RIIA) and whose wealth of knowledge on health care-related items is quite exceptional.

Dan helped me clarify some of the key differences in plan choices, which I have narrowed down into three broad categories:

---

[15]Learn more: "How to Qualify for Medicare," available online at http://ssa-custhelp.ssa.gov/app/answers/detail/a_id/400/~/how-to-qualify-for-medicare.
[16]Based on 2013 Medicare Part B premium schedules.

- *Choice of provider.* One of the big differentiators between Original Medicare and Medicare Advantage plans is the ability to choose your own provider. You may be able to reduce routine out-of-pocket costs by using a Medicare Advantage plan, but to do so you need to use the plan's in-network providers. If you want complete freedom to choose your provider, Original Medicare with a Medigap/Supplement may be your best option.

- *Extended hospital stay coverage*: Another big differentiator is the extended hospital stay coverage. Medicare Part A pays for the first 60 days of a hospital stay in full. From days 61–90, you pay a portion. For days 91–150 you pay an increased portion, and from day 151 on, the cost is yours to bear. Extended hospital stays are most likely to occur in the last year of life, and Medigap policies provide coverage for this cost. Most Medicare Advantage plans only cover up to the first 90 days.

- *Ancillary benefits*: One more differentiator among plans is the additional benefits that come with Medicare Advantage plans—things like dental, vision, and hearing. These benefits are not part of the Original Medicare + Medigap type of coverage.

▓ **Note**   With prescription drug plans, you have the choice of either picking a plan a la carte (Part D) that complements Original Medicare or choosing a Medicare Advantage plan that incorporates a drug plan. Either way, co-pays and costs for certain drugs may vary widely from plan to plan. It pays to shop around.

Your plan choice needs to be made based on your personal health situation, and it may need to be re-evaluated each year. As your health needs change, a different plan structure may prove to be more economical for you. Each year, you have the opportunity to switch Medicare health plans during an open enrollment period that occurs toward the end of the year. (For 2012 the open enrollment period ran October 15, 2012 through December 7, 2012.) Use this open enrollment period to evaluate your plan choice.

Applying for Medicare

If you are already receiving Social Security benefits when you reach age 65, you will be automatically enrolled in Medicare. Your Medicare card will be mailed to the address on record with Social Security.

If you are not receiving Social Security benefits, you need to apply online,[17] at your local Social Security office, or by phone at 1-800-772-1213. There is a seven-month open enrollment period which starts three months prior to the month you turn 65 and extends three months past the month you turn 65. You should apply even if you still have coverage through a group health plan—and if you want benefits to begin at 65, make sure you apply before you turn 65.

If you are still working, most employer-provided health plans will become secondary to Medicare once you reach age 65. If you have private insurance, it may also become secondary to Medicare when you reach 65.

TRANSITIONING TO MEDICARE

If you are covered by a group health plan as you near age 65, read Medicare.gov's Retiree Insurance page at www.medicare.gov/supplement-other-insurance/retiree-insurance/retiree-insurance.html.

If you have private insurance, read Medicare.gov's "How Medicare Works with Other Insurance" at www.medicare.gov/supplement-other-insurance/how-medicare-works-with-other-insurance/how-medicare-works-with-other-insurance.html.

You may also want to read "Should I Get Part B?" at www.medicare.gov/sign-up-change-plans/get-parts-a-and-b/should-you-get-part-b/should-i-get-part-b.html.

Medicare Part B and Medigap Policies

Medicare Part B enrollment is not mandatory, but the majority of people will want to sign up for Medicare Part B when they enroll in Medicare. However, there are exceptions. The best thing you can do is talk to your current health care provider to determine whether you should enroll in Part B at the same time you enroll in Medicare.

In limited cases, due to the coverage provided by your employer-sponsored plan, it may not be to your benefit to sign up for Part B right away. In such cases, you'll have an open enrollment period where you can sign up for Part B after your employment or employer-sponsored health coverage ends.

---

[17]Start your online application process at www.socialsecurity.gov/medicareonly/.

▒ **Note**   If you don't sign up for Part B and Part D when you're first eligible, you may have to pay a penalty to get them later. For additional details, see Understanding Medicare Enrollment Periods at www.medicare.gov/Pubs/pdf/11219.pdf.

You have six months from the time you sign up for Medicare Part B to get a guaranteed-issue[18] Medigap policy. If you wait and apply for a Medigap policy after this six-month window, you may or may not be eligible, because the terms and conditions in most states are determined after this period by the private health insurance company issuing the policy.

This makes for an interesting dilemma. At the bottom of the Medicare.gov Decide How to Get Your Medicare[19] page, it says:

> If you join a Medicare Advantage Plan, you can't use Medicare Supplement Insurance (Medigap) to pay for out-of-pocket costs you have in a Medicare Advantage Plan. If you already have a Medicare Advantage Plan, you can't be sold a Medigap policy. You can only use a Medigap policy if you disenroll from your Medicare Advantage Plan and return to Original Medicare.

When you consider that Medigap policies cover extended hospital stays, and Medicare Advantage plans don't, it's almost as if you're forced to roll the dice when you choose your plan.

One of the things to keep in mind with Medicare is that it does not cover long-term care expenses. This is the final health care cost you should examine as part of your retirement plan.

Long-Term Care

John and Cathy were in their 70s when they were referred to me by their CPA. They had been married over 50 years and they brought a smile to my face every time they came in, often still holding hands.

As they reached their early 80s I will never forget them sitting in my conference room one day, sharing with me their heartfelt thoughts on living and on dying. John was fighting a round of skin cancer, and Cathy had Parkinson's. John

---

[18]*Guaranteed issue* means you cannot be denied coverage for health reasons.
[19]Available online at www.medicare.gov/sign-up-change-plans/decide-how-to-get-medicare/decide-how-to-get-your-medicare.html.

said, "We've had a wonderful life. Our children are grown and doing well. Now, we're ready to go. Trips to the doctor and medications. Who wants all that? We're ready to go."

John had a stroke a year later and passed away quickly.

I went to visit Cathy numerous times and eventually met all their children. She was weak and frail; I honestly didn't think she'd make it more than a year past John's passing, but slowly a sparkle returned to her eye, and her strength returned. When I go see her now, we sit and have a glass of wine and I gain the most marvelous insights from this amazing 84-year-old woman.

She shared that she misses John every day and yet at the same time she realizes her opinions and thoughts had been entirely shaped by him. In the era in which she married, that was natural. In her 80s, she is now finding a new kind of independence: an independence of thought as she forms her own opinions on current events and enjoys intellectual conversations with her visitors. It has been an amazing process to watch.

Although Cathy is healthy and alert, she needs assistance around the home. Her long-term care policy covers in-home care, so she has a helper who comes each day from about 10 to 2 to offer whatever help is needed, such as running errands, preparing meals, cleaning, bathing, laundry, and so on.

Although we think of long-term care needs as being confined to a nursing home facility, Cathy's situation is quite common, and in-home care is an important feature offered by most long-term care insurance policies today.

Contrast Cathy's situation with that of my grandpa. In 2012, I flew to Des Moines, Iowa for a family reunion put together in honor of my grandpa's (on my mom's side) 90th birthday. Grandpa's short-term memory loss had started to result in things like the stove being left on and forgotten medications. This was my first time to visit him in the care facility the family had located for him.

It was a nice place with spacious, living room–like gathering areas, and grandpa expressed that he was quite happy there. There were security codes with a double door system to get in and out, and although I realize they are needed for his protection, it was still odd, as if we start in a playpen and one day end up back in one again.

Grandpa knew who I was, but other parts of his memory were jumbled up a bit. Other than memory loss, he is quite healthy and may be in this care facility for many years. Grandma passed away a number of years ago, so all of grandpa's income and assets can be used to support this need. If Grandpa still had a spouse at home, though, the financial strain of the situation would be more substantial.

Your-Long Term Care Situation

You do not know what the future may bring. Will you, like John, go quickly of a stroke, never needing any form of long-term care? Will you, like Cathy, need in-home care? Or will you, like my grandpa, need years of a full-care facility? And how will such care needs be financed?

Medicare and supplemental health insurance policies cover a minimal amount of care needed after a hospital stay, but they do not cover the cost of extended long-term care needs.

As with any insurance needs, your choices are to retain the risk, and, if needed, you will spend your assets and go on state aid or shift the risk by buying a long-term care insurance policy.

If you want to estimate the odds that you will need long-term care, start with the American Association for Long Term Care Insurance (AALTCI) web site at www.aaltci.org/long-term-care-insurance/.

From my own observations in working with retirees, it seems most people who can afford long-term care insurance policies find having them brings them greater peace of mind.

Most policies express their coverage in terms of a daily benefit amount and a number of years. For example, a policy that provides a $200 daily benefit amount for four years would provide you with a pool of $292,000 available for care ($200 × 365 days × 4 years), expressed in today's dollars. If you buy a policy that has an inflation adjustment (this is usually recommended), your daily benefit amount, and thus your pool of available dollars, will increase according to the inflation formula in the policy.

A four-year policy may last far longer than four years, depending on your care needs and how you schedule benefits. What do I mean by that? If your policy will pay up to $200 per day, and you are only spending $100 per day, your policy would last eight years instead of four using the example in the preceding paragraph. Also, some policies reimburse monthly, and some daily. A monthly reimbursement structure gives you quite a bit more flexibility when it comes to in-home care services.

For example, many people like to bundle their in-home care services. Perhaps they need help bathing and dressing every day. Let's assume the cost is $40 per hour. On Mondays, in addition to help bathing and dressing, they also like to have all the meals prepared for the week and the laundry and cleaning done. The cost of services performed on Monday might be $300. With a daily reimbursement of $200 they would exceed their limits on Monday and have to pay out-of-pocket but be under their limits on other days. With a monthly reimbursement policy, this would not be an issue.[20] The carrier would pay up to the monthly maximum of $6,000 per month, covering the higher costs of Mondays and enabling the policyholder greater flexibility in how services are scheduled.

How do you determine the amount of long-term care coverage? You could go about it in one of two ways. If you can afford a Cadillac policy, you may just decide that's what you want regardless of cost. If you're working on a limited budget, you'll have to narrow your benefits down a bit. You might go through the following exercise to determine what you need.

First, estimate hourly long-term care costs in your area. Using the Long Term Care Cost Index page[21] on the AALTCI web site, I looked up the Dallas area and got the following results:

- *Homemaker:* Average hourly rate: $18

- *Assisted living:* Lowest monthly cost: $1,450

- *Assisted living:* Highest monthly cost: $4,500

- *Assisted living:* Average monthly cost: $2,770

- *Nursing home:* Semi-private daily: $125

- *Nursing home:* Private average daily: $170

Assume you have $60,000 coming in from Social Security and investment income. That's about $164 a day, or about $4,920 a month.

However, all the income is not available for care needs, because you still need income for living expenses in addition to your long-term care costs. And if you have a spouse, they likely need a significant portion of that income to continue their own standard of living.

You may decide that of that $164 a day, $40 of it would be available for long-term care costs. That would cover about two hours a day of non-medical in-home care at $18 an hour.

If you wanted to cover a full eight hours a day of non-medical care, with the goal of enabling you to stay in your home for as long as possible, you would need an additional benefit of $108 a day.

If you decide to protect against a care need of about 2 1/2 years, then you would buy a policy that had a $110 daily benefit that would provide coverage

---

[20]Special thanks to Nicole Gurley of Gurley Long Term Care Insurance. Her input, contributions, and knowledge in helping me develop this chapter have been invaluable.

[21]Available online at www.aaltci.org/long-term-care-insurance/learning-center/cost.php#dallas.

for 2–4 years. You would also want an inflation rider, so that, if and when you needed care (likely 10–20 years after purchase of the policy,) that $110 per day would have increased.

This is just one example of how you might go about purchasing a policy to cover the risks that concern you the most.

Long-Term Care Insurance for Steve and Carol Sample

I asked Nicole Gurley of Gurley Long Term Care Insurance to put together some policy options for Steve and Carol Sample.

To acquire basic coverage, we looked at policies[22] that provide a $130 daily benefit for three years (see Table 10-1). The policies quoted have a shared rider, which gives the couple six years to share between them. This means if Carol needed care, and Steve did not, all six years could be used for Carol (or vice versa.) The policies also have a 5% compound inflation rider, so the daily benefit amount will go up over time.

Table 10-1. Long Term Care Insurance Quotes for Steve and Carol

	Carrier 1		Carrier 2		Carrier 3	
	Steve	**Carol**	**Steve**	**Carol**	**Steve**	**Carol**
Annual Premium	$3,501	$2,986	$4,187	$3,734	$4,212	$3,582
Combined Annual Premium	$6,487		$7,922		$7,794	

The quoted policies all had the following features:

- *Tax-qualified*: This means that benefits paid are not taxable, and premiums may be deductible depending on how the client files taxes.

- *Underwriting class*: These are all run at standard health status.

- *Home care daily benefit*: The coverage is applicable to all venues including home care.

---

[22]Policies quoted represent Arizona rates. Rates will vary depending on age, health status, state, and benefits chosen.

- *Facility elimination period*: All plans have a 90-day elimination period for facility care. You are responsible for the first 90 days of expense if care begins in a facility.

- *Zero day HC elimination period*: All plans have a 0-day requirement for home care. The first day of service is covered if care begins at home.

- *Spousal premium waiver*: All plans include spousal premium waiver. If one spouse/partner goes on claim, neither pays premiums during that specific claim period.

- *Monthly home care*: All plans pay home care on a monthly basis. This provides more flexibility in how services are received.

If Steve and Carol wanted to purchase a richer policy; one that provided a $150 daily benefit amount for ten years each, their combined premium could reach a whopping $15,000 a year.

In response to how people are reacting to current premiums on long-term care insurance, Nicole said, "Today, people have sticker shock... so I ask the client to define a budget that is comfortably affordable and that is consistent with the financial plan. The new normal is 'some is better than none.' And, it must be comfortably affordable because it is a life-long commitment."

To determine your needs, review family health history and longevity. Then discuss your primary concerns and financial circumstances with a knowledgeable long-term care broker and let them help you find a policy that fits your needs and your budget. I prefer working with a broker that specializes in long term-care insurance and one who can offer a full range of product offerings from a variety of carriers.

The challenge today is that long-term care insurance policies that provide unlimited benefits are incredibly expensive, and many companies do not offer them anymore. That means even with insurance that covers the average care need, if you are an outlier, you could exhaust your insurance benefits. That's why it's important to review family health history and longevity when determining coverage needs.

One option that can help protect your assets in the event of a lengthy long-term care expense is called a *Partnership* policy. A Partnership policy protects policyholders from Medicaid spend-down requirements. For every dollar that your policy pays for your care, a dollar of your assets is protected from Medicaid spend-down requirements. Two states, Indiana and New York, offer total asset protection if a required level of coverage is purchased. All but five states currently offer or are in the process of offering these policies.

WHO HAS THE GREATEST NEED FOR LONG-TERM CARE INSURANCE?

I think middle income, married couples have the greatest need for long-term care insurance. If one spouse needs care, and the other doesn't, income levels are often not sufficient to cover both the cost of care and maintaining a reasonable lifestyle for the healthier spouse. A long-term care policy that provides a few years of benefits can give you a buffer—a period of time where the healthy spouse can assess the situation and, if it looks like the long-term care event will exceed the policy limits, have time to plan. One option in this situation: meet with an elder law attorney to see what options are available to protect your remaining assets and standard of living.

PAYING FOR CARE WHEN YOU DON'T HAVE INSURANCE

What do you do when you or a loved one need care and can't afford it? Here are a few resources that may help you out:

- *Check your state's Medicaid rules*: To be eligible for Medicaid, your income and assets must be under a certain limit, and these limits vary from state-to-state. Start with your state's Medicaid office to find out your limits: www.fastemc.com/femcjom/find-your-states-medicaid-office.html.

- *Contact your local area agency on aging*: This organization can help you locate resources such as elder-abuse programs, counseling, meals on wheels, volunteers who will visit, adult day care services, and so on: www.n4a.org/about-n4a/?fa=aaa-title-VI.

- *Visit VeteranAid.org*: See if you or your loved one is eligible for a Veteran's Aid and Attendance Pension that may apply to both veterans and their surviving spouses: www.veteranaid.org/program.php.

- *Visit Eldercare.gov*: This resource can help you locate local services such as home health services, transportation resources, senior housing options, and respite care. It may be able to help you find financial assistance that you could be eligible for: www.eldercare.gov/eldercare.NET/Public/index.aspx.

Paying for Health care Costs

A crystal ball would make all of retirement planning and particularly planning for health care costs quite a bit easier. I don't know where to find one that works. The next best thing I have found is a Health Savings Account (HSA). I touched on the tax benefits of these in Chapter 5. I go into a few additional features here.

You can use money in an HSA tax-free for qualified medical expenses. What constitutes a qualified medical expense?

According to HSA Bank, that includes things like the following:[23]

- Expenses applied to your health plan deductible

- Dental care services

- Vision care services

- Prescription services

- Over-the-counter medications prescribed by your doctor

- Certain medical equipment

Once you reach age 65, you can use HSA money like an IRA—for anything! This makes it an incredibly flexible savings vehicle.

Accessing your HSA funds for medical expenses is easy. I have an HSA account that comes with a debit card. When I incur medical expenses, I use that debit card to pay for them directly from my HSA account with tax-free dollars.

HSA funds cannot normally cover insurance premiums. However, there are four exceptions:[24]

- Premiums for continuation coverage under COBRA or ERISA for the account holder, spouse, or dependents

- A qualified long-term care insurance contract

- A health plan maintained while the account holder, spouse, or dependent is receiving unemployment compensation under any federal or state law

- Premiums for those over the age of 65, including Medicare or retirement health benefits provided by a former employer

---

[23]www.hsabank.com/hsabank/Education/Eligible_Medical.aspx?sc_lang=en.
[24]Source: HSA Bank. See www.hsabank.com/hsabank/Education/Eligible_Medical.aspx?sc_lang=en.

This means HSA funds can be valuable under almost any circumstance—unemployment, buying long-term care insurance, or to use for living expenses after age 65.

To open an HSA account, you must first have an HSA-qualified health plan. Then you need to find a financial institution that offers HSA accounts.

■ **Note**   Once you reach age 65, you can no longer fund HSA accounts.

Some institutions allow you to invest your HSA money in stock, bonds, and mutual funds. For most people starting an HSA, I don't think this is wise. I'd suggest you take your deductible times five and keep this portion of your HSA in something safe and stable, like risk level 1 and 2 choices (see Chapter 4). If no medical expenses occur, your HSA balance will continue to grow, and as your balance gets larger you may consider investing amounts in excess of five times your deductible in something more aggressive.

Outside of HSA accounts, the wisest thing you can do to plan for health care expenses is build them into your budget, review your insurance coverage annually, live within your means, and do your best to live a healthy lifestyle.

Summary

If your health insurance costs are currently subsidized by your employer, you may be in for a big surprise when you go to build these expenses into your post-retirement budget.

You can break your health care expenses into two tiers: pre-age 65 and post-age 65. You'll likely want to do this when putting together your budget.

When you reach 65, you have important decisions to make about the type of health plan you choose, and the right plan for you will depend on your personal set of health circumstances. Don't be shy about seeking help when navigating through your choices at this point. And remember that your plan may need to be reviewed from year to year during the open enrollment period. As your health needs change, an alternate plan may prove to be more economical for you.

If you are eligible for an HSA-qualified plan, using it in conjunction with fully funding an HSA account each year is one of the most effective health care planning tools currently available.

### CHAPTER 11

Working Before and During Retirement

Using Your Human Capital

The best Armour of Old Age is a well spent life preceding it; a Life employed in the Pursuit of useful Knowledge, in honourable Actions and the Practice of Virtue; in which he who labours to improve himself from his Youth, will in Age reap the happiest Fruits of them; not only because these never leave a Man, not even in the extremest Old Age; but because a Conscience bearing Witness that our Life was well-spent, together with the Remembrance of past good Actions, yields an unspeakable Comfort to the Soul.

—Cicero

I had a liberating experience in 2010. I figured out what I was good at, and what I wasn't so good at. I stopped trying to be like other people and started being who I was. And a funny thing happened: work no longer felt like work. Instead, each day it felt like I got to go play. Oh sure, there were tasks that I had to do that I didn't love. It wasn't completely Goldilocks. But it was different.

I owe the difference to an assessment tool called the Kolbe A Index.[1] It helps you identify your natural, instinctive way of approaching problem solving. When you're not using your instincts, you're working against your grain. It's like bicycling against the wind; it takes more effort to get to the same place. Once you understand your instinctive talents and how to use them, the wind is almost always at your back, and work doesn't feel as worklike.

At the time I discovered Kolbe, I was feeling quite frustrated in my business situation. I always had ideas and wanted to figure out how to do things more efficiently and/or more effectively. I liked to follow the latest trends in financial planning and test out new software packages. My associates had more of the "if it ain't broke, don't fix it" mentality. One day, a colleague said something to me along the lines of, "Why can't you just be happy and leave well enough alone?"

I thought about that for awhile and wondered, "Why can't I? Is something wrong with me?" Then I found Kolbe. Through an assessment process I discovered my Natural Advantage—a Kolbe term—was that of an entrepreneur.[2] No, nothing was wrong with me. I am supposed to change things, and I am good at it. Instead of fighting myself I went full force ahead into seeing what I could create, and I haven't stopped since. I love it.

Kolbe had such a profound effect on me that, in 2011, I chose to invest in its certification class and become a Kolbe Certified Consultant, simply because I wanted to know more. The more I learned, the more I became convinced that an incredible amount of progress remains to be made in the field of human capital.

You possess human capital. It is in part your ability to earn a living. You can continue to use that capital in your retirement. You can focus on your human capital and look for ways to use it more effectively, just as you can focus on other assets on your balance sheet. As a matter of fact, for most people, their earning power is one of their biggest assets.

When focusing on human capital, you can take a strictly utilitarian approach and figure out how to make the most in the least amount of time. Or you can take a softer approach and make sure your human capital decisions align with your goals. Either way, it starts with knowing yourself.

---

[1] All terms relating to Kolbe products and service are property of Kolbe Corp.
[2] For those familiar with Kolbe, I'm a 6-5-8-2.

```
┌─────────────────────────────────────────────────────────────────┐
│                        USING KOLBE                                │
└─────────────────────────────────────────────────────────────────┘
```

Many corporations use Kolbe's tools to improve the use of their corporate human capital. Kolbe can be particularly useful in putting together teams of people that function more effectively. I use Kolbe in my business for this purpose, and it has had a significant, positive effect on how we work together and make the most of each other's strengths.

I think one of the most empowering things you can do to improve your human capital results is discover your natural instincts. You have a unique way of approaching problem solving, and someone is looking for your talents. You can start expanding on the potential of your human capital by going to www.kolbe.com and taking the Kolbe A Index. You can also use the Career MO+ to help you identify careers that most closely match your talents.

What Kind of Retirement Is for You?

There are two aspects to retirement you need to figure out. The first is: can you afford it? The second is: will it work for you?

For many people, even those who can afford it, the traditional view of retirement doesn't work. This is well illustrated in the stories of Dr. Barry, Chuck, and Ed.

Dr. Barry

Dr. Barry is 80 and still a practicing physician. He works three days a week, down from four days a week a few years ago. When he and his wife last came in for a review, I asked if he had any thoughts about fully retiring.

He said, "I am a doctor. I've been a doctor my whole life. When I go to the office, staff members are respectful to me. Students in residency come through, ask me questions, and graciously thank me for my time. Every day it's Dr. Barry, Dr. Barry. If I retire, who will I be? I'll be nobody."

Dr. Barry loves—and thrives on—his work. If you are like this, retirement can be an unfulfilling experience.

Part-time work can help ease the transition to retirement, both financially and psychologically. On the psychological side, it allows you to slowly figure out what to do with your newfound leisure time.

On the financial side, part-time work gets you used to the idea of withdrawing money from savings to live on. I have seen many people who are afraid to retire, even though the numbers say they can afford it. The thought of withdrawing money from savings on a regular basis can be frightening. A gradual transition to retirement can help you get comfortable with it.

Chuck

Contrast Dr. Barry with Chuck. Chuck and his wife were excellent savers. When Chuck reached age 55, his company offered an early retirement package. We ran through the numbers and decided that, from a financial perspective, they would be fine if he took it. Chuck was excited. A year later, he came in for a review and told me he was busier than ever. He had always been actively involved in his church and he was having a wonderful time volunteering and contributing in ways he never had the time for before.

Traditional retirement worked well for Chuck. He had activities lined up that he found fulfilling, things he and his wife had planned for years, and they knew their plan was solid financially.

Ed

Ed sidled up to me at social event. He wasn't my client, but we'd known each other for years and he knew what I did for a living. He looked around to make sure no one was listening. "Dana, I've got to tell you. I'm having trouble with this."

I instantly knew what he was talking about. I'd heard he had sold his business and retired just a few months prior.

"Yes, a lot of people do. Particularly career-oriented people such as professionals and business owners."

He continued. "It's only been a few months. And I'm thinking, is this it? I've got to find something to do."

We talked for awhile. Ed had run a successful business for years. He had carefully planned his exit strategy. He had been busy in his first few months of retirement, but it wasn't the right kind of busy. It wasn't satisfying.

Ed was used to leading a team, making decisions, and working toward goals. To be happy in retirement, he needed to find a way to continue to use these skills.

Retirement is a big life transition. It's not for everybody. It may not be for you.

QUESTIONS TO ASK YOURSELF

Before you retire, ask yourself the following:

- What does retirement mean to me?
- When will I retire?
- What will I do with my time?
- Can I describe my ideal retirement day, or week?

You will need to figure out what type of retirement will work for you. Like Dr. Barry, do you want to find a way to schedule a gradual transition into retirement? If you're like Ed, can you figure out a way to stay involved with an interest of yours so that you can continue to contribute?

If you're married, what does your spouse want? What will you do with your time in retirement? Do you have activities you are excited about pursuing?

The answers to these questions have financial implications, yet that is only one reason to think about them. Retirement may be an opportunity where you can use your talents in a new way.

Getting More Out of Your Human Capital

If you earned on average $45,000 a year from age 25 through 65, that would be $1.8 million dollars of earnings. Many people earn far more in their lifetimes but don't stop to think of their earning power as the valuable resource that it is. Your entire perspective can change when you begin to figure out how to get the most out of this resource.

There are several different views on how to effectively use your human capital. I break them into two approaches:

- The mercenary approach
- Finding work you thrive on

▒ **Tip**   Remember that your human capital—all the skills and insight you've built up over the years—doesn't go away at retirement. You can still put it to use to continue to enjoy life to the fullest and perhaps increase your income.

The Mercenary Approach

In their book *Die Broke* (HarperBusiness, 1998), authors Stephen Pollan and Mark Levine suggest a *mercenary approach* in which you maximize your career potential and offer your work to the highest bidder. You save as much as you can and put much of your savings in immediate annuities to provide guaranteed income to replace your earned income. I think this approach is interesting and, no doubt, it may work for some.

It means sacrificing current lifestyle while working, or potentially choosing work that is not fulfilling, in order to focus your financial and human capital efforts on the goal of retirement.

This mercenary-like approach can be combined with an extremely down-sized lifestyle to reach retirement far more quickly than you may think. This approach is illustrated quite effectively on a web site called Early Retirement Extreme.[3] In the About Me section, author Jacob Lund Fisker says:

> If you're new here, this blog will give you the tools to become financially independent in 5 years. . . . This is not some stupid get rich quick scheme. The method is robust and replicable (no need to win the lottery, sell your business, or win at real estate), but not easy. . . . The key is to save 75%+ of your net income and invest it in income producing assets (bonds and dividend stocks). This is done by running your personal finances much like a business.

If your goal is to get out of traditional work as quickly as possible, I'd suggest you check out the Early Retirement Extreme web site. Financial independence can be achieved in a far shorter time period than you may think, but it does require sacrifices. The advantage is that once you reach financial independence, you then have the freedom to choose what type of work you might want to do—if you want to work at all.

Another option is to spend time figuring out what academic programs, credentials, or certifications could help boost your income. Evaluate the financial cost of any program against the potential increase in income you might expect and make sure you talk to many people in your industry to find out whether they think additional education will actually translate into increased income.

Years ago, I went through this process in considering the CFA (Chartered Financial Analyst) designation. This is a designation that many investment analysts, mutual fund managers, and institutional money managers hold. I am interested in the designation even to this day, but it involves a significant time commitment. The industry leaders I spoke with said that for the career path I was choosing, they did not think it was necessary for me. Instead I have chosen other designations that more directly correlate with the work of a financial advisor who works with individuals and their money decisions.

Finding Work You Thrive On

An alternative to the mercenary approach starts with figuring out what makes you tick and what type of work puts you "in the zone." When you find a niche you thrive in, it changes everything. If you enjoy what you are doing, you are likely to work longer, and it won't feel like work. Career counseling, coaching, and tools like Kolbe can assist you in finding work you thrive on.

---

[3]http://earlyretirementextreme.com/about

A coaching process I have found beneficial is the Rediscover Your Mojo process,[4] designed by executive coach Lisa Stefan. Her process is designed to find that place "where strength meets spirit."

Lisa is one of my best friends, and I went through her process while it was in the design stage. At the time I was frustrated with the direction of my business. I was looking for answers and hoping she could help me find them. To my surprise, what I got out of the process were valuable insights that have profoundly affected the way I operate on a daily basis and have changed the way I make decisions. I didn't get a nice neat "answer" about a career decision; instead I got tuned in to my internal compass so that it has become far easier for me to find my own answers to tough decisions.

As she describes it: "Rediscover Your Mojo contains content, exercises, materials and strategies developed specifically for professional adults like you— those striving to live life based upon what inspires them, what fulfills them, and what they value most."

If your retirement income plan calls for working until 70, and you're currently 50, why wouldn't you spend some time figuring out what type of work you thrive on? In my opinion, 20 years is too long to do work you don't enjoy.

If you're near retirement but are beginning to realize that traditional retirement is not for you, you'll also want to do some soul searching. Brainstorm various ways you can use your impending free time to work on something you'll find fulfilling.

Many in the age 55–64 age range are choosing to start a business. The Start Your Own Business page at RetiredBrains says, "Data from the Kauffman Foundation shows the highest rate of entrepreneurship in America has shifted to the 55–64 age group, with people over 55 almost twice as likely to found successful companies than those between 20 and 34, and individuals between the ages of 54 and 64 represented 22.9% of the entrepreneurs who launched businesses in 2010."[5]

Starting a business isn't easy. I'll attest to that. Yet, if it is work you thrive on, even when it's hard, it is still fulfilling.

■ **Note** The Kauffman Foundation finds that those aged 55–64 now have the highest rates of business formation and are twice as likely to found successful companies as those aged 20–34. If you've always had an urge to try entrepreneurship, don't let age hold you back.

---

[4]www.mojoassociates.com/index.php/services/rediscover_your_mojo/
[5]www.retiredbrains.com/Home/Start+Your+Own+Business/default.aspx

Of course, continuing to work is not always about choice. It is often a matter of necessity. The mother of one of my close friends spent every summer in Alaska working in a dinner theater well into her 70s. In this way, she was able to save enough over the summer to supplement her Social Security throughout the remainder of the year. She had to work, yet she found a solution that got her out of the Arizona heat in the summer and allowed her to earn enough in a few months' time so that, for the rest of the year, her time was her own.

If you must supplement your income, explore every avenue you can think of. Do you have skills, hobbies, or specialized training that can be used to generate income? Can you teach part-time or turn your craft into a salable product?

A few years ago, over the Fourth of July, I stayed at a bed and breakfast in the mountains. The couple who owned it had recently retired, and this home was their retirement dream. They enjoyed people and entertaining. They wanted a beautiful house with a view, and by turning it into a business they found a way to afford it.

The town near their bed and breakfast hosts an annual arts festival. As I walked around talking with the vendors, many of them were retired. They were people who enjoyed traveling and had found a way to support their lifestyle by turning their craft into a source of income, which also enabled them to deduct many of their travel expenses.

There are numerous creative ways to use your human capital. Explore them all, just as you would explore options on how to use your financial resources.

Working in Retirement

Retirement is a relatively new concept for society. It is easy to forget that. Think about someone who works from age 20 to age 60, then retires and lives to 100. During their 40 years producing goods and services, they need to save enough to support 40 years of consumption. That is not an easy task. To support even a modest lifestyle, many will need to plan on working longer, or working part-time, well into their 70s.

Particularly for people whose plan does not leave a lot of wiggle room, it makes sense to find some way to supplement income.

As for Steve and Carol's plan, recall that Steve plans on earning about $48,000 a year from age 66 through 70. If he is not able to do this, their plan will have to be adjusted. They would have to reduce spending and/or plan on using a reverse mortgage. Steve's preference was to continue to work in a consulting capacity rather than live on an ultra-tight budget.

Whether you work in retirement because you want to or because you have to, there are two areas where retirees get themselves in trouble when they retire and then go back to work. The first often happens to those who have never been self-employed before, and the second to those who are unaware of the Social Security earnings limit.

Self-Employment in Retirement

If you have never been self-employed before and decide to venture down that path, the first thing I recommend you do is get a good accountant. Many newly self-employed people quickly get behind on their taxes. They are used to having taxes withheld from their own paychecks and don't realize that once they are self-employed, they need to do their own withholding, and sometimes it can amount to many more dollars than they thought.

In addition, a good accountant can tell you what expenses you can deduct, which ones you can't, and how to keep accurate records. The last thing you want is tax trouble disrupting your new venture.

Earnings Limit

As discussed in Chapter 3, if you begin receiving Social Security benefits before you reach full retirement age, and you have earnings that are in excess of the Social Security earnings limit, the Social Security Administration will reduce your benefits or ask you to pay back the appropriate amount.

I've seen this cause problems for those forced into early retirement. Perhaps they experience a layoff and begin Social Security benefits because they don't think they should take withdrawals from savings or retirement accounts. Then a new job opportunity presents itself. They begin work and are surprised, or even shocked, when they get a notice that they owe some of their Social Security benefits back.

If you retire before you reach your full retirement age, do a careful analysis into how your plan should be structured. Starting Social Security benefits early is often not the best solution.

▓ **Tip**   Go back and reread Chapter 3 before you decide to take Social Security at age 62. That decision will have ramifications if you then decide to go back into full-time work.

Aligning Your Plan to Your Potential Retirement Date

You can't always plan out your retirement date just the way you want to. Sometimes life has something else in mind. If you have a plan in place, you'll know what items need to be adjusted if your retirement date gets shifted (often due to health reasons, corporate restructuring, or the economy).

As you learned in Chapter 5, smart tax-planning moves can be designed around periods of time when you will have less earned income. You want to keep this in mind when you make decisions about your human capital.

For example, should your retirement date coincide with the end of the year, so that the following year you have no earned income, or should it occur mid-year? Intentionally designing your income plan to work with your intended retirement date can put more dollars back into your pocket.

In addition, if you have a plan and are forced out of your current job earlier than expected, you can quickly revisit the plan to determine whether you must continue to work, and if so, to what extent.

I've seen this occur first-hand many times. Gale and Kurt are a good example. They ran a small business and were thinking of selling it. When we put together their plan, they realized the amount they would receive was not enough to continue their desired retirement lifestyle. They rallied and focused on building the business. A few years later, Kurt passed away, rather unexpectedly. Because we had a framework in place, Gale was able to evaluate her options fairly quickly. She couldn't run the business on her own, so she located a buyer, sold the business, and went to work part-time for a former employer doing something she enjoyed. The decisions were stressful, but the stress was minimized because she and her husband had taken the time to do the planning ahead of time. She knew human capital had to be part of her plan for several more years. It was just a matter of figuring out how that was going to happen.

Summary

The traditional view of retirement is not for everyone. It is also not affordable for everyone. You need to figure out whether you are wired for traditional retirement, and whether you can afford it, and build your retirement plan around the answers.

Human capital—defined as your ability to generate income—can help fill in any gaps. Your human capital is a valuable resource. You can look for ways to make the most of this resource, just as you would look for ways to make the most of your financial resources. Explore ideas now on how to continue to use your human capital even in retirement.

Whom to Listen To

And How to Avoid Fraud

If you think it's expensive doing business with a professional, just wait until you do business with an amateur.

—Anonymous

Not everyone needs a financial advisor, but certainly everyone needs smart financial advice. So where do you find it?

The media can be a source of broad, generic advice. However, the media knows nothing about your personal situation. I'll never forget one investor calling me once and asking, "Do you have municipal bonds?"

"Yes," I replied. "Why do you ask?"

"Well," she said, "they told me I needed municipal bonds."

I was a bit confused, as I was her financial advisor, so I apprehensively said, "Do you mind telling me who 'they' is?"

"Oh," she said, "you know—the people on TV."

For numerous reasons, including her tax bracket and the types of accounts she had, other investments were more appropriate for her than municipal bonds. The TV host, however, didn't provide specifics—only an overview of municipal bonds and the fact that they paid tax-free interest.[1] This woman heard "tax-free" and thought it must be something she should pursue.

The media doesn't know you. I don't know you either. I have tried throughout this book to show you how smart planning can lead to better decisions. I have tried to avoid prescribing specific advice because I am well aware that I do not know you. Advice is personal. It is delivered after a process of data gathering and analysis, and it relates to your situation.

You can educate yourself in numerous ways. By all means, use all forms of media to educate yourself; just don't mistake what you read, watch, or hear for advice.

▓ **Tip**   Take what you hear from TV financial pundits with a grain of salt. They don't know you or your financial situation; the advice may or may not be relevant.

The Financial Advice Industry

In 1995, at age 23, I started my career as a financial advisor. I studied for 60 days and passed an exam. I was granted a Series 6 securities license. I didn't know much, and I didn't know that I didn't know much—but I was a financial advisor. This license granted me the right to sell mutual funds. That meant I could legally collect a commission on sales. I went to work.

As of 2011, there were about 350,000 financial advisors in the United States. About 94 percent of them (330,000) carry some type of insurance or securities license, which means they may legally be compensated in some way or another from selling investment or insurance products.[2] I started my career as part of this 94 percent.

I was earnest, believable, and genuine. I had never owned a home, didn't know anything about taxes, and had absolutely no perspective on what a bear market[3] could or would look like. Yet I was a financial advisor.

---

[1]Municipal bond interest is generally exempt from federal taxes, but some types of municipal bond interest may be subject to AMT (alternative minimum tax). If the bond is issued in the state you reside in, it may also be exempt from state income taxes.
[2]Stat Bank, *Journal of Financial Planning* (July 2011): 14.
[3]A bear market is defined as a period where the stock market goes down 20% or more, from peak to trough. From 1900–2008, bear markets have occurred 32 times, or about 1 out of every 3 years. The average length of a bear market is 367 days.

I believe a lot of financial advisors are like I was when I started my career: well-intentioned. Many of them are sincere, reliable, smart, and genuinely good people. However, the industry of financial advice still has a long way to go to reach maturity.

Take the CPA industry or the medical industry as an example. If you use the services of someone who is a CPA or an MD, you can be assured they have a minimum level of competence. That is currently not the case with the financial planning industry. There is fragmentation in how the industry is regulated, and there are numerous credentials and compensation structures.

As a consumer, your choices will dictate the evolution of this industry. If you demand a higher level of competence and choose to use the services of firms who provide it, then the industry will evolve and become more consumer focused. I look forward to watching this evolution and hope you make choices to help it move that direction.

This chapter covers a few practical steps you can take.

Don't Confuse Products with Advice

An investment product cannot solve a financial-planning problem any more than a drug can solve the problem of an unhealthy lifestyle. The right drug, prescribed after testing and diagnosis, may improve your health situation, and the right financial product, prescribed after testing and diagnosis, may improve your financial situation. But simply moving your money to a new slick investment is usually not going to accomplish much for you. Financial planning and investment advice are intricately intertwined, but they are not the same.

Many financial advisors—and the media—place far too much emphasis on investment selection and investment products and far too little emphasis on planning.

A 2012 paper by the Center for Retirement Research[4] concludes that financial advice

> [t]ends to focus on financial assets, applying tools that give prominence to the asset allocation decision ... and are often silent on the levers that will have a much larger effect on retirement security for the majority of Americans. These levers include delaying retirement, tapping housing equity through a reverse mortgage, and controlling spending ... for many with substantial assets, these ... levers may be as powerful as asset allocation in attaining retirement security.

---

[4]Alicia H. Munnell, Natalia Sergeyevna Orlova, and Anthony Webb, "How Important is Asset Allocation to Financial Security in Retirement?" Center for Retirement Research (April 2012). Available online at http://crr.bc.edu/wp-content/uploads/2012/04/wp-2012-13.pdf.

If planning decisions (which you can control) can be just as powerful as investment decisions (the results of which are outside of your control), it only makes sense to me that you should start by creating a plan.

A Morningstar paper titled "Alpha, Beta and Now ... Gamma" went to additional lengths to quantify the difference that smart financial planning can make, saying: "We estimate a retiree can expect to generate 29% more income" by "following an efficient financial planning strategy."[5] The efficient financial-planning strategy this Morningstar paper goes on to describe encompasses much of what I have discussed in this book.

If you decide to seek professional help in planning your retirement, and the advisor begins by discussing their investment approach, which includes buying an annuity, a real estate investment trust, a life insurance policy, or any financial product, you should quickly recognize that these are product solutions. There is nothing wrong with a product solution if it is the result of smart planning. But if the planning work has not been done, think twice before you buy.

▒ **Tip** Make sure you have planned well before you buy any financial product.

You should also understand that when it comes to investment advice, all investment advice is not alike.

The National Bureau of Economic Research (NBER) conducted a research project in which they sent undercover auditors to investigate the type of advice you might receive from a typical advisor. It published the results of its study in a paper called *The Market for Financial Advice: An Audit Study*.[6] The paper summarizes its purpose and conclusions in an excerpt that states: "We use an audit methodology where trained auditors meet with financial advisers and present different types of portfolios. . . . We document that advisers . . . encourage returns-chasing behavior and push for actively managed funds that have higher fees, even if the client starts with a well-diversified, low-fee portfolio."

This NBER study defines the typical advisor as an "advisor whom the average citizen can access via their bank, independent brokerages, or investment advisory firms."

Michael Kitces, an industry expert, took a look at this study and said, "... a look under the hood reveals a significant methodological flaw with the NBER

---

[5]David Blanchett and Paul Kaplan, "Alpha, Beta and Now . . . Gamma," Morningstar (September 8, 2012).
[6]Sendhil Mullainathan, Markus Noeth, Antoinette Schoar, *The Market for Financial Advice*, the National Bureau of Economic Research (March 2012). Available online at http://papers.nber.org/papers/w17929.

study—simply put, they failed to control for whether the people they sought out for advice actually had the training, education, experience, and regulatory standards to even be deemed advisors in the first place, and in fact appear to have sampled extensively from a pool of salespeople with little or no advisory training or focus."

Or as Wade Pfau put it, this study "tended to investigate brokers who could be better characterized as salespeople rather than advisors."

What stood out to me about NBER paper's conclusion is that when it comes to investing, there is in fact a definition of "good advice" and as a general rule much of the industry is not delivering it.

Until the industry matures, if you seek professional advice, it is going to take some work on your part to find an advisor who offers meaningful planning advice and takes an investment approach that fits the definition of "good advice."

Before you seek such services, the first question to tackle is do you need an advisor?

Do You Need an Advisor?

I am a financial advisor, and I own a firm that delivers financial advisory services. So I am clearly biased in my opinion on whether someone needs professional assistance with their retirement planning. Thus, I would like to share someone else's thoughts on this question.

I am fan of an online advice web site called Oblivious Investor,[7] written by Mike Piper. Mike also has a series of books that he describes as "somewhat akin to Cliffs Notes for personal finance topics." I've read two of his books and recommend them.

In his book *Can I Retire?,* Mike states that "… a financial planner with expertise in tax planning and Social Security benefits can be very helpful here. Spending a few hundred dollars to sit down with such a professional could quite possibly save you several thousand dollars in taxes."

He also writes: "… most investors do not need a financial advisor if they're willing to take the time to learn all the ins and outs." But he adds that "as an investor gets closer to retirement the usefulness of an advisor increases dramatically."

I agree with these comments. Not everyone needs an advisor. But I have seen first-hand that when it comes to many of the permanent and irrevocable

---

[7]www.obliviousinvestor.com

decisions you need to make as you near retirement, smart advice can provide results that are measurable in dollars and provide additional retirement security.

Another factor to consider is how you want to spend your time. I know I am perfectly capable of doing my own tax return, yet I don't. I am also capable of cleaning my own home, but I don't. I happily pay for these services and feel like I get a great value for the price. If you hire an advisor, this is the way you should feel about it—that you are getting a service that is worth the price you pay. Let's see how you can come close to ensuring you get the advice you deserve.

How to Find Advisors

How do you find an advisor who has expertise and can provide the type of planning you need? Start by understanding what credentials to look for, what compensation models an advisor may use, and what to look for when you interview an advisor.

Advisor Credentials

Last I looked, there were over 75 possible credentials, or letters, that financial advisors could place after their names. That's like looking for a doctor and having 75 different versions of MD. How do you know which credentials signify that advisors have truly taken steps to further their education and provide exemplary advice?

There are several credentials that stand out. It doesn't mean the rest are bad, but if I were looking for a financial advisor, the following are what I would look for: CFP, PFS, CFA, or RMA.

Certified Financial Planner or CFP[8]

To earn a CFP designation, professionals must pass a two-day comprehensive exam that shows they have knowledge about many areas of financial planning, including taxes, insurance, retirement planning, investments, and estate planning. To use the CFP designation, they must fulfill three years of relevant financial planning work experience. They must also agree to adhere to the CFP Board's ethics requirements. To keep their designation they must keep up with ongoing continuing education requirements.

---

[8]Author disclosure: I have been a CFP since 2003.

HOW TO FIND A CERTIFIED FINANCIAL PLANNER

The Financial Planning Association[9] (FPA) offers a PlannerSearch tool on its web site that can help you locate an advisor who has a CFP. You can narrow your search by location, compensation method, and area of specialty. To start your search visit www.fpaforfinancialplanning.org/PlannerSearch/PlannerSearch.aspx.

Personal Financial Specialist or PFS designation

If you need advanced tax advice, you may want to find an advisor who is a PFS. This designation may only be acquired by a CPA (Certified Public Accountant). To first become a CPA one must have a bachelor's degree, have passed the Uniform CPA Exam, and have two years of general accounting experience supervised by a CPA. Then, to acquire the PFS, the CPA must have an additional 80 hours of personal financial-planning education (across 9 defined areas), gain 2 years of full-time experience in personal financial planning, and pass the 6-hour comprehensive PFS exam. (Candidates who already have their CFP are exempt from the exam requirement.)

Chartered Financial Analyst or CFA

This designation is particular to the investment management piece of financial planning. If you have advanced investment-management needs—for example, you may own a big chunk of stock or stock options through your employer, be an officer of a publicly traded company, or have inherited complex investments—then you may want to find someone who either has a CFA or has a CFA as part of their team. To become a CFA, an advisor must pass three levels of exams, each requiring an estimated 250 hours of study, hold a bachelor's degree or have equivalent work experience, and have four years of acceptable professional work experience.

Searching for professionals with these designations will lead you to the highest-quality advisors. There is one additional designation I would like to mention, because it is near and dear to my heart, and this book would not have come about if I did not have it: the Retirement Management Analyst designation.

---

[9] Author disclosure: I am a member of FPA and have been since around 2003.

Retirement Management Analyst or RMA

In 2010, the Retirement Income Industry Association (RIIA)[10] began to offer a designation called an RMA. I immediately signed up, completed the education program, and was in the first class to take the RMA exam. This book would not have come about were it not for what I learned through the RMA educational materials and the presentations I have attended at RIIA conferences. Visit http://riia-usa.org/default.asp to learn more about this organization.

Once you have found an appropriately credentialed advisor, you should take steps to verify your advisor's credentials and check their complaint record.

Verify Credentials and Complaint Record

The world is full of people who are not who they say they are. Taking a few precautionary steps can help you steer clear of them. I would advise you take these steps even if you know someone well. Many prominent cases of fraud take place in close-knit groups of people where trust is automatically given— church groups or country clubs, for example.

First, verify your advisors' credentials. Ask them what regulatory agency oversees their business. If they carry a securities license, the answer will be FINRA (Financial Industry Regulatory Authority). You can use FINRA's online BrokerCheck feature to make sure your advisor is listed and make sure there are no complaints on file: www.finra.org/Investors/ToolsCalculators/BrokerCheck/.

If your advisor does not carry any securities licenses, they are probably regulated by the SEC (Securities and Exchange Commission) or a state securities commission. Either way, you can use the Investment Advisor Search feature on the SEC web site to check out both advisors and their firms at www.adviserinfo.sec.gov/IAPD/Content/Search/iapd_OrgSearch.aspx.

▒ Note Some advisors are what are called *dually registered*, which means both FINRA and the SEC or a state securities agency have oversight over their business.

If your advisor is a CFP, visit the CFP Board's search feature, type in that person's last name, and verify the advisor has the credential he or she claims to have at www.cfp.net/search/.

---

[10]Author disclosure: I am member of RIIA and serve as the Chair of its Peer Practitioner Review Committee, which reviews peer-written articles for potential publication in the *Retirement Management Journal*.

There are also specific questions you can ask to determine if your advisor has expertise in the areas that are relevant to your situation. The following questions will help you learn more about your advisor:

- *"Tell me about your ideal client":* You want someone who has expertise working with someone like you. If you're about to retire, and they tell you they work with young families, maybe this isn't the person for you. Find a financial advisor whose ideal client sounds very similar to your situation in terms of age, stage of life, and asset level.

- *"How long have you been practicing as a financial advisor?":* If any of your advisors are new to the field, find out if they are part of a team where a more experienced advisor oversees their work.

- *"Can you provide tax-planning advice?":* Many large brokerage firms and banks limit the topics their advisors may address. If you want someone who is fully aware of the tax implications of their recommendations, make sure this falls within the scope of what they can discuss with you.

Learn About Compensation Structures

Currently, there is no standard pricing model in the financial services industry. As a consumer, that can make it difficult to compare services.

I began my career as an advisor who worked on a commission basis and then transitioned to a fee-based model. When I became a partner in my own firm, I made a commitment to practice as a fee-only advisor. Let's take a look at each of these compensation models and what you might expect.

Commissions

Under a commission structure, when you buy an investment or insurance product, your financial advisor receives a commission for the sale of that product.

Take the case of something called an A share mutual fund. You may pay a 5.75% upfront sales load on this type of fund on purchase amounts up to $25,000, with the sales load dropping to 3.5–4% for purchase amounts of $100,000. That means on a $100,000 investment, you just paid $3,500–$4,000. Did you get any meaningful planning work for that fee? Do you receive ongoing tax-planning and financial counseling for that fee? Usually the answer is no.

Advisors who are compensated by commissions may have a limited set of investment products to choose from. I have met advisors under this model who sell only variable annuities, only mutual funds, only indexed annuities, or only life insurance. They know their products inside and out, but all-too-often they have limited knowledge of the choices available to you outside of their product line.

When I have a need for a specialized product, there are times—usually for the purchase of insurance products—when I refer business to commissioned advisors. If you have already determined the type of investment product you need, the right commissioned advisor may be a great resource to help you sift through the choices in that product line, but they may not be the best resource in helping you design your overall plan.

Fee-Only Methods of Compensation

Fee-only means the financial advisor cannot be compensated by commissions. You may write a check for their services, or they may debit their fees from an account that they manage on your behalf—either way it is clear that they work for you.

You will find various forms of pricing arrangements with fee-only advisors.

Hourly Rate

With an hourly pricing structure, you are paying for your advisor's time. Most advisors who charge hourly will provide you an up-front estimate of the amount of time it may take to deliver the advice you need.

When we encounter complex situations in our firm—for example, a couple who has previous marriages, each with children from previous marriages, numerous properties and/or business interests, and a plethora of investment accounts and holdings—it can easily take 50–100 hours of our time to put together a comprehensive plan.

For a single person with one retirement account and one home, it may take only five to ten hours.

With hourly pricing, much like that of an attorney or CPA, rates vary with the experience level of the advisor. You may expect to pay somewhere between $100 and $300 an hour.

TO FIND AN ADVISOR THAT USES AN HOURLY COMPENSATION STRUCTURE

If you want an advisor that charges hourly, start your search with the Garrett Planning Network (www.garrettplanningnetwork.com). This is an organization of advisors who charge an hourly rate for their professional services. The web site offers a search feature where you can seek a member advisor in your area.

Percentage of Assets

Under this method of compensation, an advisor will handle the opening and management of all your accounts and may also offer financial-planning advice along with investment advice. Their services are charged as a percentage of your account value, which may range from about .5–2% per year. Ask an advisor for their fee schedule, because usually the more assets you have, the lower their rates. Many advisors have minimum account sizes that must be met, so you may also want to inquire about minimums before you meet with an advisor.

There is often a vast difference in services delivered between brokers who want to put you in a fee-based account model (and who often can't provide tax-planning advice) and registered investment advisors,[11] who are typically more focused on holistic wealth management. At my firm we do far more than put an account into a model and rebalance once a year. We update their plan, manage assets at a household level in a way that reduces their annual taxes, provide annual tax projections, and match their investment needs to their retirement cash flow needs. It takes far more hours than most people think, and we keep people from making horrible mistakes with their money. Not everyone is cut out to do their own financial planning and investing. For those who aren't, 1% is cheap.

As you age, you must also consider your spouse. You may be well qualified to manage your finances and investments on your own, but whose hands might your spouse end up in when you are gone? It may be better for you to select the appropriate firm and build a relationship with them rather than leave such a thing up to chance.

---

[11] Not sure exactly what a registered investment advisory firm is? See Schwab's RIA Stands For You web site to learn more at www.riastandsforyou.com.

Per Plan Pricing

Some advisors charge per financial plan. They quote you a specific price that covers a particular set of services, such as $2,500 for a plan, recommendations, and a defined number of meetings.

Retainer Fees

Many boutique advisory firms charge an annual or quarterly retainer fee that includes unlimited access to them and may also include investment management services. Pricing for this type of service can vary depending on the minimums of the advisor.

FINDING A NO-COMMISSION ADVISOR

Regardless of the pricing structure, to find a fee-only advisor who cannot be compensated from the sale of investment or insurance products, visit NAPFA's (National Association of Personal Financial Advisors) web site at www.napfa.org. NAPFA is a member organization of fee-only financial advisors. They require applicants to submit documentation and a written sample of their work before becoming a member. The web site offers a search feature where you can seek such a fee-only advisor in your geographic area.[12]

Fee-Based

Many financial advisors currently practice in a structure called *fee-based*, which can be confused with *fee-only*. They are not the same.

A fee-based advisor may charge a percentage of your assets and/or collect a planning fee for putting together a financial plan for you, but may also be able to collect commissions or receive bonuses from their company depending on what type of investments or insurance products they recommend to you.

Many fee-based models have broker-dealers who put together portfolio models that dictate which funds or investments are placed in your account. In addition to the advisor's fee, you need to look at the average expense ratio of any investments that will be used in your account.

Some advisors choose to practice as fee-based rather than fee-only because the fee-based model gives them access to a suite of annuity and life insurance products that may be quite appropriate for their clients, and they can then be compensated for researching and recommending these products.

---

[12]Author disclosure: I am a member of NAPFA and have been since 2006.

TO FIND AN ADVISOR WHOSE CREDENTIALS HAVE ALREADY BEEN VERIFIED

The Paladin Registry (www.paladinregistry.com) offers a service which pre-qualifies financial advisors based on a set of specific criteria that they have developed. If an advisor meets the requirements, the Paladin Registry then verifies the advisor's credentials and compliance background. If everything checks out, the advisor becomes eligible to be listed. Advisors in the Paladin Registry are not limited to a particularly compensation method, but their compensation structure is fully disclosed in their listing.

Which Compensation Model Is Best?

I have met fabulous advisors who work under all compensation models. Personally, after practicing in all three ways, I am partial to the fee-only model. I feel that it is free of many of the conflicts of interest that come along with other compensation models. Fee-only advisors, however, are not entirely free of biases. Many commissioned advisors accuse fee-only advisors of neglecting to place enough emphasis on solutions like annuities or insurance.

Ultimately, the right advisor and compensation model for you depends on your needs. Yet sorting through various compensation models and comparing services can be challenging.

For example, one advisor may charge you 1.5% of the value of your investment portfolio per year. This price may include making limited financial planning recommendations, such as suggesting you fund a Roth or Traditional IRA. There may be additional underlying expenses in the mutual funds inside your account, so total expenses may be 2–2.5% per year.

The next advisor may charge 1% a year, use low-fee mutual funds, and include a full suite of financial-planning services in this price. With this advisor, you may be paying less and getting more in terms of meaningful planning advice.

In those two scenarios, clearly advisor number two offers a better value.

The next advisor may charge an hourly rate, but it's up to you to implement their financial-planning and investment recommendations on your own. I have had many frustrating experiences working with clients on an hourly basis, only to discover when they next came to visit me that they did not follow any of my recommendations. If you are the type of person who will follow through and implement the advice that is given, hourly advice might be appropriate.

You must determine what services you want or need and how much of it you are willing to do yourself.

▨ **Note**   According to author and consultant Bill Bacharach, "Price is only an issue in the absence of value. You may not necessarily want to say, 'I'm looking for the lowest-cost approach to achieving my dreams and goals.'"

Interviewing Advisors

Once you understand the credentials and compensation models you will encounter, the next step is the interview process.

Traditionally, people look for an advisor in their geographic area so they may meet face-to-face, but with technology today, you can work with an advisor located just about anywhere, as long as they have the proper credentials or licenses to work with people in your state. (It is the advisor's responsibility to make sure they can work with you.)

Two questions can help you gauge the financial advisor's communication and planning style.

"Can you explain [pick a financial concept] to me?"

You want to work with someone who can explain financial concepts to you in language you can understand. If an advisor speaks over your head, or their answer makes no sense and they do not respond well to additional questions, move on. Here are a few concepts you should have learned from this book that you could inquire about:

- What do you think of index funds?
- How do you determine how much of my money should be in stocks versus bonds (or high-risk versus lower-risk investments)?
- How do you help me determine what types of accounts I should contribute to, such as an IRA or Roth IRA?
- What do you think of annuities?
- What is sequence risk and what steps do you take to minimize its effects?

"What assumptions do you use when running retirement planning projections?"

All financial-planning projections are based on assumptions about the rate of return your investments will earn, the pace of inflation, taxes, and your personal spending habits.

If you prefer safer, more conservative investments, and an advisor runs a financial plan projecting your investments will grow at 10% a year, you have a problem. This assumption makes the future look rosy, but it's make-believe. You need realistic projections to make appropriate decisions.

You want to find someone who uses a conservative set of assumptions; after all, you'd rather end up with more than what is on paper, not less.

The following are a set of realistic financial-planning assumptions, which should be adjusted according to your personal circumstances and changes in the general economy:

- *Investment returns:* About 5–7% a year (this is the expected return after all investment fees) on average
- *Inflation rate:* About 3% a year on average
- *Increase in value of real estate assets:* 2–3% a year on average
- *Tax rates:* Based on your income and investment situation. For example, if you have a large sum of money in retirement accounts, you will pay taxes on that money as it is withdrawn. That puts you in a completely different tax situation than someone who has a large sum of money that is not in retirement accounts. This needs to be considered when running financial-planning projections.

In lieu of seeking professional help, you may want to do your own planning and investing. If you are comfortable with numbers and complex financial decisions, you can use Excel to lay out your plan just as I have done throughout this book.

Do It All Yourself

You can do your own planning if you are so inclined. To do it well, you'll either need to subscribe to the same types of software that professionals use or have the ability to build detailed spreadsheet models on your own.

I still find Excel to be the most versatile and useful program ever designed. You have seen samples of Excel worksheets through this book. What I like about Excel is that I can see exactly what is happening and create reports to illustrate the specific information that I think is relevant.

If you build a retirement income model in Excel, the most difficult part will be accurately assessing taxes. You could take your model and ask your accountant or CPA to help you with assessing the tax consequences of various distribution options. They have access to tax-projection software that would be useful for this type of planning.

In our firm, in addition to Excel, we use three primary tools to run retirement income projections:

- *Finance Logix:* Finance Logix offers fantastic tutorials, a dynamic interface that allows you to see the effects of different decisions, and the ability to link your investment accounts to the software so that account balances update in real time whenever you log in to review your plan. Finance Logix also offers a free downloadable app called Retire Logix that can be fun to play around with. Visit www.retirelogix.com or www.financelogix.com for details.

- *BNA Tax Planner:* BNA Tax Planner allows us to run detailed tax projections to see whether one course of action might result in a lower tax liability than another. It incorporates all the relevant state tax rules as well as AMT calculations. For additional information visit www.bnasoftware.com/ Products/BNA_Income_Tax_Planner/Index.asp.

- *Social Security Timing:* Social Security Timing helps us take a detailed look at someone's potential Social Security claiming decisions. For additional information visit www. socialsecuritytiming.com. (For consumers there are several Social Security software packages you can use to help with this decision. I keep an updated list of them in my Social Security Calculator list on About.com. Visit it at http://moneyover55.about.com/od/socialsecurity benefits/tp/Best-Social-Security-Calculators. htm.)

Anyone can subscribe to these various software packages. You will spend several thousand dollars a year to do so, and you will need to spend additional time to learn how to use them effectively.

There are also many free online retirement calculators. I think these are great tools to give you a general sense of how well prepared you may be for retirement. However, the free calculators do not offer the functionality needed to create an accurate retirement income plan.

Regardless of how you do your planning, I do hope you plan.

One additional thing you'll want to plan for is how to detect and avoid fraud.

Avoiding Fraud

People who conduct fraud are often charismatic and engaging and find it easy to gain people's trust. I could fill an entire chapter with the stories of fraud I have personally seen. I will share just a few of them with you and then provide tips you can use to avoid these situations.

The Outright Lie

If you haven't heard of him, Bernie Madoff is the former chairman of the NASDAQ stock market and the man who ran what is considered to be the largest financial scam in U.S. history. It came unraveled in December 2008 when he was arrested. Many families lost their entire life savings in this scandal.

These losses could have been avoided by following two simple rules. The first rule has to do with understanding what is and is not realistic.

There was at least one person who understood this rule and tried, unsuccessfully, to get authorities to look into the Madoff situation for many years. His name was Harry Markopolos, and he is often credited as the man who figured out Madoff's scheme.

Markopolos has said, "As we know, markets go up and down, and his only went up. He had very few down months. Only four percent of the months were down months. And that would be equivalent to a baseball player in the major leagues batting .960 for a year. Clearly impossible. You would suspect cheating immediately."[13]

I heard the story of Bernie Madoff and Harry Markopolos at a conference in March of 2012 from a man named Frank Casey. Frank worked closely with Harry Markopolos, and he was speaking at this conference to tell the story that he and Harry detail in their book *No One Would Listen: A True Financial Thriller* (Wiley, 2011). It is really a fascinating story.

As Frank Casey so aptly put it, "How do you compete with a lie?"

I've come up against the lie many times. I have not yet found an effective way to compete against it. It's difficult because it's a lie everyone wants to believe in. I can present all the logic in the world, but when some unscrupulous advisor promises 12% returns with little downside risk, it is often with a sense of helplessness that all I can do is stand by and watch a client lose money. If you understand that no one, no matter how smart, can game the system, you'll be more skeptical of people who claim they can.

The second rule investors can use to avoid the Madoff-type scam is to only use advisors that use third-party custodians. The custodian is the company that generates your account statements. In Madoff's case, he could generate his own account statements, which meant he could make up what they contained. Contrast that with the typical structure of a registered investment advisor that uses a third-party custodian, like Charles Schwab, Fidelity, T.D. Ameritrade, or Pershing. The advisor can direct the investments, but the custodian reports directly to the client. With this structure, an advisor has no ability to make up what the statement says.

---

[13]"The Man Who Figured Out Madoff's Scheme," CBS News (March 1, 2009).

Returns that are Too Good to Be True

The first lie about returns I encountered was in 2007. One of my clients, a railroad engineer, came into meet with me a month before he retired. He told me he wasn't going to need to withdraw his monthly retirement income from his IRA as we had planned.

"Why?" I asked, rather intrigued. I wondered if he'd changed his mind about retiring.

He replied that he'd invested $100,000 in a currency-trading program that was paying him $5,000 a month. He showed me the checks he had been receiving.

I got a sick feeling in my stomach. I knew the math didn't add up. At $5,000 a month, that's $60,000 a year, on a $100,000 investment. No one can deliver those kinds of returns. But how do you explain this to someone who has checks in their hand?

Within six months this client's currency trading program was discovered to be a scam, and the perpetrators were arrested. I wasn't surprised.

After netting out the checks he had received, and the tax deduction for the fraud loss, he ended up about $50,000 poorer. Luckily, the rest of his retirement money remained invested in a balanced portfolio of no-load index funds, so his overall retirement security wasn't affected.

Appealing to Your Ego

On another occasion I watched a former client of mine get scammed out of nearly $4 million. The perpetrator did what con artists are good at: they appealed to his ego. They told him he would have access to exclusive investments only available to high net worth individuals. They also told him their firm would handle everything for him: his legal work, accounting, and investments. In hindsight, this makes sense. It keeps other expert eyes from questioning what is being done.

In his case, he moved his investments to this new firm. A few years later, he came back in to see me with a stack of papers in hand asking me to help him figure out what had happened. I read, and I read some more. I turned white as chalk as I kept reading. Four million dollars—nearly all of his money—was gone. I immediately sent him to see an attorney who specialized in these types of cases.

297

The Family Friend

Con artists are skilled at finding people who are trusting and vulnerable. You may be savvy, but what about your spouse?

Henrietta's husband Frank passed away when she was 78. They had an impressive collection of original art worth millions.

Sam, a friend of Frank's, reached out to Henrietta after Frank's death. He offered to buy her art collection. Henrietta didn't seek legal counsel because she'd known Sam for a long time. Why would she need an attorney? She trusted him.

They negotiated a purchase price of $3 million to be paid to Henrietta on a schedule of $25,000 a month for the next 10 years.

About a year after this deal was finalized Henrietta was referred to me by her accountant. I reviewed the documents associated with the art sale. Something wasn't right. The sale agreement lacked professionalism, did not follow basic accounting principles, and it was missing important legal clauses. But Henrietta was receiving checks.

A year later, the checks stopped. Sam was nowhere to be found. Henrietta was finally able to track him down, at which time he told her he was going through financial difficulties, and that he would send her money as soon as he could. She waited. A few months later he sent one additional payment. Then nothing more.

It wasn't until she hadn't received a payment for two years that I was able to convince Henrietta to hire an attorney and pursue litigation. She kept telling me that Sam was a friend. She wanted to give him the benefit of the doubt. Henrietta was 82. Of course she didn't want the hassle. Who would expect to have to sue a family friend at 82?

But who would guess a family friend would prey upon a 78-year-old widow, blatantly stealing millions?

What to Look Out For

According to the Center for Retirement Research at Boston College, fraud is on the rise. Its report "The Rise of Financial Fraud,"[14] provides a list called Fraud's Red Flags. If you encounter one of these, just say no. It doesn't matter how nice the person is. Just say no.

---

[14]Kimberly Blanton, "The Rise of Financial Fraud: Scams Never Change, but Disguises Do," the Center for Retirement Research (February 2012), No. 12-5. Available online at http://crr.bc.edu/wp-content/uploads/2012/02/IB_12-5-508.pdf. Used with permission.

Fraud's Red Flags

Investments may be fraudulent if they:

- Look too good to be true.

- Offer a very high or "guaranteed" return at "no risk" to the investor.

- Require an urgent response or cash payment.

- Charge a steep up-front fee in return for making more money on an unspecified date.

- Suggest recipients do not tell family members or friends about the offer.

- Lure prospective investors with a "free lunch."

- Come unsolicited over the Internet, are of unknown origin, or come from overseas.

- Instill fear that a failure to act would be very costly.

- Cannot be questioned, inspected, or checked out further.

- Are so complex that they are difficult or impossible to understand.

In addition to protecting yourself from fraud, you may want to keep an eye out for elderly family members and neighbors. The story of one of my own family members illustrates why.

Aunt B

It was mid-summer. Dad called to give me an update on Aunt B. Aunt B, at 94, was a spirited and intelligent woman. She'd had a fulfilling career as a professor, had never married, and had managed to save a significant amount of money.

Over the past few years, her hearing and sight had become impaired, and a medical condition developed which meant Aunt B needed 24-hour-a-day in-home care.

Aunt B did not want to use an agency to provide care. She lived in a small town in a rural area and wanted local help. She found a young woman who said she and two of her friends would be willing to provide in-home care services. They started coming around to stay with Aunt B regularly.

Dad had power of attorney over Aunt B's financial affairs and lived about 15 miles away. The first problem arose when Aunt B decided it would be a great idea to write a $60,000 check to help a local failing business stay afloat. Dad investigated—and overruled. Aunt B was furious. We found out later that the business was owned by the spouse of one of the caregivers.

Dad continued to investigate and soon realized that the three caregivers had managed to drain over $300,000 out of Aunt B's accounts within a matter of months.

When Dad tried to explain the situation to Aunt B, she became angry and adamantly defended the actions of her caregivers.

Dad brought in the police and an attorney. Despite clear explanations, Aunt B insisted that the caregivers were only going through a naughty spell, and that they should be forgiven and rehired.

The attorney, who was familiar with these types of cases, explained to us how these situations develop. Homebound people often forge close bonds with their caregivers. The caregiver becomes the eyes, ears, and primary news source for the homebound person and thus can exert great influence. The caregivers can screen phone calls, mail, and outside information so their patient is only exposed to the information they want them to see.

Aunt B was nearly blind. They would present her with checks for services like lawn care or house cleaning. She would sign the checks, which were often made out directly to the caregivers. They also ordered new appliances, tools, and other household items, all delivered to their own homes, not to Aunt B's.

To perpetrate their fraud, they convinced Aunt B that Dad was out to get her money. Each time he stopped by, they would tell Aunt B that he was only there to look out for his own future inheritance. They had even talked Aunt B into changing her will to make the primary caregiver the main beneficiary (this was later remedied).

The scam would never have been discovered if Dad didn't randomly stop in at Aunt B's, ask questions, and poke around, even when she didn't want him to.

Unfortunately, because this type of crime is not a violent crime, even after law enforcement was brought in and the case went to trial, and despite the fact that the perpetrators were prior felons, they did not go to jail. They received a 15-year suspended sentence, which is like being on probation for 15 years.

The law is interesting when it comes to these things. We were told that if they had robbed a bank for the same amount they took from our aunt, they most certainly would have served time.

We also learned from the attorney general that they likely learned their techniques in prison, as strategies on how to defraud the elderly are passed along among the incarcerated. Apparently the elderly make easy prey, and someone trained to swoop in can do serious damage in a matter of weeks—then disappear.

Numerous people out there are trying to part you from your money. I found one book about them, *Snakes in Suits* by Paul Babiak and Robert D. Hare (HarperBusiness, 2006), to be most insightful in providing tips on how to identify these types of people in advance.

■ **Tip** Keep an eye on your elderly friends and relatives. They can be easy prey for financial predators.

Snakes in Suits

If I mention the word *psychopath*, most likely a known killer such as Ted Bundy comes to mind. We think of psychopaths as deviants who maim and kill others for pleasure. The book *Snakes in Suits* provides insight into a different kind of psychopath—the kind found in the business world. These psychopaths may not be physically violent, but the destruction they cause is just as unthinkable.

According to the book, the psychopath's first goal is "to convince others of their honesty, integrity, and sincerity." Trust is often easy for a con artist to gain because they come across as charismatic, charming, and grandiose. My own experience with someone who was quite grandiose has changed my understanding of the word.

I used to think that if someone made grand claims, there must be some truth to them. After all, how could someone blatantly lie about such things when the truth would come out later? I've since learned that these types of people often lie because it is in their nature—they simply can't help it. They may have some type of mental illness that causes their destructive behavior. They also frequently believe their own lies, which makes it all the harder to detect them.

A good business con artist will appear passionate and give the illusion of having high ethical standards. They may ingratiate themselves with a church group and say they are on a mission, either for God or for the company or industry they work in. They'll often be a newcomer to a community you are involved in. They'll build trust quickly and say and do all the right things. They can make you feel incredibly special, and after they feel they've earned your trust, they may turn on you and question your own morality and values in an attempt to manipulate you. When they get what they want, they leave chaos behind.

How can you recognize them?

Snakes in Suits offers the following insights into the typical behavior of a business con artist:

- When challenged or asked questions about details, "he or she will simply shift gears, subtly change the topic and generally weave an altered tale" that is quite believable.

- They avoid answering direct questions.

- Their banter and dialogue is filled with "jargon, clichés, and flowery phrases" as well as inconsistencies and bad logic.

- They avoid taking responsibility for things that go wrong, always placing blame on something external—other people, circumstances, fate.

- They "spread disinformation in the effort of protecting their scam and furthering their own career" and "seize opportunities to bring harm to others' careers or professional standing."

Con artists are particularly skilled at eliciting emotional reactions in people. If you find yourself experiencing strong emotions around someone new in your life, be wary. Slow things down a bit. Get away from them so you can think clearly.

In addition, if someone you care about seems too quick to place unwarranted trust in someone new in *their* life, ask questions. If they get defensive, keep investigating.

Summary

Education is good, and I encourage you to learn all you can, but education is not advice. Investment and insurance products are needed solutions, but they in and of themselves are also not advice.

Advice is personal and appropriate to your individual circumstances, including your attitudes about risk. As I have often told my clients, I can have two families with identical financial circumstances, and after going through the same planning process they will make different decisions. That is exactly as it should be.

If you need professional advice, decide what type of advice you need and be sure to do a thorough job of selecting and interviewing the person you will hire. Investigate their credentials and make sure you understand their compensation model.

In addition, take steps to avoid fraud and teach others how to do the same. Scam artists could not get away with their cons if we were all trained to recognize the tell-tale signs.

Finally, however you do it, engage in the planning process. People don't ever plan to fail; instead they simply fail to plan.

I

Index

W, X, Y, Z

Windfall Elimination Provision
  (WEP), 55, 82

Withdrawal strategy
  required minimum distributions
    joint and last survivor table, 153
    large retirement account
    balances, 153
    retirement plans, 154

single life expectancy table, 153
uniform lifetime table, 153
Roth and traditional IRA, 148
social security benefits
  claiming options, after-tax basis, 151
  combined income, 149
  taxable income and liability, 150–151
  tax minimization, 152
  three-part test, 149–150
  threshold amounts, 149

Other Apress Business Titles You Will Find Useful